Creative Writing Pedagogies for the Twenty-First Century

Creative Writing Pedagogies for the Twenty-First Century

Edited by Alexandria Peary and Tom C. Hunley

Southern Illinois University Press
Carbondale

Cover illustration: "To Infinity and Beyond," iStockphoto LP

Library of Congress Cataloging-in-Publication Data
Creative writing pedagogies for the twenty-first century / edited by
Alexandria Peary and Tom C. Hunley.
    pages cm
Includes bibliographical references and index.
    ISBN 978-0-8093-3403-2 (pbk.)
    ISBN 0-8093-3403-8 (paperback)
    ISBN 978-0-8093-3404-9 (ebook)
1. Creative writing. 2. English language—Rhetoric—Study and teaching.
I. Peary, Alexandria, [date] editor. II. Hunley, Tom C., editor.
PE1404.C726 2015
808'.04207—dc23   2014036154

The paper used in this publication meets the minimum requirements of
American National Standard for Information Sciences—Permanence of
Paper for Printed Library Materials, ANSI Z39.48-1992. ∞

To Laura Mullen and Ira Sadoff, my teachers

To my wife, Ralaina, and to my mentor,
the late Wendy Bishop

Contents

Contents

Creative Writing Pedagogies for the Twenty-First Century

Prologue

PEDAGOGY IS ONE of three essential legs of any academic discipline. To become a recognized academic discipline or simply to evolve, a branch of study works purposefully on developing its pedagogy, research, and theory. Pedagogy, of the three, arguably has the most bearing on and the greatest interest for students. When we put learners at the center of our endeavors, at the core of our employment at colleges or universities, pedagogy is not an intellectual lawn game with ideas passed leisurely back and forth by scholars just for the sake of thinking. Instead, it becomes a professional responsibility. Increasingly, there's been a call inside creative writing studies for a greater focus on pedagogy. As Steve Healey, one of the contributors to this book, wrote in 2009 in the Association of Writers and Writing Programs' publication *The Writer's Chronicle*: "What has been missing from the impressive success story of Creative Writing is an equally strong attention to its pedagogy and theory; in other words, the field has tended to avoid thinking about how it teaches and what assumptions it has about language and literature" (30). Happily, this situation has begun to change. A growing body of work is devoted to creative writing pedagogy, and people are beginning to take notice. This discussion about how to best teach creative writing is even finding an audience outside of academia—on February 4, 2012, the *Huffington Post* published "Creative Writing Can Be Taught: Creative Writing Professors Answer More Important Questions," an article co-written by Dinty Moore and five other authors of books on creative writing pedagogy.

Prologue

Over the past few decades, efforts to advance the pedagogy of writing have led to groundbreaking developments in academia—including the formation of a whole new discipline, composition studies, which, as Tim Mayers has pointed out, rose as a response to a "series of apparently intractable pedagogical problems" ("One Simple Word" 218). A whole approach to writing—called *process pedagogy*—came to the forefront in the 1960s and early 1970s in the United States to counter the mechanistic and stultifying ways in which writing was being taught. Composition teachers at the time eagerly latched onto the idea of the student as writer and of writing as a rich process, which transformed their classrooms and led to a revolution in teaching. One prominent scholar in the field, Theresa Enos, described the impact of this wave of pedagogical awareness on her when she was a graduate student, saying that it "kind of [blew me] away. . . . It was a 100 percent turnaround, and I could see the engagement of the students. I could see the cognitive process. I could see their minds working" (Alexandria's interview with Enos). However, the reason composition studies *continued* to evolve as a discipline is that it did not settle on this single albeit exciting new pedagogy, process pedagogy, but instead went on to develop a wide range of pedagogies. Pedagogy in an academic discipline refers to a range—not just one or two types but multiple options. So far, the brunt of work on pedagogy inside creative writing studies has been focused on dealing with the blessings and limitations of just one pedagogic model: the workshop. Academics who identify both as scholars and as creative writers, including Mary Ann Cain, Lynn Domina, Anna Leahy, Eve Shelnutt, and David Starkey—just to name a few—have endeavored to help instructors understand the best workshop methods and, significantly, the conversation is turning toward various alternatives to workshop pedagogy. Like Dianne Donnelly, we believe that "Those of us in creative writing must, *if* we are to move beyond questions of whether the workshop model works or does not work . . . come to better visualize what *else* is possible in this workshop space" (1).

The chapters in this book offer a dozen different pedagogical avenues for the creative writing classroom—many of which were initiated in composition studies. We first want to be clear, however, that both of us feel thankful for the instruction we received in workshop-style courses from many dedicated creative writers who also teach. Workshop has its merits (especially in its student-centered approach to learning), but workshop can become detrimental when allowed to function as the only pedagogy in a creative writing program. We also want to be clear that what we are not advocating is that creative writers merely mime compositionists. Like Patrick Bizzaro, Tim Mayers, and others, we maintain that the adaptation of pedagogy from composition studies must be a careful one for it to be productive. The author of each chapter uses a "take what we need and leave the rest" approach when importing ideas of compositionists to the very different needs of creative writing instructors. *Creative Writing Pedagogies for the Twenty-First Century* seeks to enter the "productive dialogue" with composition studies which Mayers advocates in his chapter in *Can It Really Be Taught? Resisting Lore in Creative Writing Pedagogy* (2007):

> I would like to see creative writing enter into a productive dialogue with other fields of English studies, especially composition. This will require significant changes in the way most creative writers view themselves and their students as writers, and in their willingness to question and challenge their place within the hierarchies of English studies. Creative writers in academia must be willing to reassess the conventional wisdom—the lore—that has long provided a foundation for both theory and practice in creative writing classrooms. (7)

The examination of existent composition pedagogies is one stage in the continuing evolution of creative writing studies: the next step would be for the field to use these established pedagogies to initiate brand-new ones—as composition studies has done in a flurry over the past thirty-five years. It is highly possible, too, that in trying on established composition pedagogies, creative writers will perceive even more clearly what makes their field unique and be inspired to form a new tier of nuanced pedagogies. Our inclusion of Steve Healey's chapter on creative literacy pedagogy points to the beginning of that next tier. Who knows, perhaps the pendulum of borrowing will swing in a few years in the opposite direction, with composition scholars peeking over their disciplinary boundary to borrow once again from creative writers. Creative writing studies has a lot already going for it; what's holding it back is its recalcitrance to developing more pedagogies and taking this step into disciplinarity.

Creative Writing Pedagogies for the Twenty-First Century is modeled largely on Gary Tate, Amy Rupiper, and Kurt Schick's 2001 *A Guide to Composition Pedagogies*, which we discovered in graduate courses in composition theory (Alexandria at University of New Hampshire, Tom at Florida State University). Several of the pedagogies we're suggesting are discussed in that book. These pedagogies have established histories inside composition studies—they're not passing fads. In its own way, each of these pedagogies is devoted to the process and success of writers in and often out of the classroom. We won't detail here the histories of all of the pedagogies that we have included, but suffice it to say that each of them is well established—with its own journals, conferences, websites, and even presses.

Tom recalls a class discussion of *A Guide to Composition Pedagogies* in which the professor, Wendy Bishop, said that she hoped that some students would base their future teaching on a single pedagogical approach in that book while others would take more of a "smorgasbord approach," combining and synthesizing elements of various pedagogies presented in the book. We have the same hopes for readers of our book. As an example of the first option, a new teacher who wishes to take a service learning approach could begin by replicating Cathy Day's syllabus, included in Stephanie Vanderslice and Carey Smitherman's contribution to this book. Another new teacher might model her syllabus after the ideas in the "Designing the Course in Creative Writing" section of Patrick Bizzaro's chapter on mutuality.

An example of a smorgasbord approach would be to develop a service learning unit, a collaborative unit based on the ideas expressed in Jen Webb and Andrew Melrose's chapter, and a unit on digital technology that nods to the research presented here by Bronwyn Williams. In such a course, students would explore a great variety of methods of composing and presenting their creative writing. Another productive combination might join the generative exercises advocated in the rhetorical theory chapter (co-written by Tom and Sandra Giles) to response theories in Patrick Bizzaro's chapter on mutuality and Kate Kostelnik's chapter on writing center pedagogy. Such a course would provide a wealth of invention exercises and other activities designed to help students produce creative works as well as some thoughtful approaches for teachers and peers to respond to those works in progress. Or someone who wishes to design a course that challenges traditional notions of genre might combine elements of digital technology, creative literacy, and creative writing across the curriculum. Or an instructor who wishes to train writers to be socially conscious might combine elements of James Engelhardt and Jeremy Schraffenberger's chapter on ecopedagogy with elements of the chapters on service learning and mutuality.

Our target audience consists of graduate students, new creative writing teachers, and others who understand that teaching is no less of an art or skill than creative writing. We hope our book reaches those who believe that students deserve classroom practices derived from serious scholarship rather than from repeated viewings of *Dead Poet's Society* (on the one hand) or (on the other hand) from the macho, toxic "Bobby Knight School of writing pedagogy" that Stephanie Vanderslice describes in her chapter of *Does the Writing Workshop Still Work?*, edited by Dianne Donnelly (31). It is good for individual teachers, good for the profession, and above all good for students to have creative writing instructors reflecting upon and refining their practices. We are heartened to note that more new instructors are joining the conversation about creative writing pedagogy, as evidenced by the recent release of *Dispatches from the Classroom: Graduate Students on Creative Writing Pedagogy*, edited by Chris Drew, Joseph Rein, and David Yost. As more creative writing teachers take the time to consciously, carefully reflect on their teaching methods and course design, students will be more likely to develop as writers, and they will be more confident that their teachers are "in their corner instead of at the opposite side of the ring," as Clyde Moneyhun says, quoting John Butler, in the chapter on basic writing pedagogy. In addition to being good for students, this kind of dialog is good for instructors. In their chapter on collaborative pedagogy, Jen Webb and Andrew Melrose scrutinize the Romantic myth of the writer as "a solitary individual, shut away with typewriter or laptop," and they show how writers can flourish in community. Just as writers and their work can actually suffer from unhealthy social isolation, so can teachers of creative writing, and our target audience consists of those who seek the company and counsel of other writing teachers. In her chapter on writing center pedagogy, Kate Kostelnik recalls a prospective student asking her about "the product," what kind of work gets "produced" in her classes. We love her answer: "I explained that students are the products and that I don't fix drafts in a workshop; I give students the tools to work into their drafts." Similarly, we hope that the product of this book will be a cadre of new creative writing instructors who are more clear about their goals in the classroom, more confident in their ability to meet those goals, and happier and more excited about this discipline, this profession, than they were before turning these pages.

Alexandria Peary and Tom C. Hunley

Works Cited

Donnelly, Dianne, Tom C. Hunley, Anna Leahy, Tim Mayers, Dinty W. Moore, and Stephanie Vanderslice. "Creative Writing Can Be Taught: Creative Writing Professors Answer More Important Questions." *Huffington Post*. Web. 4 Feb. 2012.

Donnelly, Dianne, ed. *Does The Writing Workshop Still Work?* Bristol: New Writing Viewpoints, 2010. Print.

Drew, Chris, Joseph Rein, David Yost. *Dispatches from the Classroom: Graduate Students on Creative Writing Pedagogy.* London: Bloomsbury Academic, 2011.

Enos, Theresa. Telephone interview. 15 July 2010.

Mayers, Tim. "One Simple Word: From Creative Writing to Creative Writing Studies." *College English* 71.3 (Jan. 2009): 217–28. Print.

———. "Figuring the Future: Lore and/in Creative Writing." *Can It Really Be Taught? Resisting Lore in Creative Writing Pedagogy.* Ed. Kelly Ritter and Stephanie Vanderslice. Portsmouth, NH: Boynton/Cook, 2007. 1–13. Print.

Tate, Gary, Amy Rupiper, and Kurt Schick, eds. *A Guide to Composition Pedagogies.* Oxford, UK: Oxford UP, 2001. Print.

Vanderslice, Stephanie. "Once More to the Workshop: A Myth Caught in Time." *Does the Writing Workshop Still Work?* Ed. Dianne Donnelly. Bristol, UK: New Writing Viewpoints, 2010. 30–35.

1
Rhetorical Pedagogy

Tom C. Hunley and Sandra Giles

LET'S SAY THAT rhetoric is the art of persuasion. Or maybe it's the art of speaking well. Or maybe it concerns itself with the effects of language. Of meaning. Of how we humans convey meaning. And interpret it. Or misinterpret. Simple enough, huh?

Even the ancients didn't agree on a pinpointed definition. Many of them, including Aristotle and Cicero, emphasized persuasion, while Quintilian broadened it to speaking well in general (see Kennedy's *New History of Classical Rhetoric*). These days, the study of rhetoric includes not only genres of language use but also visual rhetoric, the rhetoric of advertising, the rhetoric of place. It has to do with meaning—the making of it and the interpreting of it. As Sandra tells her students, it's the study of how we humans construct and construe meaning. Of course, defining it that way is a deliberate rhetorical move that allows her to design a course to cover the genres of meaning-making she wants to cover.

When we in English departments define our subfields as creative writing *or* literature *or* cultural studies *or* composition *and/or* rhetoric— when we separate them the way they've come to be separated—we make a rhetorical move that has allowed us to reach a depth of development in each area, the kind of depth that specialization does foster. But there are drawbacks. Turf wars. Jockeying for position. Reinventing of the wheel. And, what should strike us creative writers in our hearts, failures of the imagination.

When a fellow writer and teacher says he doesn't need to know "all that theory stuff," by which he means practically everything except writing and reading poetry and fiction, what is it he's really saying? If rhetoric is the study of meaning, even in the particular sense of language use, then he's basically making the same argument (making the same rhetorical move) as an art student, for example, who says she doesn't need to know about the various types of brushes, or how paint is made. Or that she doesn't need to know how viewers will respond to this kind of color or that sort of texture. Who needs viewers, she says. All she needs to do is express her feelings and that's all there is to it.

Creative writing instructors struggle against such arguments daily, arguments which come not just from our students, but from our colleagues and administrators. We have to defend ourselves and our work, justify our place in the academy. Grounding what we do in rhetorical theory is one way to accomplish such a task. And grounding our pedagogy in both Greco-Roman rhetoric and the work of more recent rhetoricians would provide for our students a framework for deeper, richer training and understanding of the tools, the messages and methods and media, of their chosen art. This pedagogy is valuable because, to writers, rhetoric is, simply, everything.

A Short History of Creative Writing Studies
(and Its Relationship to Rhetoric)

Rhetoric, composition, and creative writing were not always considered separate fields. According to D. G. Myers, author of *The Elephants Teach: Creative Writing Since 1880*, creative writing and composition studies emerged together in academia and soon parted ways, pursuing separate goals and separate pedagogies. Interestingly, Myers locates the seeds of today's creative writing programs in the first modern composition courses, the "Advanced Composition" courses taught at Harvard in the late nineteenth century by Dean Le Baron Briggs, Charles Townsend Copeland, Adams Sherman Hill, and Barrett Wendell. He goes on to describe a push-back against the production of literary texts in composition courses. As a result of this push-back, "English Composition was pulled in the direction of proficiency, starting to become what we would now call a service course" (66). This left a void that would be filled by the emergence of creative writing programs. The influence of rhetoric on composition studies, sometimes referred to as rhet/comp or comp/rhet, has ebbed and flowed since the 1880s. The same

8

is true for rhetoric's influence on creative writing studies. At the moment, rhetoric holds a good deal of sway over composition studies but is generally seen as peripheral to creative writing studies.

It seems evident to us that rhetoric has positively impacted composition studies in recent decades, and we believe that creative writing studies could also benefit greatly from conscious applications of rhetoric. In his essay "Rhetorical Pedagogy," a chapter in *A Guide to Composition Pedagogies*, William A Covino writes that "a 'return' to *rhetoric*, specifically, the history of rhetoric" has recently taken place within composition studies, a dialectic pendulum swing away from expressivist pedagogy, with its "language games, koans, epigrams, and psychedelic pictures" (36). Something like expressivism is the dominant mode of creative writing instruction, and Wendy Bishop shows, in *Released into Language*, how conscious applications of expressivist pedagogy can benefit workshop leaders who are inclined to use it. More often, we're concerned that the similarity between workshop practice and expressivist pedagogy is coincidental. While we may not go as far as Jed Rasula, who has suggested that the emphasis on self-expression in many workshops owes more to "the rise of the self-help publishing market" than to any legitimate pedagogical theories (Dawson 121), we have each witnessed creative writing courses that devolved into extended exercises in navel gazing rather than rigorous training in challenging art forms. As creative writing instructors, we're interested in exploring all avenues that challenge our students to see how much discipline and craft is involved in the undertaking. We find that many young poets, apprentice writers of creative nonfiction, and even some novice fiction writers think it's enough to write diary entries about their important thoughts and feelings. We believe that a return to rhetoric could be one way of showing that creative writers have to master as much technique as ballet dancers or oboists.

In this chapter, we intend to show how creative writing has been treated as a branch of rhetoric in other eras and what today's classrooms can gain from a return to the practice. In her 2009 study, "The Licensing of the Poetic in Nineteenth-Century Composition-Rhetoric Textbooks," Alexandria Peary notes that Samuel P. Newman's 1839 *A Practical System of Rhetoric: Or the Rules and Principles of Style* "links imagination to the study of rhetoric" (W162). Peary goes on to argue that the road to today's creative writing courses was paved, in part, by increased attention to figurative language in late-nineteenth-century composition courses (W150). The study of figurative language, the cataloguing of tropes, schemes, and figures, has been a favorite pastime of rhetoricians going as far back as Aristotle—so rhetoric

9

had a hand in the early development of creative writing as an academic discipline. Additionally, from roughly 1890 to 1910, Brander Matthews taught a course at Columbia called "metrical rhetoric," which, he said, "was designed to parallel the prescribed courses in the theory and practice of rhetoric, my intention being to tempt the students into various kinds of verse-making" (Myers 70). Again we see one of the forerunners of creative writing studies treating the subject as a branch of rhetoric.

Myers recognizes rhetorical underpinnings in George Pierce Baker's famous "47 Workshop" in playwriting taught at Harvard from 1906 until 1925 and satirized by Thomas Wolfe in *Of Time and the River.* "The problem facing a current dramatist is how to adapt the essentials to the public of his time. If this sounds rhetorical Baker does not flinch: 'the dramatist shapes his material more and more in relation to the public he wishes to address, for a dramatist is, after all, a sort of public speaker'" (69). We believe that creative writers of all sorts could potentially reach larger audiences if they were taught to think of themselves this way, as public speakers of sorts. But, as Myers shows, the traces of rhetorical theory evident in Baker's statement above were erased in the first courses labeled "Creative Writing," which were taught in junior high schools, circa 1920s, by William Hughes Mearns, one of Baker's pupils. Mearns promoted a more holistic, expressivist pedagogy, impacted, according to Myers, by progressive educational reformer Thomas Dewey's belief that "self-expression is of vital necessity to the human being" (105). Like the proto-creative writing taught at Harvard in advanced composition courses, which aimed not to train professional creative writers but rather viewed itself as a means to teach literature by showing students what kinds of decisions literary artists make (109, 111, 123), the goal of Mearns's pedagogy was something other than professional training:

> Schoolchildren everywhere were invited to try their hands at poetry, but the business of making professional poets—something with which Hughes Mearns had never had the least interest—was left to take care of itself. Other people were more interested, but they did not believe it sufficient merely to liberate the talent of young poets. They also believed in criticism. And so they started the business of making professional poets by drawing up a partnership between criticism and creative writing. (121)

That's the workshop model, as we know it, in a nutshell: a combination of the self-expression taught in junior high school by William Hughes Mearns in the 1920s and the New Critical practices, such as close reading, that were *au courant* in literary studies in the 1940s and 1950s.

In *The Iowa Writers' Workshop: Origins, Emergence, and Growth*, Stephen Wilbers shows this movement away from rhetoric in favor of a more artist-centered workshop approach that applied New Critical principles to student-generated texts. Wilbers credits Iowa City's nineteenth-century nonacademic literary societies and writers' clubs devoted to "the development of rhetorical and oratorical skills" (19), in part, with paving the way for the Workshop. Wilbers refers to these activities as "peripheral to the actual creation of literature" (19) and recalls that they were overtaken by writers' clubs who pioneered the workshop method "by allowing each member to have a turn reading his or her original work, after which the group would respond with suggestions and literary criticism" (20). How might the history of creative writing studies look if some writers' club leader or one of the Workshop's founding professors had applied some of the literary societies' rhetorical principles to creative writing instruction? Although we concede that the literary societies themselves were probably not producing publishing writers (or even attempting to do so), it does not follow that some of their methods could not have been conducive to that end, that these methods could not, in fact, have proven far superior to the workshop method that grew out of the writers' clubs.

"But creative writing is new" Myers insists (13), pointing out the nineteenth-century origins of the term, which he traces to one of Emerson's essays. To us, that's a little like arguing that the English language didn't exist until "English" made its first appearance in the Harvard course catalogue in 1868–69 (20). Myers concedes that an earlier tradition of teaching verse writing existed, but oddly argues that these efforts were not creative writing per se because the goal "was to produce human beings, not poets" (14). Be that as it may, Greek, Roman, Elizabethan, and Metaphysical poets alike studied tropes and figures, wrote stylistic imitations, and learned complex memory systems using pedagogical applications of rhetorical theory.

Perhaps what's truly new about creative writing and its role in academia is the notion that it provides a relatively painless way for publishing writers to earn a living, a kind of replacement for the patronage system of previous eras. Myers quotes Kingsley Amis and others lamenting the way creative writing has been "ridiculed" by other academics who perceive it as a soft discipline (3). Paul Dawson observes the same phenomenon in *Creative Writing and the New Humanities*, wherein he quotes a 2002 article by

Marjorie Perloff in which that leading poetry critic dismisses creative writing programs as "anti-intellectual and separatist" (125) and Myers cites "an antischolarly animus" (16) as a precipitating factor in the development of the first creative writing programs. Many MFA programs have stayed true to these antischolarly origins, churning out graduates who don't want to be scholars, academics, or intellectuals—although a large percentage do aspire to become professors. The strange antiacademic stance adopted by many university workshop leaders is evident in statements by some of the pioneering founders of graduate-level creative writing programs. For example, Norman Foerster, to whom Stephen Wilbers and D. G. Myers give the most credit for the establishment of the Iowa Writers' Workshop in the 1930s, said "I would have the writer go to college, but I would not have him become what we call an 'academic'" (Myers 134). To this day, the official position of the Iowa Writers' Workshop is, according to a recent brochure, "Though we agree in part with the popular insistence that writing cannot be taught, we exist and proceed on the assumption that talent can be developed, and we see our possibilities and limitations as a school in that light" (Dawson 11). We believe this sort of disclaimer is designed to give creative writing instructors an easy way out. Claiming that creative writing can't be taught frees instructors from the rigors of figuring out how to articulate and pass on what they know about it. Freed from that responsibility, they can teach their unteachable subject in the most expedient ways possible and turn the bulk of their time to their all-important novels, short stories, and poems. We believe that the pervasive view that creative writing teachers are writers first and teachers second (a distant second) has led to a lot of unreflective, destructive pedagogy that has let students down, made teachers' jobs unnecessarily frustrating, and hurt the reputation of creative writing studies as an academic discipline. One way out of this mess, in our view, is to consciously study rhetoric and seek ways to apply it to our field, just as folks in composition studies have done.

According to Dawson, some apologists for creative writing programs have attempted to answer their detractors by tracing the discipline back to "the composition of Latin and Greek verses as part of rhetorical instruction in the classical languages" (48). We view most contemporary creative writing instruction as decisively severed from that tradition, but we're heartened to see traces of an emerging understanding that a return to the rhetorical tradition will benefit creative writing students and add legitimacy to creative writing as an academic discipline.

Old School: Greco-Roman Rhetoric, Medieval Rhetoric, and the Creative Writing Classroom

How, specifically, would a return to rhetoric affect creative writing studies? What would a rhetoric-based creative writing class look like? Can we really base our pedagogy on the ideas of long-gone folks like Isocrates, Aristotle, Cicero, and Quintilian—thinkers who lived in a very different world from our own? In "Notes on Rhetorical History as a Guide to the Salvation of American Reading: A Plea for Curricular Change," James J. Murphy points out that "Shakespeare as a schoolboy studied in a way that would have been familiar to Cicero, Seneca, Tacitus, Horace, and Vergil. In the next century the poet John Milton did the same" (6). The main thrust of Murphy's essay is that reading instruction and writing instruction have, fairly recently, been severed, and his plea is for a return to rhetoric as a way to stitch reading and writing instruction back together. In *Classical Rhetoric in English Poetry*, Brian Vickers argues that canonized writers from Ovid to Shakespeare and John Dryden "believed that rhetoric was *the* important discipline for a writer" (15). It's not hard to see why these great poets might have taken this position. The study of rhetoric can help poets think of the relationship between audience and purpose; it can help them become more sophisticated and imaginative in their use of tropes and schemes; it can provide a means to developing a poetic voice and synthesizing an original style; it can help poets think of new ways to begin, shape, and revise poems; and it can teach them to give more dynamic public readings of their work.

To readers who object that these writers lived in an entirely different world from our own, we offer Walt Whitman's self-education as a more recent example of a literary writer whose training was based on rhetoric. Whitman's poetry differs so greatly from that of his contemporaries largely because he ignored them, choosing instead to model his work on the oratorical stylings of political orators such as Daniel Webster, suffragists such as Fanny Wright, and preachers such as Henry Ward Beecher (Reynolds, 168–69, 219, 173). We wonder if those twentieth- and twenty-first-century writers who have developed in writing workshops would have been even better if a rhetoric-based pedagogy were in place. We also wonder how many would-be Whitmans, Shakespeares, Drydens, Ovids, and Miltons gave up writing because the teaching methods of their workshop leaders didn't serve them well.

For some instructors, a return to rhetoric might mean a minor change for creative writing studies, such as continuing to workshop stories and poems during most class sessions while adjusting our terminology to include frequent considerations of Aristotle's appeals (ethos/ethical appeal, logos/ rational appeal, and pathos/emotional appeal). It might mean coaching workshop participants on how to focus on a literary work's impact on its potential audience, the "inter-relationships among a speaker, a writer, and his [or her] message" (Corbett, "Enabling Discipline" 27). For other instructors, a return to the ancient art of rhetoric as a parent discipline might mean chucking the workshop model altogether. For these instructors, a return to rhetoric could mean, among other things, developing writing prompts based on Cicero's *Topica*, an elaboration on Aristotle's checklist of ways to "turn up any material for the development of one's subject" (Corbett, *Classical Rhetoric* 97). They may also find it beneficial to develop creative writing exercises based on the progymnasmata, "a highly structured, approved way of narrowing, amplifying, describing, praising, criticizing, comparing, proving, and refuting something" (Kennedy 27).

The "cornerstone of the study of rhetoric" (Bizzell and Herzberg 3) is a taxonomy known as the *five canons* (sometimes alternatively called the *five domains, five parts,* or *five offices*). The five canons are ubiquitous in textbooks on rhetoric. In her essay "Classical Practice and Contemporary Basics," Susan Miller offers a brief summary of this taxonomy:

> The five domains of rhetoric, for Aristotle and for all the other ancients, were invention, or the discovery of the content of a discourse; arrangement, or deciding in what order to present the content invented; style, or the diction, schemes, tropes, and figures of elegant sentences; memory, or the skill of memorizing what would later be spontaneous and engaging; and delivery, or the control of stance, voice, posture, and audience contact. (50)

We will now briefly examine each of the five canons and consider their possible applications to creative writing pedagogy. (Readers interested in a fuller exploration of what a five-canon creative writing class might look like—specifically a course in poetry writing—are encouraged to check out Tom's 2007 *Teaching Poetry Writing: A Five-Canon Approach.*)

First up is invention (Latin *inventio*, Greek *heuresis*). Aristotle's three modes of persuasion (ethos/ethical appeal, logos/rational appeal, and pathos/emotional appeal) fall under this heading. These are the three ways that a rhetor, whether in oratory or in composition, attempts to persuade audiences or readers to accept his or her point of view. Aristotle famously defined rhetoric as "an ability, in each case, to see the available means of persuasion" (36). The purpose of a literary work is rarely simply to persuade someone to hold a different belief about a given subject; however, we would argue that literary works do aim to persuade, in a sense. The purpose of a lyric poem might be to evoke a particular feeling in readers, and that is a form of persuasion. Similarly, a fiction writer must persuade his or her readers to suspend disbelief. Some awareness of Aristotle's modes of persuasion could help in that regard.

The ancient rhetoricians considered rhetoric "an offshoot of logic, the science of human reasoning" (Corbett, *Classical Rhetoric* 97) and they held the first appeal, *logos*, higher than the others. While literary writing is not necessarily bound by syllogistic reasoning, a poem or story will not be persuasive if its internal logic isn't consistent, and creative writers could benefit from some consideration of logical fallacies. The second appeal, *ethos*, consists of efforts to win favor with audiences or readers by showing that you are an authority and/or a person of good will. In his *Institutes of Oratory*, Quintilian put it this way: "For he who would have all men trust his judgment as to what is expedient and honorable, should possess and be regarded as possessing genuine wisdom and excellence of character" (Corbett, *Classical Rhetoric* 80). Ethos in a poem might come from the deft handling of a difficult form or from an apt allusion. In fiction, ethos could refer to the believability of characters and their actions, the authority of being able to create a story so that readers willingly suspend belief. Also, fiction writers and writers of creative nonfiction derive their ethos from their ability to get the details right—what Eudora Welty, in *One Writer's Beginnings*, calls "getting your moon in the right part of the sky." Finally, the third appeal, *pathos*, would seem to have a particularly strong role in making a literary work persuasive, as pathos is the appeal to those faculties that are beyond the conscious will of readers. If creative writing instructors want their students to write poems that give readers goose bumps or stories that transport readers to strange, new worlds, it makes sense for them to devote some class time to discussions of pathos.

The topics (or *topoi*) laid out in Aristotle's *Topica* and Cicero's *Topica* are used as invention strategies in composition courses. In her composition textbook, *Work in Progress: A Guide to Academic Writing and Revising*, one of Lisa Ede's recommended strategies for invention is to use five of Aristotle's topics (definition, comparison, relationship, circumstance, and testimony) as "a means to confront an intellectual problem" and "to discover and explore ideas about a subject." Perhaps the topoi could help creative writing students tap their imaginations in the same way they help composition students clarify their intellectual arguments.

Earlier we mentioned the progymnasmata, a group of invention exercises that were part of the Greek technê, handbooks dating at least far back as the first century A.D. (Kennedy 26–27). Of the fourteen categories of progymnasmata, at least six could easily be applied in creative writing classrooms: *mythos*, or fable (think of Anne Sexton's *Transformations*); *gnome* (Latin *sententia*) in which students recommend or disprove an aphorism; *enkomiom*, or praise (likely the origin of the ode); *psogos*, or blame (as in the now little-used poetic subgenre of curse poems); and *ekphrasis* or description (most often of a work of art). In addition to their uses as means for kick-starting poems, these could work as starting points for works of fiction. In fact, they were used that way in the ancient world. Graham Anderson has observed that "From the very first exercise in the progymnasmata, sophists could expect to be trained in the art of telling stories" (156).

The second canon is arrangement (Latin *disposition*, Greek *taxis*). If invention has to do with forming arguments, arrangement involves putting them in the order that gets them across most clearly and forcefully. We see tons of possible applications to creative writing courses in the form of classroom exercises and discussions about topics ranging from whether to structure a story chronologically or to begin a story *in medias res*; how to effectively open and end a poem or story; whether to write about a given subject in free verse or in a fixed form; and how to arrange stories or poems into coherent, publishable manuscripts.

The third canon, style (Latin *elocutio*, Greek *lexis*), is not about what you say but how you say it. When Robert Frost wrote "All the fun's in how you say a thing" in his poem "The Mountain," he was, in a sense, addressing the third canon of rhetoric. Under the heading of style are such considerations as diction, syntax, word choice, virtues (such as clarity and decorum) and vices (such as archaic language and willful obscurity), sentence length and type, stylistic imitation, and the study of tropes and figures. In *Copia: Foundation of the Abundant Style*, Desiderius Erasmus demonstrates that there are an almost infinite number of different ways to make any given utterance by writing 150 variations on the sentiment "Your letter pleased me very much." Erasmus, a poet as well as a rhetorician, remarked that "this exercise is designed for the composition of verse as well" (609). We have found that excerpts from *Copia: Foundation of the Abundant Style* and *Exercises in Style* by Raymond Queneau (in which Queneau tells the same simple story ninety-nine very different ways) are eye-opening for apprentice poets and budding fiction writers alike.

The study of figurative language has been largely neglected in both composition studies and creative writing studies. In "Ciceronian Rhetoric and the Rise of Science: The Plain Style Reconsidered," S. Michael Halloran and Merrill D. Whitburn note that, despite the noble efforts of Richard Lanham, Edward P. J. Corbett, and others to restore "old fashioned rhetorical devices" to the curriculum, "most books omit even such basic stylistic techniques as antithesis, parenthesis, ellipsis, and climax" (68). Contemporary creative writing textbooks that do address figurative language typically give it short shrift, covering a few figures such as metaphor, simile, personification, and hyperbole, but little else. In contrast, Elizabethan-era poets such as Sidney, Spenser, and Shakespeare had at their disposal such treasure troves as Henry Peacham's 1577 *The Garden of Eloquence*, which listed 184 tropes and schemes. It's not that similar books aren't being compiled today; it's that they're not being utilized much in college writing classes. Richard Lanham's *A Handlist of Rhetorical Terms* is a wonderful resource that we would like to see used, to some extent, in creative writing courses. Another is Robert A. Harris's *Writing with Clarity and Style: A Guide to Rhetorical Devices for Contemporary Writers*.

More knowledge of tropes and schemes means more tools in a writer's toolkit. This is especially true for poets, for many of whom figurative language is a mother tongue. For example, a poetry instructor might ask students to write a poem that contains examples of *anaphora* (repetition at the beginnings of lines), *epistrophe* (repetition at the ends of lines), and *symploce* (repetition both at the beginnings and the ends of lines). Writers of creative prose, too, can benefit from more training in this area. For example, a fiction writing instructor skimming Lanham's book might quickly devise an assignment in which students begin a story with *diazeugma* (one subject with many verbs: e.g., "The dog trotted, leaped, barked, and landed") and end the same story with *antanagoge* (balancing an unfavorable aspect with a favorable one: e.g., "a flawed and broken man, but a happy one nonetheless"). As with any creative writing exercises, these may or may not lead to polished, publishable literary works, but we would argue that the process is more important than the literary product. That is, even if students abandon the works written via these means, they will have spent some time learning different ways to use language figuratively and different ways to construct sentences and/or lines while constructing arguments in time-honored ways.

Malcolm X, Benjamin Franklin, and Somerset Maugham are just a few American writers who learned to write via one of the staple techniques of the ancient rhetorical treatises: conscious stylistic imitation (Latin *imitatio*, Greek *mimesis*). In "Teaching Style: A Possible Anatomy," compositionist Winston Weathers outlines a four-step format for imitation exercises: *recognize, copy, understand,* and *imitate* creatively. Daniel Alderson recommends a very similar format in his 1996 poetry writing textbook, *Talking Back to Poems,* as does in Nicholas Delbanco in the fiction writing textbook *The Sincerest Form: Writing Fiction by Imitation.* Like painters, musicians, and other artists, writers frequently have animated conversations with one another about their influences. The ancient art of stylistic imitation provides a mechanism for consciously learning aspects of craft from other writers. It makes our reading time more productive, enabling us to read as writers.

With a little ingenuity, creative writing instructors should be able to find applications for the fourth canon, memory (Latin *memoria*, Greek *mnēmē*). In 1235, Boncompagno da Signa declared "that memory did not belong to rhetoric alone but was useful for all subjects" (Yates 4). Medieval rhetoricians devised the loci mnemonic, an amazing system for memorizing huge chunks of text. We don't think today's creative writing instructors need to get carried away and burden their students with that complex memory system, but they could spend some class time having students memorize poems and favorite passages of prose. This could help them more easily make allusions, it could pack the rhythms of excellent writings into their heads and enable them to subconsciously reproduce those rhythms in their own writing, and it could help them consider what features make writing (their own writing and that of others) more memorable.

Finally, we arrive at the fifth canon of rhetoric, delivery (Latin *pronuntiatio*, Greek *hypokrisis*). Creative writing instructors can spend class time on delivery, showing students how to better declaim literary works orally, as in public readings. They can also use this fifth canon as a lens for considering concerns with how literary works look on the virtual or real page. What book aficionado hasn't attended a public reading by a favorite author, hoping that an inhabited, animated presentation by the writer would bring the text even closer to home, only to be disappointed by the author's fidgeting, lack of eye contact, and/or monotone? Who hasn't opened a literary journal with excitement, only to immediately slam it shut after seeing tiny fonts and off-putting illustrations? Training in delivery to the rescue!

Modern and Contemporary Rhetoric

From Classical times through the nineteenth century, rhetoric went through a number of promotions and then demotions (see chapter 1 of Foss, Foss, and Trapp's *Contemporary Perspectives on Rhetoric* for a particularly good encapsulation). By the nineteenth century, rhetoric gained the reputation of being mostly a study of style (Foss, Foss, and Trapp 13) with long lists of tropes and sentence styles to be memorized. We don't necessarily care that students memorize lists of names of the tropes and sentence styles, but they need to be able to write and interpret them.

Contemporary rhetorical theorists, particularly I. A. Richards, Ernesto Grassi, Richard Weaver, and Kenneth Burke have argued that content and style are inseparable, that style is part of content and vice versa. Change one and you change the other. In other words, style is not decoration like the sprinkles on a cupcake's icing, but a fundamental part of the cupcake itself. We need classroom discussions and activities to help students see this principle in action.

Ivor Armstrong (I. A.) Richards, whose rhetorical theories involve the study of what causes understanding or misunderstanding, argues that metaphor is of central importance to understanding. Contrary to Aristotle, who considered metaphor a special and exceptional use of language, something that could not be taught but was a knack a rhetor either had or didn't, Richards defines metaphor as part of the human thought process itself. His semantic triangle (see Ogden and Richards) consists of a Referent (dog, for example) and a Symbol (the word *dog*), with a Thought or Reference at the top (the connotations in the listener's mind, based on previous experience). If misunderstanding occurs when a listener lacks the same connotations or common experience, then metaphor can signal to the listener what the communicator intends. As presented in works such as *Principles of Literary Criticism* and *The Philosophy of Rhetoric*, metaphor to Richards is "the means by which meaning is developed" and also "a method by which a communicator may provide listeners with the experience needed to elicit similar references for a particular symbol" (Foss, Foss, Trapp 33). Richards presents the terms literary critics still use to deepen discussion of metaphor—*tenor* and *vehicle*—and the idea that metaphor works "through disparity as well as through likeness" (*Interpretation in Teaching* 133). Fill-in-the-blank exercises seem to indicate metaphor as simple decoration, without the depth and grounding that are possible with more thoughtful, more fully developed activities.

Ernesto Grassi also rehabilitates our view of metaphor. In medieval rhetoric, he argues in *The Primordial Metaphor*, metaphor was seen as obscuring or obstructing truth, attaching itself to the superficial image. But in the humanist tradition, according to Grassi, metaphor discloses "what rational thought and discourse are unable to unveil" (*Renaissance Humanism* 114). For him, metaphor is a basic function inherent in language: "Language is fundamentally a process of connecting a symbol to an experience" (paraphrased in Foss, Foss, Trapp 67). Metaphor performs an inventive function that rational speech cannot, a function that allows the seeing of new relationships and always engages the particulars of situations rather than universals and generalizations. How often do we ask our writers to be concrete rather than abstract? How difficult is it for the rational, academically trained mind to do that? Metaphor, Grassi argues, is an apt, perhaps the most apt, method. Again, those fill-in-the-blank exercises simply aren't up to the task because they lack depth and complexity.

As stated before, what we need are activities dealing with all sorts of figurative language, not just metaphor, that ground the learning writer in a deeper experience of how the trope functions in a writing situation, how it creates meaning. This is true not just of tropes but also of grammatical study itself. When it comes to sentence styles, a study of Richard Weaver's grammatical categories will help the writer attune to varieties of meaning that result from choosing one type of sentence over the others. For example, a simple sentence "tends to emphasize the discreteness of phenomena within the structural unity" (*The Ethics of Rhetoric* 119), while a complex sentence "does not stop with seeing discrete classes as co-existing, but distinguishes them according to rank or value, or places them in an order of cause and effect" (120–21). Weaver also examines the rhetorical effect of parts of speech: "Nouns deal with essences, which have a higher degree of being than actions or qualities" (127–28), while adjectives do not have as much force and are secondary in importance. To Weaver, a style that relies heavily on adjectives indicates "a lack of confidence about essences and reality on the part of the rhetor" (129). A writing style that uses a lot of verbs is vigorous because "it reflects the rhetor's ability to label the quality of an action while at the same time recognizing the essence of a state of being" (135–36). A rhetor's choice of sentence style and part of speech directly creates the degree of force desired. It would be much more useful to design class activities and discussions around the rhetorical functions of grammatical choices rather than memorizing and naming the categories. This is applicable, we argue, not just for the creative writing class, but for composition and other writing and communication courses as well. Style is often ignored in these other settings, too, or it gets bogged down in lessons on terminology and taxonomy.

Richards's work on the causes of misunderstanding can lead to refinements on existing exercises dealing with dialogue and scene, which are obviously relevant to fiction writing but could also be made relevant to the other creative genres. In an interview with Reuben Brower, Richards posits that people "could not possibly *say* what they *meant*" (20). This is something dialogue writers know all too well. But in class, instead of throwing students into "write a scene in which two characters misunderstand each other," we can ground the exercise with a preparatory discussion of what conditions can cause what kinds of misunderstanding. Keith Jensen explains:

> Misunderstanding may occur . . . if the communicators do not agree about the subject of their interaction (indicating), do not realize the implications of what is being said (realizing), do not accept the proposals that are offered (influencing), do not understand or will not agree about the way in which a proposal should be carried forward (controlling), or do not agree about the purpose of their interaction (purposing). (paraphrased in Foss, Foss, and Trapp 31)

A creative writing instructor could design a series of dialogue and scene exercises based on the above conditions for misunderstanding.

We could ask students to use irony and/or humor very deliberately to undercut some aspect of the society about which they are writing, say the pressure for conformity, for example. In speech-act theory, every speech act, every utterance—whether verbal or nonverbal—has intention, and one cannot know the meaning of the speech act until one knows the context and the intention. For Jürgen Habermas, a number of criteria must be met for a speech act to be competent or successful: equal access and equal ability to use speech; lack of constraints on the discussion; free ability for self-expression of attitudes, feelings, intentions, and motives; and rules, obligations, and norms that all participants make and abide by equally. Habermas admits that such would be the ideal situation, rarely occurring in life (Horster and van Reijen 97). So what would happen if one or more of these criteria were not met in a scene or dialogue? This provides another rich basis for a set of scene and dialogue activities. Critics of Habermas bring up a question that could be yet another springboard for an exercise: what happens for individuals whose preferred mode of "managing differences" is not discussion (see Foss, Foss, and Trapp 252)? These theories could ground a common exercise into which students are often thrown without much preparation: to design a "dialogue" where nothing is actually said between the characters. One particular critic of Habermas, John Peters, points out that Habermas ignores how use of tropes such as humor, irony, and metaphor "have the capability of sensitizing us to the oppressiveness of whatever categorical distinctions are dominating our thought and social interaction" (qtd. in Foss, Foss, Trapp 253). It seems that the critics of Habermas have almost as much to offer us as he does himself. Here is another opportunity to delve deeply into the rhetorical effects of figures and to approach style as part of content.

These are just a few ways in which contemporary rhetoric could be used in creative writing instruction. There are more, of course. Kenneth Burke's pentad could easily be adapted for idea generation or scene-building. When it comes to fiction's building of characters and worlds, the works of Burke, Jean Baudrillard, and Mikhail Bakhtin would be helpful, as well as additional work by Richard Weaver and Ernesto Grassi. Creative nonfiction writers could learn from these folks how to render and think on the worlds and people about which they're writing. Our section here on dialogue construction could also address the issue of argumentation, where the works of Chaim Perelman and Lucie Olbrechts-Tyteca, Stephen Toulmin, and Burke are relevant. Toulmin and his colleague Jonsen provide advice and justification to poets and prose writers who wish to address topical issues: "moral experience does not lie in a mastery of general rules and theoretical principles." Instead, it "comes from seeing how the ideas behind those rules work out in the course of people's lives" (*The Abuse of Casuistry* 314). An idea for a dialogue or scene exercise would be to explore "what is involved in insisting on (or waiving) this or that [moral] rule in one or another set of circumstances" (314). This is what we creative writing instructors mean when we tell students to *explore* a topical issue, such as when an abortion might be justifiable, and not try to *persuade* the reader. But contemporary takes on the issue of how to define and what constitutes persuasion are complex.

And, of course, anyone serious about teaching narrative technique should see Wayne Booth's *The Rhetoric of Fiction* and "Distance and Point of View," where he argues that types of narrators are a better focus for both writers and critics than point of view. Beginning writers often struggle to understand the varied effects of point of view on style, scene, narration, etc., perhaps because first/second/third person is too simplistic to be of much help.

In this chapter we address the question of what a rhetorically informed creative writing pedagogy might look like, how it might function in the writing course. Our limited space here allows us only to scratch the surface of the wealth of possibilities. In addition to inspiring invention and drafting activities, many of these rhetorical theories could also stimulate revision, leading writers back into their works by providing analytical frameworks as an antidote to the dictum teachers often give to "go revise," which seems to mean "go fix everything all at once," which is overwhelming at best.

Rhetoric has been defined numerous ways. In *The Philosophy of Rhetoric*, I. A. Richards defines it as "a philosophic discipline aiming at a mastery of the fundamental laws of the use of language" (7). In *The Ethics of Rhetoric*, Richard Weaver defines it as "truth plus its artful presentation" (15). For bell hooks, rhetoric should help eradicate "the ideology of domination that pervades Western culture" (*Talking Back* 19). For Kenneth Burke it is "the use of words by human agents to form attitudes or to induce actions in other human agents" (*A Rhetoric of Motives* 41). Burke also sees rhetoric as *"rooted in an essential function of language itself . . . the use of language as a symbolic means of inducing cooperation in beings that by nature respond to symbols"* (43, emphasis ours). For him, the field serves to name and define situations. A speech or story or poem, then, is "a *strategy for encompassing a situation*" (*The Philosophy of Literary Form* 109, emphasis ours). Situations, intentions, motives, power, language, words, sentences, metaphors—these are the tools in the writer's toolbox, a common metaphor we use to describe the "tools" of our trade. In *On Writing: A Memoir of the Craft*, Stephen King presents several layers of such tools available to use in our boxes and laments, echoing Amy Tan, that no one much talks about the language anymore. He's right. But, to echo Richards, our toolbox metaphor tells us as much by disparity as anything else: our writer's tools are not tangible objects that exist outside of us in some objective "reality." Situations, intentions, motives, power, and language are what we do as writers, and what we do becomes what we are made of, which becomes what we are (see Habermas). Contemporary rhetoricians posit that we are symbol-using creatures, and as such, once we created the symbol system, we can never be free of it (see Burke). We read the world mediated through language, not directly through our senses, and so literature becomes a project in rescuing for us the concrete. According to Grassi, "the problem of every philosophical system is to make its reasonings concrete, to keep the system in touch with the world" and so literature is "thus a way of forming meaning without losing the details of an event" (qtd. in Foss, Foss,

Trapp 64). Students of nonfiction writing often ask what the difference is between what we do in the way of nonfiction, in a creative writing class, as opposed to what they may have done in composition or journalism class. Sometimes, there is no difference. Sometimes, there is overlap. But what makes creative nonfiction creative? Grassi provides an answer for us here. It is to render a meaning through the concrete, through the particular experience in all its particular details. This is also the technique that renders good fiction and good poetry.

As language-wielding creatures, also constituted by language, writers should be grounded in rhetorical theory, which should be as much a part of our education as reading the great works of the past or present. A thorough grounding in rhetoric would, as discussed in our introduction, add legitimacy to the field of creative writing by adding a lengthy history and a tradition of theory. Contemporary rhetoric does not make the same distinction between literature and other forms of writing that the *belles lettres* tradition of the nineteenth century did. In fact, contemporary rhetoric is sometimes faulted for supposedly overreaching its boundaries and addressing not only informative and persuasive rhetoric, but also literature, and shading over into the fields of history, psychology, sociology, and anthropology. It's syncretic. Creative writing, then, put together with this syncretic tradition of rhetoric and the tradition of literary critical studies, could help reunite "English Studies" in our colleges and universities.

But even if our point here overreaches a bit, we at the very least argue this: that rhetoric adds depth not only to the learning writer in learning his craft, but to the willing teacher in learning hers. This depth has often been missing in both aspects in the history of creative writing pedagogy.

Appendix: Classroom Applications

- Have students work on their writing styles through the ancient practice of *imitatio* or *mimesis*. First, have them copy a passage of poetry or prose that they admire. Next, have them write a brief rhetorical analysis, identifying the features of the piece of writing that draw them to it. After that, have them create a self-exercise based on what they noticed about the model text. Finally, have them write an original work, trying out the techniques that they observed in the model text.
- Provide students with a list of aphorisms such as "No good deed goes unpunished" (Ambrose Bierce) and "Genius is one percent inspiration and ninety-nine percent perspiration" (Thomas Alva Edison). Then, in

the spirit of *gnome* or *sententia* from the progymnasmata, ask them to write a poem, story, or piece of nonfiction that contradicts the aphorism.

- In *Copia: Foundations of the Abundant Style*, Renaissance-era rhetorician Desiderius Erasmus demonstrates the range of available styles by writing "Your letter pleased me very much" in 150 different styles. Show that to your students; then have them write a poem in which they make the statement fifteen or twenty different ways.

- Provide students with a list of tropes (such as *zeugma* and *antanaclasis*) and schemes (such as *symploce* and *hypallage*). Also give them some published poems that contain these tropes and schemes, and ask them to locate the tropes and schemes in the poems. Then have them write a poem in which they try out several tropes and/or schemes.

- Teach the fifth canon of rhetoric, delivery, by coaching students on appropriate physical gestures and vocal inflections to employ while reading their poems in public.

- First, freewrite or draft a poem or scene. Then go back, see what's happening in the piece, and feel where a periodic and/or cumulative sentence would create a desired effect (see Harris, *Writing with Clarity and Style: A Guide to Rhetorical Devices for Contemporary Writers* for lists and examples). Write it in.

- First, read Orwell's essay "Shooting an Elephant," paying careful attention to his use of metaphor, particularly when he tells us the dead man is lying with "arms crucified" (44). Discuss how that metaphor was already built into the situation and Orwell simply had to recognize the possibilities and bring it to our attention with words. Then draft a poem, essay, or story (or take one you've already written) and find areas of meaning that are already there and can be deepened, brought more to the fore, by a metaphor or simile.

- Read the first two sentences of June Jordan's "Requiem for the Champ" and imagine other ways she could have punctuated them. Think about the differences in effect. Alternately, here's something your instructor could do for you. Instructors, take the first paragraph of that same essay. Retype it, removing all capital letters and punctuation. Have students re-punctuate the paragraph as they would like it to read. Have them compare and contrast their re-punctuated versions with each other. (For similar activities, see Wendy Bishop's *Acts of Revising: A Guide for Writers*).

- Here is a list of situations in which people can misunderstand each other (after Richards): They disagree on the topic they're discussing,

25

do not realize the implications of their actions or beliefs, do not want to do the same thing, do not agree about how to do something or how something should be done, or do not agree about why something should or should not be done. Write a dialogue that illustrates one or more of the above.

- Write a dialogue in which one person is very good at expressing himself or herself verbally but the other is not.
- Write a dialogue in which the verbal arguing has already played itself out, and what's left is all nonverbal.
- In the play *Tartuffe*, Moliere uses various forms of irony and humor to satirize some of the dominant pressures of late-seventeenth-century French society—religious conformity and hypocrisy, arranged marriages, rule by divine right, etc. What would you say are the dominant pressures in our society? Your hometown? Your school? Write a poem, story, essay, or play in which you use humor and various forms of irony to satirize some of these pressures.
- Take one of your works, maybe a poem, in which your impulse to write came from wanting to express your feelings. Write a reflection in which you first explore why you wanted to write it. Then, put yourself in the reader's shoes and explore why the reader would want to read it. What will he or she get from reading it? What writing techniques have you used to help the reader feel that experience?

Works Cited

Alderson, Daniel. *Talking Back to Poems: A Working Guide for the Aspiring Poet.* Berkeley: Celestial Arts Publishing, 1996. Print.

Anderson, Graham. *The Second Sophistic: A Cultural Phenomenon in the Roman Empire.* New York: Routledge, 1993. Print.

Aristotle. *On Rhetoric: A Theory of Civic Discourse.* Trans. George A. Kennedy. New York: Oxford UP, 1991. Print.

Bishop, Wendy, ed. *Acts of Revision: A Guide for Writers.* Portsmouth, NH: Boynton/Cook Heinemann, 2004. Print.

———. *Released into Language.* Urbana, IL: NCTE, 1991. Print.

Bizzell, Patricia, and Bruce Herzberg, eds. *The Rhetorical Tradition: Readings from Classical Times to the Present.* 2nd ed. Boston/New York: Bedford/ St. Martin's, 2001. Print.

Booth, Wayne. "Distance and Point of View: An Essay in Classification." *Essentials of the Theory of Fiction.* 2nd ed. Ed. Michael J. Hoffman and Patrick D. Murphy. Durham, NC: Duke UP, 1996. 116–33. Print.

———. *The Rhetoric of Fiction.* 2nd ed. Chicago: U of Chicago P, 1983. Print.

Brower, Reuben. "Beginnings and Transitions: I. A. Richards Interviewed by Reuben Brower." *I. A. Richards: Essays in His Honor.* Ed. Reuben Brower, Helen Vendler, and John Hollander. New York: Oxford UP, 1973. 17–41. Print.

Burke, Kenneth. *A Rhetoric of Motives.* New York: Prentice Hall, 1950. Print.

———. *The Philosophy of Literary Form: Studies in Symbolic Action.* Baton Rouge: Louisiana State UP, 1941. Print.

Corbett, Edward P. J. *Classical Rhetoric for the Modern Student.* 3rd ed. New York: Oxford UP, 1990. Print.

———. "Rhetoric, the Enabling Discipline." *The Writing Teacher's Sourcebook.* Ed. Edward P. J. Corbett, Nancy Myers, and Gary Tate. 4th ed. New York: Oxford UP, 2000. 26–35. Print.

Dawson, Scott. *Creative Writing and the New Humanities.* London: Routledge, 2005.

Delbanco, Nicholas. *The Sincerest Form: Writing Fiction by Imitation.* Boston: McGraw Hill, 2004. Print.

Ede, Lisa. *Work in Progress: A Guide to Academic Writing and Revising.* Boston: Bedford/St. Martin's, 2001. Print.

Erasmus, Desiderius. *Copia: Foundations of the Abundant Style.* Excerpted in Bizzell, Patricia, and Bruce Herzberg, eds. *The Rhetorical Tradition: Readings from Classical Times to the Present.* 2nd ed. Boston/New York: Bedford/St. Martin's, 2001.

Foss, Sonja K., Karen A. Foss, and Robert Trapp. *Contemporary Perspectives on Rhetoric.* 3rd ed. Prospect Heights, IL: Waveland, 2002. Print.

Grassi, Ernesto. *Renaissance Humanism: Studies in Philosophy and Poetics.* Trans. Walter F. Veit. Binghamton, NY: Medieval and Renaissance Texts and Studies, 1988. Print.

———. *The Primordial Metaphor.* Trans. Laura Pietropaulo and Manuela Scarci. Binghamton, NY: Medieval and Renaissance Texts and Studies, 1994. Print.

Halloran, Michael S. and Merrill D. Whitburn. "Ciceronian Rhetoric and the Rise of Science: The Plain Style Reconsidered." *The Rhetorical Tradition and Modern Writing.* Ed. James J. Murphy. New York: The Modern Language Association of America, 1982. 58–71. Print.

Harris, Robert A. *Writing with Clarity and Style: A Guide to Rhetorical Devices for Contemporary Writers.* Los Angeles: Pyrczak Publishing, 2003. Print.

hooks, bell. *Talking Back: Thinking Feminist, Thinking Black.* Boston: South End, 1989. Print.

Horster, Detlev, and Willem van Reijen. "Interview with Jürgen Habermas: Starnberg, March 23, 1979." Trans. Ron Smith. *New German Critique* 18 (Fall 1979): 29–43. Print.

Hunley, Tom C. *Teaching Poetry Writing: A Five-Canon Approach.* Clevedon, UK: Multilingual Matters LTD., 2007. Print.

———. *The Poetry Gymnasium: 94 Proven Exercises to Shape Your Best Verse.* Jefferson, NC: McFarland and Co., Inc., 2012. Print.

Jensen, Keith. "I. A. Richards and His Models." *Southern Speech Communication Journal* 37 (Spring 1972): 312. Print.

Jonsen, Albert R., and Stephen Toulmin. *The Abuse of Casuistry.* Berkeley: U of California P, 1988. Print.

Jordan, June. "Requiem for the Champ." *The Progressive* 1992. Print.

Kennedy, George A. *Classical Rhetoric and Its Christian and Secular Tradition from Ancient to Modern Times.* 2nd ed. Chapel Hill: U of North Carolina P, 1999. Print.

———. *A New History of Classical Rhetoric.* Princeton, NJ: Princeton UP, 1994. Print.

Kesey, Ken. *One Flew over the Cuckoo's Nest: Text and Criticism.* Ed. John Clark Pratt. New York: Viking Critical Library/Penguin, 1996. Print.

King, Stephen. *On Writing: A Memoir of the Craft.* New York: Pocket, 2001. Print.

Lahnam, Richard A. *A Handlist of Rhetorical Terms.* 2nd ed. Berkeley: U of California P, 1991. Print.

Miller, Susan. "Classical Rhetoric and Contemporary Basics." *The Rhetorical Tradition and Modern Writing.* Ed. James J. Murphy. New York: The Modern Language Association of America, 1982. 46–57. Print.

Murphy, James J. "Rhetorical History as a Guide to the Salvation of American Reading and Writing: A Plea for Curricular Courage." *The Rhetorical Tradition and Modern Writing.* Ed. James J. Murphy. New York: The Modern Language Association of America, 1982. 3–14. Print.

Myers, D. G. *The Elephants Teach: Creative Writing Since 1880.* 2nd ed. Chicago: U of Chicago P, 2006. Print.

Ogden, C. K., and I. A. Richards. *The Meaning of Meaning: A Study of the Influence of Language upon Thought and of the Science of Symbolism.* London: Kegan Paul, Trench, Trubner, 1923. Print.

Orwell, George. "Shooting an Elephant." *Creative Nonfiction: A Guide to Form, Content, and Style, with Readings.* Ed. Eileen Pollack. Boston: Wadsworth Cengage, 2010. 43–47. Print.

Peary, Alexandria. "The Licensing of the Poetic in Nineteenth-Century Composition-Rhetoric Textbooks." *College Composition and Communication* 61.2 (2009): W149–W176. Print.

Richards, I. A. *Interpretation in Teaching.* New York: Harcourt Brace. 1938.

——. *Principles of Literary Criticism.* London: Kegan Paul, Trench, Trubner, 1924. Print.

——. *The Philosophy of Rhetoric.* New York: Oxford UP, 1936. Print.

Reynolds, David S. *Walt Whitman's America: A Cultural Biography.* New York: A. A. Knopf, 1995. Print.

Vickers, Brian. *Classical Rhetoric in English Poetry.* London: MacMillan. 1970. Print.

Weathers, Winston. "Teaching Style: A Possible Anatomy." *College Composition and Communication* 21 (1970): 144–49. Print.

Weaver, Richard. *The Ethics of Rhetoric.* South Bend, IN: Henry Regnery, 1953. Print.

Welty, Eudora. *One Writer's Beginnings.* Boston: Harvard University Press, 1983.

Wilbers, Stephen. *The Iowa Writers' Workshop: Origins, Emergence, and Growth.* Iowa City: U of Iowa P, 1980.

Yates, Frances. *The Art of Memory.* Chicago: U of Chicago P, 1966.

Creative Writing and Process Pedagogy

Tim Mayers

"THERE IS AN ambiguity in the term *writing*," notes composition scholar Bruce Horner, "arising from its use to designate both an activity and the product of that activity" (209, italics in original). Creative writer and scholar Graeme Harper also notes this ambiguity: "When speaking about Creative Writing it is sometimes the case that we are speaking about two things. That is: the activities of Creative Writing *and* the finished works that emerge from the activities of Creative Writing" (2, italics in original). A rich and productive understanding of writing requires that we keep this ambiguity always in mind. Writing can be both a noun and a verb; writing harbors both static and dynamic dimensions; it is both *product* and *process*.

The product/process ambiguity is reflected in the way college and university English departments—as well as the scholarly field at large—are often divided into subfields. Literary studies is a product-oriented subfield. Its scholars and teachers approach texts as stable and static entities to be interpreted. And while literary studies can also produce new texts, such texts almost always exist in service to the notion that the "primary" texts being interpreted are stable, meaning-bearing entities. In literary studies, the writing of scholars and practitioners is regarded largely as an instrument for transmitting interpretive knowledge of *other* texts. Composition and creative writing, on the other hand, are process-oriented subfields. Their teachers, scholars, and practitioners approach texts—very often *students'* texts—as dynamic, unstable, and usually unfinished entities. Sometimes, in fact, creative writing and composition concern themselves with the very beginnings of writers' processes: those chaotic and often mysterious places where texts first emerge in the form of inspiration, idea, image, or sound. The process of writing, then, (at least at first glance) should be a concern shared by creative writing and composition, perhaps a strong enough connection to create a scholarly and practical alliance between them. Yet because creative writing and composition—especially in the United States—have developed in largely separate ways as part of the larger field of English studies, shared concerns cannot merely be acknowledged or wished for; they must be understood within the larger contexts of disciplinary and institutional history and politics. Without such considerations, inter- and intradisciplinary collaborations may not be fully and productively realized, since institutional history has erected certain barriers that cannot simply be ignored. This chapter aims to explore the possibilities that "process theory" as it has come to be known and articulated in composition studies might have something to offer for practitioners and teachers in creative writing, and that creative writers' understandings of process might be illuminating for teachers and scholars of composition. In order to realize those possibilities, we must first delve into a bit of institutional and scholarly history.

Process Theory, Pedagogy, and Composition: A Whirlwind History

"Process," it could be argued, is the concept upon which scholars and teachers founded the fledgling field of inquiry called "composition studies" in the United States. As with any such argument, there is a risk of oversimplifying the matter. On the other hand, though, it would be impossible to consider the formation of composition as an academic field without acknowledging the crucial conceptual power that *process* wielded.

In order to understand the emergence of composition studies as a scholarly field, it is important to grasp the "problem" its scholars and practitioners originally sought (and in some cases, still seek) to address. Put bluntly, the problem was (and is) that college students do not write well enough. Or, to be more specific, the problem was that a significant number of college and university faculty, administrators, and potential employers of college graduates *believed* that college students do not write well enough: not well enough to produce the kinds of academic papers their professors expect, not well enough to produce the varied forms and genres of writing their future (or present) employers expect. This problem started to become apparent after

31

the Civil War, when college and university curricula began to shift from a common core model (in which all students took exactly the same courses, often in the same order) to an elective model (in which students chose the area or areas in which they wished to focus their study, supplemented by "general education" requirements). As the core model slowly transformed into the elective model, the methods for assessing student learning changed as well. Oral declamations and disputations were slowly replaced by written assignments. And as students did more and more writing, professors and administrators became more and more dismayed. The students—nearly all of whom had come from the United States' most prestigious private preparatory schools—struck professors and administrators as so poorly prepared in writing that they bordered on "illiteracy."

During the last quarter of the nineteenth century, Harvard University sought to address the perceived problem of student writing by requiring all entering students to take a writing course. (Essentially what they did was to take an existing sophomore-level rhetoric course, focus it more on writing than on oral argumentation, and move it down to the freshman level.) Harvard's faculty and administration hoped this would be a temporary measure; they assumed that the existence of such a requirement at one of America's most prestigious universities would exert downward pressure on high schools and prep schools to do a better job of preparing students to write at the college level. What happened instead, though, was that by 1900 most other U.S. colleges and universities had followed Harvard's lead and established a required first-year composition course for all students. This course remained a fixture of American higher education throughout the twentieth century, and it remains so today. At any given time, there are probably fewer than two dozen institutions of higher learning in the United States that do *not* require all first-year students to take a composition course or to demonstrate writing proficiency deemed sufficient to exempt them from such a course.[1]

From the latter decades of the nineteenth century until the middle of the twentieth, college and university writing instructors in the United States approached the "problem" of student writing by trying to eliminate errors (usually grammatical ones) in students' assignments. The composition handbook—a compendium of grammar rules, sometimes with chapters on style, paragraph structures, and the rudiments of academic research conventions like the citation and listing of bibliographic sources—became a staple of collegiate writing instruction. Instructors often used numeric and alphabetic codes (keyed to chapters and sections in the handbook) to mark errors on student writing assignments. The underlying assumption seemed to be that students could use these codes to find their errors in the handbook, read or reread the relevant sections, and learn to correct and avoid these errors. Such instruction was often supplemented with grammatical and mechanical drills, sometimes replete with workbook fill-in-the-blank exercises that reminded many students of high school and elementary school.[2]

For a number of decades, it did not seem to matter to many teachers that this sort of instruction was not working; students continued to make grammatical errors in spite of the handbook codes and workbook drills. Educational research had long cast doubt on the value of such pedagogies anyway, at least since a study by Franklin Hoyt, published in 1906, that discovered only a tiny and statistically insignificant correlation between elementary school grammar instruction and the grammatical fluency of students when they reached high school (Rose 6). But it was probably not until the 1950s that public questioning of these accepted pedagogies by a few college professors began to emerge.

In 1953, a Purdue English professor named Barriss Mills (who was also a published poet and translator) published a *College English* article entitled "Writing as Process." Mills argued that college-level writing ped-agogy in the United States had failed largely because it treated writing in a "static, atomistic, and non-functional" way (19). Outside of classroom settings, Mills asserted, writers and readers are always guided by *purpose*; writers have specific reasons for writing, and these reasons guide virtually every choice they make, from the genres in which they write to the topics they write about to the stylistic and mechanical conventions they follow. Readers likewise have their own purposes for reading, and these purposes shape the expectations they have when approaching texts. In far too much school writing, however, this sense of purpose is missing. Writing seems intended only to display grammatical correctness and stylistic fluency, and these matters are divorced from any genuine sense of purpose, treated in isolation, and regarded as ends in and of themselves. A genuine rethinking of writing pedagogy, argued Mills, was the only way out of this malaise. Such a rethinking would have to focus first and foremost on *purpose*, and it would have to attend closely to the *processes* by which writers—estab-lished writers as well as student writers—produced their work. The "mass methods" of the past would not work. As much as possible, individualized instruction would have to be undertaken, attending to issues of grammar and style in the same manner as all other issues: as part of students' unique and evolving writing processes (25). In other words, any "problems" that appeared in student writing would ideally be treated *as they emerged*. A problem like subject-verb disagreement, for example, should be "treated" only for those students who consistently exhibited it in their own writing. And it would be dealt with not through drills and handbook study, but by attending to the specific situations in which it arose.

At least a decade would pass, though, before this concern with process gained a secure foothold within the professional discourses of composition teaching, and perhaps another decade still before any significant changes in pedagogy found their way into American college composition classrooms—at least on any widespread basis. Many historians of composition studies point to the 1963 meeting of the Conference on College Composition and Communication (CCCC) or the 1966 Anglo-American Seminar on the Teaching of English (held at Dartmouth College, and often referred to as "The Dartmouth Conference") as watershed moments in the development of a disciplinary identity for composition. At these meetings, scholars and teachers questioned received modes of pedagogy—and the assumptions behind them—more seriously than ever before, and the "process movement" was underway.

In the latter half of the 1960s and the entire decade of the 1970s, new modes of teaching writing—often guided by theory and research, but sometimes guided only by instructors' yearning for something new—began to appear in some classrooms. Handbooks and workbooks were discarded or pushed to the margins; invention exercises were used to help students generate ideas, begin texts, and work through writer's block; red-penned corrections of errors were replaced by individual conferences between instructors and students or peer-editing groups in which students themselves worked together through the processes of drafting, revising, and proofreading; students' papers were used as texts for the class, sometimes alongside the older models of "classic" essays, sometimes replacing those models entirely.

Two of the most visible figures in this process movement were Donald Murray and Peter Elbow, both of whom rose to prominence in the 1970s. In 1972, Murray (a newspaper reporter and fiction writer who taught at the University of New Hampshire) published "Teach Writing as a Process Not Product," a manifesto that neatly summed up some of the emerging practices and principles, including "The student should have the opportunity to write all the drafts necessary . . . to discover what he [sic] has to say on this particular subject" (6–7). The idea that drafting allows a writer to discover or clarify meaning, as opposed to having it completely grasped before writing begins, was crucial to the early process movement in composition. In 1973, Peter Elbow published his widely influential *Writing without Teachers*. In that book and elsewhere, Elbow championed "freewriting," an early drafting procedure in which the writer commits to writing without stopping for a period of time (usually ten to fifteen minutes) and without any immediate concern for grammar, spelling, coherence, or any of the other conventions of finished, polished writing. Many teachers and students found freewriting helpful in alleviating "writer's block." But even writers who did not feel "blocked" sometimes benefited from the texts generated through freewriting, which could later be revised, edited, and expanded.

In a 1982 *College Composition and Communication* article, Maxine Hairston of the University of Texas argued that the teaching of composition was in the beginning stages of a "paradigm shift." She borrowed this notion from the historian of science Thomas S. Kuhn, who in 1963 had published his groundbreaking *The Structure of Scientific Revolutions*. Acknowledging that Kuhn had not originally intended for the concept of the paradigm shift to apply to the social sciences or humanities, Hairston nonetheless asserted that it was useful as an analogy that would help teachers and scholars understand ongoing developments in composition ("Winds" 76). Basically, a paradigm shift starts to occur when a long-accepted way of looking at the discipline's object of study, or of looking at the world in general, begins to break down because new problems have emerged—or old problems have become more insistent—that cause practitioners to question conventional wisdom. A new paradigm takes hold because it can answer current questions or solve current problems in ways that the old one could not. In the teaching of composition, according to Hairston, the process movement, championed by a vanguard of teachers and theorists, had all the markings of a revolution in the making.

There were two related problems, though, according to Hairston, that prevented this revolution from progressing as quickly as it otherwise might. She put the matter quite bluntly:

> [T]he overwhelming majority of college writing teachers in the United States are not *professional* writing teachers. They do not research on rhetoric or composition, and they do not know the scholarship in the field. . . . They are trained as literary critics first and teachers of literature second, yet out of necessity most of them are doing half or more of their teaching in composition.

> And they teach it by the traditional paradigm, just as they did
> when they were untrained teaching assistants ten or twenty
> or forty years ago. Often they use a newer edition of the same
> book they used as teaching assistants. (78–79, emphasis mine)

The old paradigm to which Hairston refers is commonly called the "current traditional" view of writing, characterized by an excessive focus on grammar and style, as well as the underlying assumption that writers know everything about their topics before they begin to write. In other words, writing under this paradigm is conceived as an act of "translating" what one knows about an external reality in words (and in a format) that makes sense to readers. This stands in stark contrast to what researchers on the writing process have learned, namely that writers most often *discover* their meanings, or at least portions of them, only *as* they write. Hairston is essentially arguing—though she does not articulate the point in much detail in this particular article, beyond what I have cited here—that the very history of the discipline of English in the United States has hindered the development of a rich and pedagogically useful composition theory. That was the first problem: literature professors and the graduate students they produced had no real professional stake or interest in studying rhetoric and composition. The second problem, deeply related to the first, was that so many of these graduate students could only find jobs teaching composition, and once in the classroom they found themselves thoroughly unprepared for the problems they would face, and without the intellectual tools even to begin figuring a way out of the problem. Scholars in English had struggled mightily to establish literary study as the professional core of their discipline (replacing the older German-influenced philology) at the end of the nineteenth century and the beginning of the twentieth. But they had also grown the discipline largely on the strength of the fact that English departments were responsible for the teaching of composition. Half a century later, this left many English departments in a quandary. They were producing far more literary scholars than there were academic jobs teaching literature, and the old methods of teaching writing were not working, even as the problem of student writing grew more and more insistent.

Hairston was confident that the emergence of doctoral programs in rhetoric and composition, and the explosion of new writing research and knowledge they were producing, would begin to solve these problems. More people trained in the relevant scholarship and theory would go out into the world as writing program directors, and more graduate students in

English would receive training in composition pedagogy and theory, even if only as part of practica related to their teaching assistantships. By 1985, though, Hairston still saw the dominance of literary critics and theorists within English departments as a problem, and speculated that perhaps the goals of the process movement could best be fulfilled if rhetoric and composition specialists made a break with English and formed their own departments ("Breaking").

Sharon Crowley, looking back at the process movement during the 1990s, shared Hairston's concern with the dominance of literary study within English departments, but was far less cheerful about what had been accomplished by process-oriented writing theorists and teachers: "A truly paradigmatic alternative to current-traditionalism would question the modernism in which it is immersed and the institutional structure by means of which it is administered. Process pedagogy does neither" (212–13). In Crowley's view, process pedagogy and theory were not nearly as revolutionary as Hairston had hoped and believed they could be. They were, instead, too often grafted onto current-traditionalism and proved to be quite compatible with it. They did not challenge the underlying—and for Crowley, deeply flawed and suspect—assumptions about language upon which current-traditionalism rested.

While Crowley is certainly correct that ideas from the process movement were often shoehorned into an apparent compatibility with older and less palatable modes of pedagogy, she perhaps gives short shrift to the positive changes that the process movement did usher in to composition classrooms. In many classrooms after the process movement took hold, students were given more responsibility for their own writing, and they and their teachers worked together to understand writing processes and harness that understanding to help produce better texts. In many cases, students came to understand and experience writing as an active, dynamic field of endeavor as opposed to a mere medium of display and evaluation. Students became more attuned to context and audience, and in the best process-oriented classrooms, came to understand grammar and style not as static and isolated bodies of rules, but as essential (and often malleable) elements of the communicative, expressive, and inventive power of language.

The process movement may have faded into the background—or become a standard but no longer much noticed part of the scene—in the late 1980s and early 1990s, when composition scholars turned their attention toward institutional history, cultural studies, poststructuralist theory, and the political dimensions of language. Yet there can be little doubt that without the process movement, there would have been no composition studies in the first place, and that an understanding of the process movement is therefore crucial to any general appreciation of what composition studies is, has been, and might become.

The History of Creative Writing and the Problem of Process

As I noted earlier, creative writing at first glance appears to be a field that would naturally be concerned with process. If literary study is concerned with interpreting and appreciating texts whereas creative writing is concerned with making texts, wouldn't process be an inevitable concern for creative writing? If creative writing is a field of practice as much as it is a field of knowledge and inquiry, shouldn't process be a natural—perhaps even a central—concern?

A quick survey of the history of creative writing as an academic field—especially in the United States—should demonstrate that the answers to these questions are not so obvious as they appear at first.[3] Such a survey should also illustrate that creative writing, like composition, had a "traditional" way of doing things that went largely unquestioned for decades until new situations and new problems (or newly insistent old problems) caused it to be questioned and challenged. If composition's "old way" was current-traditionalism, then creative writing's old way was—and in many instances still is—the workshop.

At the University of Iowa, creative writing first became accepted for academic credit—that is, it first became possible for graduate students to write "creative" theses—during the 1930s, largely due to the influence of Norman Foerster.[4] As director of the university's School of Letters, Foerster believed that students studying literature should know something about how literature is made. He thus saw creative writing as an essential counterpart to interpretive criticism, and believed that students should have practice in both. Foerster was never able to fully reconfigure the literary curriculum as he saw fit, and eventually left Iowa in 1944. After that, the creative writing program moved quickly to become its own entity, and the world-famous Iowa Writers' Workshop, replete with its prestigious MFA program, was born. The workshop pedagogy, in which student writers submit pieces of work (usually stories or poems) for classroom critique by fellow students and the instructor, was a staple at Iowa, and at the handful of other graduate creative writing programs that sprang up in the United

States around the same time. Graduates of Iowa and these other programs fanned out around the country, getting jobs in college and university English departments. Once there, they often developed new courses—and occasionally whole programs—in creative writing on both the graduate and undergraduate levels. And they brought creative writing's workshop pedagogy with them.

This workshop pedagogy had a number of widely recognized features. Usually, a creative writing class—especially at the graduate level—was composed entirely of workshops. During a workshop meeting, one or more pieces of student writing were under consideration, having previously been photocopied and distributed to all class members. In most cases, the student writer whose work was being discussed had to remain silent for the duration of the discussion. In some cases, though, the student would be allowed to speak briefly either at the beginning or the end of that discussion. The other students and the instructor would discuss what they liked and disliked about the work in question, focusing often on what they believed "worked" or did not work in the poem or story. Once the discussion was finished, the student writer presumably had much to think about, and often would go off to digest what had been heard and, in many cases, revise or edit the work based upon the commentary received. For courses at the graduate level especially, it was often assumed that the student would use the workshop commentary in order to make the work more "publishable."

The workshop model was believed to offer the student writer a number of benefits, the most obvious of which was a ready and engaged audience of other aspiring writers and the instructor (who was often a well-published writer). Presumably, the commentary offered by such an audience would constitute a kind of apprenticeship for the would-be writer, saving him or her valuable time in development. In its idealized sense, the workshop could be conceived as a miniature writing community. Just as many of the famous writers of the past had sometimes congregated in large cities (Paris being the paradigmatic example) to be around other writers and draw upon their insight and energy, the aspiring writer could now join a workshop and share a similar experience.

For some writers at the graduate level, the workshop functioned in exactly this way. An Iowa MFA, for some, marked the beginning of a rich and rewarding career in writing and teaching—the latter being a necessary part of the writer's life since so few (even those who published prolifically) were able to make a living by writing alone. But as the decades passed, and as the number of creative writing courses and programs proliferated, questions began to emerge. Perhaps some of these questions had been circulating for some time behind the scenes. Eventually they got asked in more prominent and public forums—at conferences and in professional publications. The workshop model that had seemed for so long to work at the graduate level seemed, in the experience of many instructors, not to work nearly as well on the undergraduate level—or perhaps not to work at all. What was going on? Other, deeper questions emerged too: What was the purpose of creative writing programs in the first place? What were they trying to achieve? Were graduates of such programs expected to find success in the publishing market? Were they supposed to follow in the footsteps of their teachers and get academic jobs of their own? If that was the case, what could be done about the apparent oversupply of MFA graduates in an academic job market where only a relative few of them could succeed?

In 1989, a volume of essays edited by Joseph M. Moxley appeared, published by the National Council of Teachers of English. *Creative Writing in America: Theory and Pedagogy* aimed to begin answering some of the questions about creative writing that had emerged—or at least to acknowledge that such questions were being asked, and were worth thinking about. In the preface to this collection, Moxley notes,

> Despite the rapid growth and popularity of courses and programs in creative writing, pedagogical techniques have not evolved all that much. In fact, perhaps because they studied at Iowa or were trained by graduates of the Iowa Writers Workshop, most creative writing teachers at the undergraduate and graduate levels follow the same studio method established at Oregon and Iowa over ninety years ago. (xiii)

Five years later, NCTE published another collection of essays, this one edited by Wendy Bishop and Hans Ostrom. *Colors of a Different Horse: Rethinking Creative Writing Theory and Pedagogy*, like Moxley's collection, gathered together scholars and teachers who wondered if creative writing had perhaps reached a point at which it was necessary to take a step back, survey the scene, and begin asking and answering difficult questions.

Chief among these questions was whether the workshop, as a staple of creative writing pedagogy, needed to be redesigned or perhaps abandoned entirely. (The first section of Bishop's and Ostrom's collection is called "Reconsidering the Workshop," and the very first chapter is called "The Workshop and Its Discontents.") One of the things that seemed to have gone unnoticed for so long about the workshop (or at least not to have presented itself as a significant problem) was that the workshop as traditionally organized is a primarily *product*-oriented endeavor. Student texts as read in the workshop were not exactly "finished" texts like stories in literature anthologies or poems in literary magazines and journals. But they were most often "finished" as drafts, and in many cases the writer had gone through numerous drafts before the piece ever appeared in a workshop. (This can be especially true in classrooms with competitive atmospheres in which students attempt to impress the instructor and each other—to be the best or second best writer in the room.) Creative writing as an activity is undoubtedly enmeshed with process. But workshop pedagogy often focused only on a single, frozen moment in that process; all of the real work (the "process," if you will) took place before and after that moment.

Another (and an older) question became insistent as well: can creative writing even be taught at all? Perhaps the most remarkable (and on some levels, unbelievable) aspect of creative writing's development as academic field in the United States is that the early stages of that development were undertaken by many people who accepted—axiomatically—that creative writing cannot be taught, that "genius" is a talent or gift granted long before one ever enters a writers' workshop, and that only technical elements of writing (often, though not always, referred to as "craft") could ever be imparted through instruction. In describing key aspects of the "new [process] paradigm" in composition studies, Maxine Hairston had noted, "It views writing as a disciplined creative activity that can be analyzed and described; its practitioners believe that writing can be taught" ("Winds" 86). This, according to Hairston, stood in sharp contrast to the assumptions of the older, current-traditional paradigm. Yet in creative writing, it might be more likely to find views like those of Mary Oliver, who asserted in 1994: "Everyone knows that poets are born and not made in school. . . . Something that is essential can't be taught; it can only be given, or earned, or formulated in a manner too mysterious to be picked apart and redesigned for the next person" (1). Oliver's views are not universal among creative writers, but they are certainly widespread enough to constitute a significant obstacle to the development of new and innovative pedagogies. The workshop pedagogy that already existed—especially when it tended to hone in on almost-but-not-yet-quite-finished student texts—was in most cases compatible with the notion that creative genius and invention are unteachable.

During the 1980s and 1990s, the kind of work published in collections like those by Moxley, and by Bishop and Ostrom, was more the exception than the rule. Creative writers in academia did not publish scholarship about creative writing and its pedagogy. They published their own creative works—poems, stories, novels, memoirs, etc. Such work was considered much more important (and for many writers, much more fun) than scholarly prose and pedagogical theory. The first decade of the twenty-first century, though, saw a virtual explosion of scholarship on creative writing in the United States, as well as a significant body of scholarship from Australia and the United Kingdom, where creative writing programs had mostly gotten underway during the 1990s, and where the institutional dynamics of such programs are quite different than they are in creative writing programs in the United States.[5] (The appearance of such scholarship may signal the beginning of a major reorientation in creative writing, but just as Maxine Hairston cautioned in the 1980s that many composition teachers were not aware of the then-current scholarship on writing processes, I would caution today that many who teach creative writing are unaware of the emergence of new scholarship in the field, and many MFA programs do not include it as part of their curricula.) The time seems ripe to examine or reexamine creative writing's potential points of overlap with other areas of scholarly inquiry and pedagogical development. And for the purposes of this chapter, two key questions remain: First, in what ways can the history of the process movement in composition illuminate key current issues in creative writing? Second, can creative writing teachers draw upon process pedagogy from composition in their own classrooms and assignments?

Process and the Creative Writing Classroom

At the outset I must acknowledge that a thorough exploration of the relevance of composition process theory and pedagogy to the creative writing classroom already exists, and has for some time. Wendy Bishop's *Released into Language: Options for Teaching Creative Writing* (originally published by NCTE in 1990, republished by Calendar Islands Publishers in 1998) is a book-length treatment of many issues discussed in this chapter. Readers interested in these issues would be well advised to familiarize themselves with Bishop's work, if they have not done so already. Bishop's book may not have gotten as much attention as it deserved because it was published at a time when composition scholars were moving away from process theory in order to pursue other areas of research. My own arguments in the rest of this chapter might be considered a supplement to Bishop's work, although they are also informed by developments in both composition and creative writing that took place after the publication of *Released into Language*.

The first step toward making composition process theory and pedagogy applicable to creative writing would be to reject the twin notions that, on the one hand, writers' processes are too mysterious to describe, and on the other hand, that the attempt to describe and analyze writers' processes is harmful or destructive to those processes. This is not to say that all writing processes can be described and demystified down to the last detail. The finer points of process can be elusive, even for the writers who engage in them. Nor is it to say that the description and analysis of writers' processes will always yield useful theoretical or practical knowledge. Sometimes these descriptions and analyses may raise more questions than they answer. But because the possibility exists that new knowledge or practical benefits *may* emerge from inquiry into writers' processes, the activity is well worth the time and effort required, especially for those whose jobs involve teaching creative writing.

One specific way to create a more process-oriented creative writing classroom is to develop assignment sequences that include invention exercises. (The fifth chapter of Bishop's *Released into Language* focuses on in-class invention exercises.) Invention exercises can be useful for a number of reasons, not the least of which is that they focus classroom attention on the very earliest stages of student writers' processes, thus bypassing the traditional workshop dynamic in which the earliest stages of the process are ignored or mentioned only in passing. One assignment sequence I currently use in my creative writing classes[6] (I call it "The Three Elements Story") begins with the following in-class writing prompt:

> This exercise will begin in class on Wednesday, January 25. On Friday, February 3, you will submit *at least five word-processed, double-spaced pages* of a complete or incomplete story draft. The story must contain the three elements listed on this page. In other words, each of these things must either *happen* or *be referred to* in your story. The elements may be included in any order, and one or two of them may be much more significant than the other(s). Here are the three elements:
>
> 1. A young woman (in her early twenties), while repairing a framed photograph, finds another photograph underneath the one that was displayed. In this photo, her father (as a young man) has his arm around a woman the daughter does not recognize.
> 2. A man, walking out of a pizza place, discovers that he has received more money in change than he should have.

3. A child, four years old, has an imaginary friend. The child
sits on a picnic bench and watches a plane fly overhead.

During the class session in which the prompt is presented, students are invited to begin the story however they wish. They may start writing the opening paragraphs of a story draft, for example, or begin with an outline or character sketch, or try to imagine a key scene in their story and work forward or backward from there. They have been presented with something like a puzzle, and their immediate task is to figure out some way in which they might begin to solve it; for many of them, that first step involves diving headlong into the story itself. For others, it involves what composition scholars have called "prewriting."

I usually give students about twenty-five minutes to work on the prompt in class, and during the remainder of the period, I invite students to talk about the different ways in which they dealt with the prompt. This discussion continues during the next class meeting, sometimes in richer detail because by then students have had more time to work on their stories. What almost always becomes obvious through these discussions is that writers can begin working on stories (both successfully and unsuccessfully) in a wide variety of ways. Among the class members sometimes, two very similar stories will arise through dramatically different processes; in other instances, two very similar processes produce two dramatically different stories.

Because I often use this exercise at the beginning of the semester, issues of process move to the foreground. All of the students are working on the same kind of story at the same time, and most of the classroom discussions are not evaluative in nature; in other words, I try to steer the discourse away from whether a particular story is "good" or "bad" and focus instead on how it is coming into being and what some of its alternative possibilities are. Once the students submit their five or more pages of prose, the class engages in its first round of writing workshops. Students choose to submit their stories-in-process to an online "workshop" folder or a "no workshop" folder, and I choose workshop pieces from among the former (most of the time, the class is able to conduct face-to-face workshops, over approximately a two-week time period, for all of the stories submitted to that folder). I try to lead these workshop discussions so that they focus at least as much on the processes of how these stories came (and are coming) into being as they do on static features of the texts. Inevitably, though, such features find their way into the discussion because students notice them; evaluative concerns enter the discussions here also, because students invariably like some of the stories more than they do others. As much as possible, though, I try to contextualize such issues within the larger discussion of process. I frequently find myself sprinkling in bits of creative writing's conventional wisdom—for example, if a particular story contains an obvious example of using dialogue for exposition, or if a passage suits itself well to a discussion of "showing" vs. "telling." I introduce these concepts not for the purpose of prescription or proscription, but to demonstrate that in the course of most stories, moments will arise where the author must make choices: Is this bit of information absolutely necessary to the progress of the story? If so, is it wise to introduce the information via dialogue or in some other way? If it does seem feasible to introduce this information via dialogue, what are the possible ways to do it? Of these possibilities, which ones add the most (or detract the most) from readers' understandings of the characters and the plot?

After this first part of the assignment, and the first round of workshops, students have the option to continue and/or revise their Three Elements Stories if they wish, and those who do choose to continue are then freed to eliminate one or more of the elements from the original prompt. My creative writing classes also usually involve at least two poetry assignment sequences that follow the same arc—from in-class invention exercise to first draft to workshops to optional continuation and/or revision. Probably my favorite one of these involves the random selection of ten words from books students have brought to class with them (usually textbooks or required readings from some of their other classes). These words become the skeleton of a twenty line poem: the words, in the exact order they were chosen, must be used at the ends of the poem's even-numbered lines. Each line must be between eight and seventeen syllables long, and no more than eight end-stopped lines are allowed. Students are required to generate a full first draft of this poem during the initial fifty-minute class period, then they are allowed one week to polish and revise it before submitting it online. After that, they have the option to continue working on this poem, and at this point they are allowed to remove some of the original randomly selected words if they so desire.

I have noticed over the semesters that there is rarely any student resistance to the attempt to break down and analyze their writing processes in these sequences (the attempt, metaphorically speaking, to "get under the hood" and see what is going on). There is, on the other hand, occasionally some reticence toward discussing process when the works in question are the students' "own"—that is, when the ideas originated outside of an assignment prompt for the class. When process *is* discussed, students usually seem to find it interesting and helpful, especially because it constitutes a way of looking at poetry and fiction that differs dramatically from what they encounter in their literature classes. As the semester moves along, I frequently bring in (if they seem to connect with ongoing discussion in the class) published writers' accounts of their own writing that focus wholly or partly on issues of process, like Edgar Allan Poe's "The Philosophy of Composition," William Wordsworth's 1802 Preface to *Lyrical Ballads*, T. S. Eliot's "Tradition and the Individual Talent," and other pieces by more contemporary writers, like Sherod Santos's "Eating the Angel, Conceiving the Sun."

Does attention to process in the creative writing course shed any light on the persistent question of whether or not creative writing can be taught? Does it merely shift one of the most common answers to that question from "We cannot teach writing but we can teach *craft*" to "We cannot teach writing but we can teach *process*"? I do not think the matter is quite so simple. So much depends upon how we choose to define—or how we implicitly or unconsciously define—crucial terms like *writing* and *teaching*. In perhaps the most extensive available current philosophical meditation on the subject—*On Creative Writing*—Graeme Harper illustrates that the term "creative writing" has never been clearly defined, that it serves as the site for an ongoing contest of possible meanings. One of his central arguments is that creative writing is a complex collection of *activities* that have too often been approached from a standpoint of "post-event analysis" in which readers or critics try to find evidence of the creative writer's actions and intentions (or brushes with fortuitous "un-intentions") only in the *product* of those actions. Harper goes so far as to suggest that perhaps "process" is too neat and restrictive a term to refer to all the various activities that constitute creative writing (59–65). While this is an important point to keep in mind, it seems likely that the word "process," given its frequent use in the discourses of both creative writing and composition, will remain with us for some time. And perhaps rather than arguing about whether or not writing processes can be taught, we would do well to shift the focus to another question: Is it possible in the classroom, and in assignments intended for students to work on outside the classroom, to *create the conditions* whereby students *experience* the diverse and dynamic activities and actions that constitute so much of creative writing? I believe the answer to that question is an emphatic *yes*. And I believe it is important—though at times also quite difficult—to make these processual experiences a key part of the discussion that takes place in creative writing classrooms.

Some creative writing instructors might reasonably ask how it is possible to *grade* students' work in a process-oriented class. I would respond that it certainly *is* possible to grade students' work in such a class. But before I explain how, I would like to lay some groundwork for my response. First, I have long felt that grades are a very poor motivator for students' writing improvement (in creative writing or any other kind of writing, for that matter) because it is easy for students to focus so intently on grades that their view of writing becomes myopic, and their long-term development is actually inhibited. In an ideal world, I believe, writing courses would not have to be graded at all. Students would get extensive (and sometimes evaluative) feedback on their writing, but that feedback would be focused solely on making the student a better writer in the long run, and in helping the student understand, in a very personal way, *what it might mean* to become a better writer in the long run. Grades, at best, are only snapshots of a very brief window of time in a student's long-term development. Yet we do not live in an ideal world, and grades are often an institutional and administrative necessity for those who teach creative writing. Second, I see the question of how it is possible to grade creative writing in a process-oriented classroom as related to a question that has plagued some creative writing teachers, and some of those who aspire to teach creative writing, for decades or longer: How does one grade *creative writing* in the first place? The very existence of this question, I would assert, points to some prevalent assumptions about the nature of creative writing that are too often left unarticulated and unquestioned. There is not room in this chapter to unearth and question those assumptions in great detail, but I will mention two of them briefly here: First is the assumption that because different readers' responses to any given piece of creative writing can vary, the evaluation of creative writing must be inherently "subjective," in a very simplistic sense of that term, and therefore a teacher's grade on a piece of student writing is not an "objective" measure of the text's quality, but rather a mere expression of the teacher's idiosyncratic personal preferences.[7] Second is the assumption that creative writing—much more so than other kinds of writing—is so deeply connected to the writer's *personal* identity that to grade someone's writing is, in effect, to pass judgment on his or her value as a person. Though writers *as writers* may enjoy great success without ever digging deeply into their assumptions about what writing is and how it works, and engaging in critical analysis of those assumptions, writers *as teachers* will eventually experience failures if they do not do so. This is one among many reasons why I believe the emerging field of creative writing studies, to which this chapter and this book both aim to contribute, is so crucially important in our time. And I would suggest that anyone who reflexively believes it is not possible to grade creative writing should engage in some sustained reflection about why that is.

To the more insistently practical question of how one assigns grades in a process-oriented creative writing class, I would say the answer is fairly simple: students should be evaluated on whether or not they *do the work*, on whether or not they *engage in the processes and activities of creative writing* as defined in individual assignments and in the larger structure of the course. If an assignment requires that students incorporate certain things into a story draft (as in the Three Elements Story described above), then students can be graded on whether or not they have actually done so. If the assignment is to write a sonnet, then students can be graded on how well they manage (or do not manage) a sonnet's complex metrical and rhyming scheme. If the assignment is to write a brief fictional scene in the first-person voice of a person dramatically different in some way (like age, gender, nationality, or historical time period) from the student, then the students' work can be graded on whether or not (and perhaps in the teacher's professional judgment, how well) they do so. In my own classes, portions of students' grades are also based upon how well they engage in classroom discussions of their own and others' writing, and also on reflective essays— submitted at the end of the semester—in which they articulate how their own writing processes work (or occasionally do not work) and evaluate their own progress as writers, and articulate their future writing goals.

To focus on process in the creative writing classroom is—at least in part—to deemphasize product, though it is certainly possible to shift the focus back and forth so that attention is paid to both. More advanced students, especially those seeking or soon to be seeking publication, may desire more attention to product. But in most undergraduate courses, especially those at the introductory level, I would argue that the focus should be mostly on process. One of the most important things an undergraduate creative writing course can offer to students as part of a well-rounded literary or liberal arts education is a *way of looking* at fiction, poetry, and literature that differs from the way in which such things are often looked at in school settings. Another way to articulate this is that creative writing courses can introduce students to (or enhance their prior experiences of) an epistemological—perhaps even ontological—orientation toward textuality and the world. Creative writing offers ways of knowing and ways of being that are active, dynamic, and participatory. Creative writing courses, especially at the

undergraduate level, may not necessarily produce the world's next generation of literary geniuses. As I see it, that is not the purpose of such courses
anyway. A deeper and more important purpose is to afford students at least
a glimpse of what it is like to *be* a creative writer. And that purpose cannot
be accomplished without significant and sustained attention to process.

Notes

1. This history of the origins of the required first-year composition course
in American colleges and universities is distilled from a number of sources.
Composition scholars like James Berlin, Robert Connors, and Susan Miller
have all chronicled important details of this history. D. G. Myers, a major
historian of creative writing, also provides a detailed account of the early
days of composition at Harvard, highlighting some of the ways in which both
composition and creative writing emerged together as rivals to the philological model of literary and linguistic research, which had held sway in the late
nineteenth century. Sharon Crowley's *Composition in the University* mines
much of this history as well, in a sustained attempt to uncover the ideological assumptions that helped to create and sustain the dominance of literary
study, and the subservience of composition, within the larger structure of
English studies. And the first chapter of Mike Rose's *Lives on the Boundary*
provides another brief but excellent overview of the history that led to the
creation of the required first-year college composition course.

2. For a much more detailed treatment of this history, see the second and
third chapters of Robert J. Connors's *Composition-Rhetoric: Backgrounds,
Theory, and Pedagogy.*

3. The two key sources for this history are Myers and Wilbers.

4. Undergraduate courses in verse writing and short story writing had
been in existence at Iowa since the last decade of the nineteenth century
(see Wilbers).

5. To note just a few examples: My *(Re)Writing Craft: Composition, Creative Writing, and the Future of English Studies* was published in 2005, the
same year as Paul Dawson's *Creative Writing and the New Humanities.* And
the "New Writing Viewpoints" series from Multilingual Matters Press has
published an impressive collection of books about creative writing theory
and pedagogy.

6. The university where I teach offers only one undergraduate course
devoted exclusively to creative writing. In some ways, it is much like the
typical introductory multigenre course. It is, however, a 400-level course, and
therefore considered "advanced." Many of the students who take this course

have already taken composition and advanced composition, and many also have taken numerous courses in literary studies.

7. Many veteran creative writing teachers can report something like the following having happened at least once in their careers (if not with great regularity) if they assign grades to individual pieces of student writing: An indignant student challenges a grade on a story or poem by saying something like this: "All my friends and family who read this thought it was great. How can you not give it an 'A' just because *you* don't like it as much as they do?" If you have not experienced this yet, or if you have been stumped by it in the past, you might do well to think seriously about how you would respond to such a challenge.

Works Cited

Bishop, Wendy. *Released into Language: Options for Teaching Creative Writing.* 1990. Portland, ME: Calendar Islands Publishers, 1998. Print.

Bishop, Wendy, and Hans Ostrom, eds. *Colors of a Different Horse: Rethinking Creative Writing Theory and Pedagogy.* Urbana, IL: NCTE, 1994. Print.

Connors, Robert J. *Composition-Rhetoric: Backgrounds, Theory, and Pedagogy.* Pittsburgh: U of Pittsburgh P, 1997. Print.

Crowley, Sharon. *Composition in the University: Historical and Polemical Essays.* Pittsburgh: U of Pittsburgh P. 1998. Print.

Dawson, Paul. *Creative Writing and the New Humanities.* London: Routledge, 2005. Print.

Elbow, Peter. *Writing without Teachers.* 25th anniversary ed. New York: Oxford UP, 1998. Print.

Hairston, Maxine. "Breaking Our Bonds and Reaffirming Our Connections." *College Composition and Communication* 36.3 (1985): 272–82. *JSTOR.* Web. 10 Feb. 2012.

———. "The Winds of Change: Thomas Kuhn and the Revolution in the Teaching of Writing." *College Composition and Communication* 33.1 (1982): 76–88. *JSTOR.* Web. 20 Jan. 2012.

Harper, Graeme. *On Creative Writing.* Bristol, UK: Multilingual Matters, 2010. Print.

Horner, Bruce. *Terms of Work for Composition: A Materialist Critique.* Albany, NY: SUNY Press, 2000. Print.

Mills, Barriss. "Writing as Process." *College English* 15.1 (1953): 19–26. *JSTOR.* Web. 21 Dec. 2011.

Moxley, Joseph M., ed. *Creative Writing in America: Theory and Pedagogy.* Urbana, IL: NCTE, 1989. Print.

Murray, Donald M. "Teach Writing as a Process Not Product." *Cross-Talk in Comp Theory.* 2nd ed. Ed. Victor Villanueva. Urbana, IL: NCTE, 2003. 3–6. Print.

Myers, D. G. *The Elephants Teach: Creative Writing Since 1880.* New York: Prentice-Hall. 1996. Print.

Oliver, Mary. *A Poetry Handbook.* San Diego: Harcourt Brace, 1994. Print.

Rose, Mike. *Lives on the Boundary.* New York: Penguin, 1989. Print.

Wilbers, Stephen. *The Iowa Writers' Workshop: Origins, Emergence, and Growth.* Iowa City: U of Iowa P, 1980. Print.

Mutuality and the Teaching of the Introductory Creative Writing Course

Patrick Bizzaro

THOUGH HE WAS not a classroom teacher of mine, William Stafford greatly influenced my thinking about the teaching of creative writing. In occasional workshops I had the good fortune to attend, but especially through my reading of *Writing the Australian Crawl*, I noted that Stafford took a critical stance toward teaching creative writing that empowered young writers to take control of the conditions of their educations as writers and thereby to find their own visions.

The Australian Crawl

"Poems are nothing special," Stafford claims,
nothing special,
the kind of *thing*
you have to see
from "the corner
of your eye."
Like very faint
stars, Stafford says, if you look straight
at them, you can't see them at all.
No doubt he is right:
Teachers of young poets
are not astronomers
and shouldn't be.

"No interest" in this vision of the stars
is better than the "conscientious interest" of a scientist.
That's why even learn'd
astronomers are most often failed poets.
A poem is a joke, a very serious joke,
"a truth that has learned *jujitsu*."

Years ago I had hoped, against the wishes of my editor, to title what eventually became *Responding to Student Poems* in honor of Stafford's advocacy for what he calls "the second kind of company." The passage from which that sense of humble teacherly identity comes echoes the goals of what in time came to be known as *liberatory* or *critical pedagogy*, though we can be fairly certain Stafford did not see anything overtly political in the way he taught.[1] Stafford writes,

> First, suppose you had a chance to work with someone who would correct your writing into publishability. This person would be efficient, knowing, memorable, valid: an accomplished writer. In the company of this person you could go confidently into the center of current acceptance; you would quickly learn what brings success in the literary scene.
>
> Now suppose another kind of associate. This one would accompany you as you discovered for yourself whatever it is that most satisfyingly links to your own life and writings. You would be living out of your own self into its expression, almost without regard to the slant or expectation or demands of editors and the public.
>
> Let there be no mistake about it: a large and significant, and I believe most significant, group of writers today would prefer the second kind of company. (80)

A more contemporary version of critical pedagogy, and the subject of this essay, "mutuality," shares the goals implied by Stafford's pedagogical stance in the quote above.

Mutuality is not quite critical pedagogy. But in the past ten years, it has emerged as a way to salvage critical pedagogy, which itself is a long-standing approach to teaching that many still believe holds the promise for achieving social equality in our writing classrooms. Difficulties over the years in successfully employing critical pedagogy have been at the center of recent debate in our most visible journals (see Gorzelsky; Lu and

Horner). It seems especially important to note that no one ever promised a perfect translation of critical pedagogy from the use Paulo Freire made of it in Brazil to the efforts to improve the living conditions of the American poor. Indeed, the translation of critical pedagogy from first-year writing to the introductory creative writing classroom, promising though it may be, still needs to be implemented in that adaptation of critical pedagogy called mutuality.

Adaptation of critical pedagogy has given hope to scholars that its principles may be used in various ways Freire had not envisioned. On the global level, Richard Shaull, in his "Foreword" to the 1989 edition of *Pedagogy of the Oppressed*, wrote about the possible adaptation of the Brazilian project to the conditions of the poor in the United States. Shaull believes such a translation is at least possible:

> At first sight, Paulo Freire's method of teaching illiterates in Latin America seems to belong to a different world from that in which we find ourselves in this country (the USA). Certainly, it would be absurd to claim that it should be copied here. But there are certain parallels in the two situations which should not be overlooked. Our advanced technological society is rapidly making objects of most of us and subtly programming us into conformity to the logic of its system. To the degree that this happens, we are also becoming submerged in a new "culture of silence." (14)

In 1987, Shor and Freire addressed the problematic notion of whether a direct correspondence existed between liberatory education in Brazil and the possibility of employing that pedagogy in the United States: "Is it possible for us here in North America to use a dialogical method that came from the Third World? How do you use this kind of liberating pedagogy here?" (24). A liberatory pedagogy as Freire employed it and wrote about is not simply a theory, as it still seems to be in this country today. Rather, as Freire describes liberation in *Pedagogy of the Oppressed*, it is an action or a set of actions informed by a theory of inclusion, not just a theory that without practice exists in isolation: "just as the oppressor, in order to oppress, needs a theory of oppressive action, so the oppressed in order to become free, also needs a theory of action" (185). We might call the theory of action that best characterizes Freirean pedagogy "a theory of liberation," as Freire did. Circumstances to which Freire's pedagogy of liberation have been applied in the United States, for example, are similar but certainly not identical to those Freire encountered in Brazil. Nonetheless, some believe we have a moral obligation to apply this theory in every arena we can. No doubt, from this perspective, we should use everything at our disposal to teach literacy skills and do so in every course where it is possible to do so.

On a more local level, we note that while critical pedagogy has been used with varying degrees of success in first-year composition, no one to my knowledge has publicly argued for the adaptation of critical pedagogy to the creative writing classroom. In doing so in this essay, I will first argue for the value of assessing *how* we teach in a creative writing course rather than *what* we teach in it. Then I will consider the more tangible tactics of mutuality and how they reflect not only practices that could be used in a creative writing context but also methods that are already a part of standard approaches to the teaching of creative writing. Clearly, mutuality has emerged over the past ten years as an adaptation of critical theory to circumstances specific to the United States and complementary to the teaching of a range of writing courses that focus largely on discourse relations. But mutuality as a pedagogy and a metaphor for teacher/student relationships still has not been successfully articulated as practices, specific tactics, in any of these courses, including creative writing (see Wallace and Ewald 2000). Therefore, we must step back and take a panoramic view of critical-pedagogy-turned-mutuality while noting that many of the practices typically employed in creative writing classrooms (e.g., the workshop method) have long mirrored the intentions of critical pedagogy. However, further adaptation of these tactics must focus on the teacher/student relationship as it is defined by discourse opportunities and less on traditional emphases that stress genre and its various elements, a holdover of the New Criticism.[2]

Mutuality and Critical Pedagogy

Let's briefly articulate the goals of mutuality and critical pedagogy and, by doing so, consider their application in the teaching of introductory creative writing courses. It may be useful to consider the views of Gorzelsky alongside those of Wallace and Ewald when they assert their belief that mutuality is a possible solution to problems recently attributed to critical pedagogy. In "Working Boundaries: From Student Resistance to Student Agency," Gorzelsky notes that "Composition studies' use of critical pedagogy has been fundamentally called into question" (64). Some students resist the blatant politicizing done by some critical pedagogues. It might be that ethical teaching requires us to ignore our own political positions (see Smith); if we choose to do so, we may still disguise our personal political beliefs and thereby not impose them on our students while maintaining a classroom that values equally the cultures of all the students in attendance. Such an effort to construct the architecture of liberation in the classroom without blatantly proselytizing one political view or another requires that teachers participate in the *performance* of a pedagogy that masks their political views (see Davis, Kopelson). Performance pedagogy has two related and predictable scenarios. In one, teachers may thus feel silenced as political beings in their classrooms, and the goal of instruction becomes for many the preparation of students for positions in the professions (Lu and Horner), a position I believe to be parallel in first year writing to the goal of producing the next generation of published authors in creative writing courses. In the other, students often come to view teachers who advocate one political view or another as intrusive and, thus, resist those teachers' pedagogies altogether (Trainor).

Wallace and Ewald's solution to the problem of enacting overt politics in the classroom is to view discourse relations as potential sites of social equality: "it is . . . common to underestimate the power of classroom language to both construct and reflect knowledge as well as social relations in the classroom" (2). Wallace and Ewald echo Gorzelsky when they note that "the impetus to empower students by engaging them in liberatory and emancipatory pedagogies is simply not enough" (3). Rather, "The impetus to engage in *alternative pedagogy* must be worked out in language—in discourse among teachers and students that transforms traditional classroom roles" (emphasis in original, 2). They insist,

> [V]aluing students' interpretive agency is a definite step in achieving mutuality. From this perspective, strategies such as abandoning lecture in favor of class discussions, teacher-student conferences, peer group work, tutoring sessions, and other methodologies have the potential to focus classroom discourse on the intersections between disciplinary knowledge and students' unique subjectivities as the starting point for learning.

My perspective requires that we also consider the kind and amount of information students bring to the classroom as an aid to interpretive agency. Concerns over what we might expect students to know when they enter our classrooms seem as well to be at the heart of Freire's answer to his own question about how to adapt critical pedagogy to conditions for which it did not at first seem relevant: "my comprehension of empowerment [is] 'social class empowerment.' *Not* individual, *not* community, *not* merely social empowerment, but a concept of 'social class empowerment'" (111). Those who have advocated for mutuality believe such empowerment can only occur through discourse. How might changes in the way we use language in our classrooms with our students best accommodate students from varying social classes and cultures in an introductory creative writing class? Clearly, Freire is not concerned with the teaching of various genres, literary or professional. Knowledge about traditional genres may be outside the experience (what Bourdieu calls *habitus)* of students who might most benefit from a creative writing course shaped by critical pedagogy. In short, genre knowledge may be brought to a creative writing course by some students but not by others. It constitutes cultural capital in creative writing.

If it is true that Freire's notion of liberation is the emancipation of members of certain *social classes*, then those of us interested in following his lead in developing emancipatory pedagogical practices in our creative writing classes and elsewhere must learn to use methods that do not privilege one social class over another, including understanding genres unique to cultures from which those students come (Pough). For example, spoken word in my experience as a teacher is a greater influence on some students than, let's say, genres such as flash fiction or the sestina. And genre is culturally situated: research in using poetry with English language learners suggests Japanese students might write haiku or Korean students sijo without much class instruction in doing so. I believe we should teach genre as socially and culturally situated. The task of reorienting ourselves to genre as creative writing teachers is complicated by the fact that teachers themselves aspire as writers and come from certain social classes and may resist the critical pedagogy themselves because it just doesn't make any sense to them to employ it. How can we teach creative writing without teaching the traditional genres? Many think knowledge about storytelling, for instance, is common to all cultures. It may not be, however, even if it is common in the cultures from which most teachers originate. The thrust of this essay, then, is to argue for the position that we can, indeed, employ methods of discourse in creative writing that resist social class emphases by giving interpretive agency to all students, regardless of their backgrounds. For some teachers, use of these methods amounts to relearning how to teach creative writing altogether, and perhaps this is not too much to ask. My starting point in saying so, as it must be, is my conviction that relearning how to teach in an effort to establish equal power relations among our students in our classrooms is a discursive act—that is, an act that may take place whenever teacher language intersects with opportunities for students to use language, as well. We must start with language because, as Bourdieu insists, language functions as symbolic power, and our goal is to focus less on the teaching of genres than on the equity potential in discourse relations. What's more, as Delpit might insist, we must learn to value genres from historically excluded cultures alongside those from the privileged groups that have always shown up in creative writing classes.

Among such specific discursive acts teachers routinely perform are the acts of designing courses (course architecture), making writing assignments, responding to student writing, and employing teacher-talk in the classroom. As in first-year writing, creative writing pedagogy holds as its highest goal the fostering of mutuality, that is, the development of strategies I describe as *emancipatory*, echoing Freire. My goal is to justify a theory of emancipation for the teaching of creative writing based upon Freirean notions of social class equality and the *ways* equality can be enacted in the creative writing classroom.

What should such strategies attempt to achieve in a mutuality-driven creative writing classroom? From the perspective Freire offers and, thus, from the one advocated here, they should *not* emphasize the individual, a community (e.g., members of a profession), or only serve to advance the capitalistic agenda of certain groups (e.g., white, middle-class male poets, fiction writers, essayists, or dramatists). Instead, teaching strategies must enable all students to challenge and thus change the class structure, perhaps by providing insight into how social class functions (including who benefits from a class system and who ends up oppressed by it) or perhaps by inviting students to see what they have in common with others, regardless of their varied social classes. Although "class analysis" is difficult for Freire to define when his efforts are applied in the United States, the remedy nonetheless is in educating the masses, including (perhaps especially) the poor. In *A Pedagogy for Liberation*, Freire reflects on his notion of social class empowerment, the goal of his pedagogy as it might be applied in the United States, and the difficulty of teaching for such empowerment:

> [I]t is *one* thing to make a class analysis in Latin America, and it is something altogether different to make the same kind of analysis in the States. . . . It does not mean that U.S. society is without social classes. There are classes here, but not with the almost geographical frontier, the powerful reality we have

as social classes in Latin America. I always say that in doing class analysis in the U.S., Marxist instruments of analysis were valid once but now need to be refined, in order to be useful to such a complex society like the American one. (111)

The process of developing our teaching methods for those of us who choose to do so begins with theory and involves a process of what Freire calls *refinement*.

Refinement makes possible discursive moments that enable students to analyze social class distinctions and human commonalities. Many scholars have made this case for first-year writing; I want to make this case for introductory courses in creative writing as well and, for reasons discussed below, I believe it is important that we do so. This refinement could be done in any class, of course, but I believe creative writing classes are especially adaptable for the ends of social equality or no less so than first-year writing courses. Nonetheless, I do not believe this refinement has yet occurred widely in the American educational system, in first-year writing, really, or certainly in creative writing. And there are good reasons for that, not the least of which is Freire's own concern over how exactly that refinement might occur. When Freire concludes, "I recognize that this preoccupation I have with 'class' has to be recreated for the States" (112), he also seems to suggest that our definition of what it means to teach to students of different social classes needs to be revised. In my mind, we must focus on *how* we teach our students, not only on *what* we teach them. And each time we teach a course, because it is to a new group of students, teachers must relearn how to teach. What makes social class analysis relevant is that, in Shor's words, it "is a problem of analysis as well as a problem of pedagogy" (111). We are prone to error if we believe social class can be measured by the income of our students' parents, for instance. Social class issues are easy to miss or misconstrue. Henry Giroux addresses this very problem in his 1995 essay "Who Writes in a Cultural Studies Class? Or, Where Is the Pedagogy?":

[M]y overriding pedagogical project was rooted in an . . . education whose aim was to advance the ideological and lived relations necessary for students to interrogate the possibility of addressing schooling as a site of ongoing struggle over the "social and political task of transformation, resistance, and radical democratization" (Butler 13). . . . By not paying more attention to what it meant to give students more control over

> the conditions of their own knowledge production, I reproduced the binarism of being politically enlightened in my theorizing and pedagogically wrong in my organization of concrete class relations. (10–11)

What makes class a problem in this analysis is that certain features of pedagogy influenced by class are hidden from us, so that it is quite easy to fall into the binarism to which Giroux refers. And that particular blindness is what makes it possible for otherwise well-intentioned educators to empower one group while inadvertently oppressing another. As Amy Lee points out so pertinently, "Hegemony is working best precisely where we begin to perceive the world as given, natural, or just common sense" (9). As teachers we may see school as the site of class conflict but think that we do not have the tools to resolve that conflict in our effort to liberate our students. Thus, in the absence of appropriate tools, Lee makes the same request in 2000 that Freire and Shor made in 1987, as though very little had been accomplished in the intervening years; although we have debated and attempted to employ critical pedagogy, we have not yet developed acts made possible by that theory: "From claiming a pedagogy, we must move to reflecting on the challenges and possibilities of actualizing it" (Lee 5). I believe mutuality is a timely restatement of this call for action in our classrooms; this essay is just one effort to reflect upon the challenges posed by mutuality, especially as they influence how we teach creative writing.

Most people nowadays agree that discourse is at the core of power in the classroom. Based on the premise that language symbolizes power relations, Bourdieu labels as *habitus* the various combinations of experience from home life that influence a student's "readiness" for advanced study, as in our first year writing classes but also, as I will argue, with a similar group of students in our introductory creative writing classes. Like Delpit before me but in a slightly different context, I note with alarm the number of teachers who, having completed all the requirements to become teachers of writing, go off to teach armed with methods that prove ultimately ineffective in their dealings with those who have been excluded historically in our classrooms; traditional methods of instruction do not work well with nontraditional students because of the disconnect between the students' habitus and the habitus required for success in their classrooms. Delpit's position on instruction, before the advent of postprocess theories, surprised many people in the profession and threatened many others:

"Process writing" and "whole language" advocates believed me to be attacking their "progressive" and "child-centered" methods of instruction, while *I saw myself as struggling to figure out why some children of color in classrooms utilizing these methodologies were not learning to read and write*, not acquiring the "codes of power" necessary for success in this society. (my emphasis, xxvi)

"Process writing" and "whole language" instruction are examples of "standard" approaches to teaching language skills that, in Lee's words, arise from "the world as given, natural, or just common sense" (13). We do not always "see" how these approaches might disenfranchise one group while they simultaneously empower another.

Although Delpit does not refer directly to Bourdieu, whose ideas seem now to have been absorbed into the jargon of education, she easily could have. In the passage above, Delpit refers to the hegemony of standard approaches to educational practice in writing classes. While the advice of process and whole language advocates works well for some groups of students, Delpit rightly notes that the advice does not work well for everyone. Likewise, while the advice we give our young poets and story writers seems to work well for some students, it is a form of insult to others. Common sense is common only in particular groups and in specific, sanctioned ways of thinking. In a creative writing class, when we teach genre without regard for social class—because, after all, we believe and have believed for a long time that students first and foremost need to learn the elements of different genres—we likewise do so blind to its social consequences. This assertion is true when we teach students to hear their "voices" in their writings, as well.

An excellent example of how wrong we can be, often when we think we are being inclusive, even open-minded, is given by bell hooks:

When I became a student in college creative writing classes, I learned a notion of "voice" as embodying the distinctive expression of an individual writer. Our efforts to become poets were to be realized in this coming into awareness and expression of one's voice. In all my writing classes, I was the only black student. Whenever I read a poem written in the particular dialect of southern black speech, the teacher and fellow students would praise me for using my "true," authentic voice, and encouraged me to develop this "voice," to write more of these poems. From the onset this troubled me. Such comments seemed to mask racial biases about what my authentic voice would or should be. (11)

Voice, when it is at the heart of creative writing instruction, is a "natural" way to enforce some concepts related to social class that may be debilitating for some students. I think hooks's analysis of this event clarifies this point:

In part, attending all-black segregated schools with black teachers meant that I had come to understand black poets as being capable of speaking in many voices, that the Dunbar of a poem written in dialect was no more or less authentic than the Dunbar writing a sonnet. Yet it was listening to black musicians like Duke Ellington, Louis Armstrong, and later John Coltrane that impressed upon our consciousness a sense of versatility—they played all kinds of music, had multiple voices. So it was with poetry. The black poet, as exemplified by Gwendolyn Brooks and later Amiri Baraka, had many voices—with no single voice being identified as more or less authentic. (11)

At the center of ongoing thinking concerning power in the classroom and at the heart of hooks's concern about voice is the notion that power is symbolized through language (i.e., the way we talk to students in class, the way we respond to their writing, the kinds of reading and writing assignments we give). We might even say that the language of our syllabi and other written materials signals our relationships with our students. Because language may exclude certain specific groups of students or, in hooks's example, pigeonhole and thereby limit them, finding out how to include them is an ongoing and difficult matter because it involves social class relations that make some teachers uncomfortable and that others just don't see as relevant. Nonetheless, we hear Delpit clearly as she rearticulates, and thus recontextualizes, Bourdieu: "even while teachers provide access to the 'codes of power' represented by acquiring facility in 'standard edited English,' they must also value and make use in the classroom of the language and culture children bring from home" (xxvi). We might adopt Delpit's important observation by saying the codes of power in creative writing, in addition to voice, are the elements of poetry and fiction, genres valued by the New Criticism and still taught as the centerpieces of most creative writing courses. We certainly still see the elements as chapter titles in many of our creative writing textbooks. This, indeed, is the challenge in any classroom that aspires to mutuality: to "value and make use in the classroom of the language and culture children bring from home" (Delpit xxvi; also see Pough).

In their definition of mutuality, Wallace and Ewald say much the same thing Delpit does but with a slightly different emphasis that merits examination here because it refocuses our sense of class and class relations to be more inclusive than Delpit or even Freire ask us to be. In Wallace and Ewald's words, "mutuality can be understood as teachers and students sharing the potential to adopt a range of subject positions and to establish reciprocal discourse relations as they negotiate meaning in the classroom" (3). In her earliest work, Delpit refers chiefly to race relations in the classroom while Wallace and Ewald use the concept of subject positions and acknowledge that there might be a variety of them to negotiate, "a range of subject positions," including race, gender, economic class, sexual orientation, disability, and ethnicity. In these explanations of what should happen in the classroom, discourse stands as the power that is either transferred to and shared with or denied our students, unless their subject position is the one appropriate for the classroom, a position typically white and middle income and heterosexual and abled and male. In truth, Freire and Ira Shor, one of his American advocates, might be less interested in whiteness and maleness and hetero-ness than in middle economic classes.

As we see each semester in our first-year writing classes, some students have it (*habitus*), others get it, but still others don't stand much of a chance at success. The breakdown of these groups is fairly predictable. As Delpit asserts,

> [P]ower plays a critical role in our society and in our educational system. The worldviews of those with privileged positions are taken as the only reality, while the worldviews of those less powerful are dismissed as inconsequential. Indeed, in the educational institutions of this country, the possibilities for poor people and for people of color to define themselves, to determine the self each should be, involve a power that lies outside of the self. (xxv)

In spite of the differences in readiness demonstrated by diverse groups of students, factors typically associated with the language and even the preconceptions of the dominant social class, when we employ the good and standard advice found in any number of well-intentioned sources available these days for use in our teaching of writing courses (Lindemann), we exclude many of our students. I think we must still acknowledge that even those who aspire to become teachers of creative writing are instructed in their graduate programs' teaching of writing course by compositionists. This difficulty cuts in two directions. Resistance to certain pedagogical matters comes from students, but it also comes from teachers. Delpit describes her own breakthrough moment as her realization of "the need to step outside of [her] self and [her] beliefs in order to allow the perspectives of others to filter in" (xxvi). I contend that we must also learn to step outside the pedagogy of our narrowly defined disciplines to find strategies that empower students if properly enacted in the classroom.

Mutuality, Literacy, and the Invitation to Write: Toward Social Equity in Creative Writing

Some teachers will inevitably ask, why should we be concerned with social equity in creative writing? Isn't teaching for social equity better suited to activities we might use in first-year writing? I believe the introductory creative writing course is an excellent place to employ alternative pedagogies. After all, in addition to the failings of critical pedagogy in first-year composition that Gorzelsky points out, we are increasingly certain that our students in an introductory creative writing class are not much different from those we've had in first-year writing. Elizabeth Wardle, for one, has told us convincingly what we have long suspected, that we should not expect much carryover from first-year writing to any writing course we might teach, and I think that must include creative writing, though she does not single out that course. Nonetheless, she writes,

> The gist of the critiques against FYC [first-year composition] as a general writing skills course is this: the goal of teaching students to write across the university in other academic courses assumes that students in FYC can be taught ways of writing (genre and genre knowledge) that they can then transfer to the writing they do in other courses across the university. (766)

Wardle's critique probably provides some comfort for creative writing instructors if Donald Murray is correct when he insists in "Unlearning to Write" that, if our students have learned skills in their composition courses that carry over into the creative writing class, we probably need to be prepared to unteach some of those skills: "They bring with them (into their creative writing classes) knowledge which may be true for some of the writing they have done but which makes the writing of fiction difficult"

(103). When I think about the observations of Wardle and Murray side by side, I am reminded that we are at an early stage in understanding how to teach creative writing but, of equal importance, that we should seize the opportunity whenever we can in creative writing or in other writing courses we might teach to avoid replicating the class system of the dominant culture which, if enforced in our classrooms, may disenfranchise many of our students.

No doubt, the relationship between composition and creative writing at a meeting such as Conference on College Composition and Communication assumes that creative writing is a subdiscipline of composition studies. An important article by Doug Hesse that appeared in the September 2010 *College Composition and Communication* is titled "The Place of Creative Writing in Composition Studies," a title that orients us quite clearly to the view of creative writing as it is held by many compositionists. This we have come to accept axiomatically: creative writing has indeed learned a lot about itself from composition. As a result of that fact, there is an increasingly large group of teachers everywhere around the country, like myself, who try to live comfortably in both worlds, teaching comp at 9 A.M. and creative writing at 10. But while I'm convinced I do a better job of teaching creative writing when I employ skills I've learned from my colleagues in composition, I also believe that composition has been slow to learn from creative writing. For one thing, as a teacher of composition I believe there's more I can do to use the best elements of creative writing instruction in making my first-year composition course socially equitable.

Designing the Course in Creative Writing

As I have already noted, creative writing has long used methods that advance the notion of mutuality as a sharing of subject positions. The workshop is one of those methods. The use of genres from traditionally excluded groups (haiku, sijo, spoken word) is another.

The workshop has long assisted teachers of creative writing, when it has been used to help teachers resist the authority they have been granted through tradition and privilege. In my opinion, it can be used incorrectly, too, as when we keep authors silent while others talk about their work, a procedure that surely is not dialogic. This statement, even as I write it, brings to mind for me the title of Dianne Donnelly's much-needed book, *Does the Writing Workshop Still Work?*

I am reminded especially of Mary Ann Cain's observation about her use of workshops not only in creative writing but in rhetorical studies, as well. She says the workshop "is geared towards re-visioning the question of 'what works,' to make the resulting comments, written and spoken, more dialogical, and thus more 'open' to other, previously unthinkable alternatives" (224). For me the key word Cain uses is "dialogical." The workshop is potentially inclusive and consistent with the goals of mutuality.

In the same important collection of essays, Stephanie Vanderslice calls the workshop "the Bobby Knight School of writing pedagogy, so named for the famously abusive, chair-throwing college basketball coach" because "the workshop was also designed as a kind of 'boot camp,' which would 'toughen' students so that they could withstand inevitable adversity and criticism as an artist" (31). Vanderslice makes the observation, important to my argument here, that "the creative writing landscape has changed since the early days of the Iowa workshop" and that "the overwhelming majority of creative writing workshop students bear no resemblance to the cadre of graduate students, the 'polished' writers who populated the workshop as it took hold in creative writing mythology" (32). I find it easy to agree with Vanderslice when she says: "the creative writing workshop is a victim of its own success." By most reports, creative writing has never been more popular to college students than it is now, populated as it is by a new, previously excluded body of students. But that popularity also makes it essential that we reexamine methods for teaching that course.

Nonetheless, I think the workshop nicely exemplifies a space where mutuality might be fostered. For me, the starting point in any effort to establish equal power relationships in the classroom, creative writing or composition, is in the effort to create those relationships through the language we use. We have those opportunities in designing the architecture of the course, for instance, in our decision to employ a wider range of genres (possibly focusing on ways of thinking rather than genres), the workshop model of instruction, and response methods during workshop of the sort described below.

One last point about course architecture. Because we rarely know the backgrounds and habitus of our students until we meet them, I think there is a benefit to withholding decisions about what will be read in a course until after the class begins. That way, teachers can enlist help in constructing a reading list that is relevant to all the students in attendance. In this way, students can recommend selections that reflect their cultural backgrounds, genres such as haiku and sijo discussed earlier as but two of many.

Assigning Writing

I read Richard Hugo's *The Triggering Town* nearly thirty years ago. He won my trust with this statement in his very first chapter: "You'll never be a poet until you realize that everything I say today . . . is wrong. It may be right for me, but it is wrong for you" (3).

Hugo's advice on composing may sound familiar to you: "The poem is always in your hometown, but you have a better chance of finding it in another" (12). This statement, though familiar, is always open to interpretation. Let me offer mine: You drive into Pittsburgh, for example, and remember you've been told to stay on Route 386 to get downtown. In writing a good composition, the successful composition student might stay right on a figurative route 386 and not deviate from that plan. But the good poet might see a sign for a street called Olive Street. Associations with the word Olive pass through the poet's brain: Popeye, olive loaf sandwiches, martinis with three olives. The essay might be down Route 386, but the poem is more likely to be somewhere down Olive Street.

To me, an assignment in a creative writing class needs to begin, as Hugo says, in your students' hometowns but through imagining end up someplace else entirely, someplace that does not adhere to all the known things we remember exactly about our hometowns, such as the fact the Olive Garden near the Monroeville Mall has cold restrooms. I believe the subject of a poem, and, therefore, the assignment that triggers it, must eventually become focused on the words themselves.

Let me give an example. Here's an exercise from the Behn and Twichell book *The Practice of Poetry* that I believe starts on Route 386 but then takes the Olive Street exit. Poet Roger Mitchell offers this three-part activity:

> Describe an object or scene that particularly interests you without making any comparisons of one thing to another. Rewrite it, if necessary, until it is as free of comparisons as possible. Then take the same object or scene and use it to describe one of your parents. In other words, indulge yourself in comparisons. Finally, write a poem which, though it is a description of the object or scene above, is really about your parents.

I like this exercise because it works well in a writing course that stresses mutuality; it does not dictate a specific end but rather lets students find their own way, even if it takes the student down a side street. The activity triggers a poem without requiring the student to write the exact poem the teacher has in mind. This is what I believe our assignments should do for our students.

Responding to Writing

I may have already said everything I will ever think of about response twenty years ago in *Responding to Student Poems*. I wrote that book because I had shown a short story of mine to a creative writing colleague who appropriated it, all the way from the subject to the very words the narrator spoke. He did allow me to keep my original dedication, which was to him. I'd been teaching myself theory at the time and thought one characteristic of some theories is that they serve as alternatives to the ways teachers typically respond to student writing. In fact, when I applied them in my own classes I saw how difficult it would be for me to appropriate my students' writing if I used those theories instead of the one I had been brought up to use, the New Criticism. I believe teachers of creative writing have thought through the issue of appropriation in ways teachers of composition have not, with the possible exception of the work of Nancy Welch whose advocacy of "side-shadowing" is intentionally dialogic, in spite of the fact that sideshadowing privileges the writer in the making of meaning, not the reader.

Sadly, there haven't been very many innovative response methods proffered in our most influential journals. But in studying the few available, Nancy Welch's "Sideshadowing Teacher Response" seems important to consider in light of the fact that it promises mutuality in its treatment of student writing. Welch's method offers us the kind of discourse relation with students we should strive for in creative writing classes if our goal is social equality.

Welch develops a method of response that, on the advice of Brannon and Knoblauch, encourages teachers to "resist the 'Ideal Texts' they bring to their reading of students' work" (375). To be clear on this point, let me add that Brannon and Knoblauch argue that teachers respond to student writing by comparing the student text to the Ideal Text they have in their minds, "where it often resides secretly as a guide to judging" (18).

In her critique of Thomas Recchio's essay, Welch, in commenting on Recchio's narrative about discussing an undergraduate student's draft of an essay in a graduate seminar, offers her view: "the student might contribute to and gain from such rich discussion about her text" (375). Indeed, the goal of commenting on student writing during workshops should, from the perspective mutuality offers, give students the chance to enter this "rich discussion" with their peers. Envisioning how this belief might be adapted to the situation of the teacher reading student writing, Welch advocates a procedure she calls "sideshadowing," borrowing "from the Bakhtinian theorist Gary Saul Morson's examination of narrative technique" (326). According to Welch, "[i]n contrast with the much more common narrative device of foreshadowing, which fixes our attention on a predetermined future, sideshadowing redirects our attention to the present moment, its multiple conflicts, its multiple possibilities" (376–77). By using sideshadowing, we disrupt "the pattern of student-composes-and-teacher-comments" (377). Students, thus, interact with their own texts.

The example of a sideshadowed text that Welch offers shows her student, Bill, offering "marginal comments, brackets, and arrows" that indicate his critique of what he had written. The comments Bill writes in the margins of his essay include those that reveal how he reads his own text. Bill's comments are both strategic and affective, as for example in the following: "effect of listing advantages first?" and "struggled with how personal, vulnerable [I] wanted to be" (386). From the perspective offered in her essay, Welch has indeed helped us move beyond the baseline of commentary found in the examples offered by Richard Straub.

No doubt we continue to work with a limited range of response styles, a predicament perhaps best identified in the scholarship of Straub and his colleague Ronald F. Lunsford, both in Straub's well-known essay concerning varieties of "Directive" and "Facilitative" response, and in several other books that focus on the way well-known composition scholars respond to student writing. The response methods modeled in these sources, whether directive or facilitative, to use Straub's terms, continues to see writing as an activity in which meaning adheres to the words on the page and the teacher as an authority for the outcome of the text itself. I want to see the methods Straub and Lunsford put before us as a baseline from which Welch wisely deviates.

Still, one might rightly conclude about sideshadowing that, while it helps us better envision ways of carrying on a dialog with our student/ authors, it privileges the author as the maker of meaning. Reading theorists for nearly fifty years have argued that the locus of meaning should instead be in the reader. As a result, let me reintroduce my best contribution to any conversation on responding to student writing, the *Parallel Text*. In bringing the Parallel Text to your attention, I forward the view that reader response criticism provides valuable insights into a teacher's reading processes and, perhaps, encourages a method of response consistent with the goals of mutuality.

Parallel Text Response is a method of responding to drafts of student writing that, instead of focusing on analysis of a text's features, gives teachers an opportunity to demonstrate to students *how one reader reads the text*—that is, how the reader implied by the text comes to construe meaning. In making a Parallel Text Response, teachers employ a double-entry format reminiscent of Ann Berthoff's double-entry journal. This strategy enables the teacher to function as a reader carrying on a written conversation with an author and the author's text in an effort to reveal to the author how the essay was read.[3]

Rather than acting out the role of expert reader by making comments that give students directions as to how to write on a specific subject to a particular audience, a teacher employing Parallel Text Response reflects to students/authors how one willing and receptive reader—the reader invoked by the author, the "implied reader"—constructs the text's meaning. Since the reader's text appears alongside rather than on top of the author's, teachers can reveal to their students how the student text was read by responding to various textual cues as the reader encounters them. By doing so, teachers can offer comments that either predict what will come next in the student text or indicate to the student what additional information the reader needs if the teacher is to become the reader the student hopes to create.

Where the teacher/reader construes a meaning different from what the author intends, the teacher has created by means of the parallel text an *area of dissonance* that students might choose to revise. I say "might choose to revise" because the student might also decide that the reader has not read correctly and the student might opt, as a result, to not revise those areas of dissonance in the expectation that the reader will read more carefully next time. Or, the student may decide to show that same draft of an essay to a peer to see if the peer likewise creates an area of dissonance. In any case, the primary goal of this kind of commentary is to read drafts of student papers in a manner consistent with the strategies currently being explored by critical theorists, particularly reading theorists. The resulting commentary is aimed at returning responsibility for revision—beyond simply doing what the teacher says to do in the student's effort to write the text the teacher would have written had the teacher done the assignment—to the student/author, where that responsibility belongs in a mutuality-driven classroom.

Use of Parallel Text Response, then, signals to students a teacher's interest in the reading process itself rather than in the features of a text. Here is an example of a student poem to which the teacher has made a Parallel Text Response.

Your Poem	*My Reading of Your Poem*
Back to the Ole Drawing Board The picture was drawn simple black and white. I thought it needed something more. You didn't.	—title is a cliché for starting over. Is that what you want? —picture? drawing? line drawing? Which do you mean? I take this as metaphor, right?
If only you had let me paint it, add some shading, definition. You were content to leave it untinged. (no stanza break) Just the outline, you said. Nothing more.	—Here's a contrast in views as to what should be added to the skeletal drawing: "You" wants less; the speaker wants more. Is this the central tension of your poem?
You controlled the drawing board. I allowed it once. You teased the sketch with splashes of red, purple, even green then left it alone looking empty, tainted.	—What does it mean to control a drawing board? Can it be controlled? How? If the speaker allows it, did "you" really have control? "You teased" sets me up for some upcoming contradiction, right?
Now you're back, paintbrush in hand, ready to create a masterpiece. The outline has been erased. The easel—thrown away. You were stuffed in the back of my portfolio. I have begun to paint again.	—Where did "you" go to make it possible for him/her to be "back"? Okay. The outline and easel are gone. How, if this is metaphor, does "you" get stuffed in a portfolio? You have a new relationship and have painted this time rather than drawn?

Teacher Talk in the Syllabus

I'd like to begin this section with another poem I've written because it is pertinent to my topic and because by its very nature it invites us to think about the ways we employ language in addressing our students, what I think of as "teacher-talk."

Falling Asleep While Reading "Mutuality and the Teaching of the Introductory Creative Writing Course"

Okay, you're right. From here
I can't tell if you're sleeping
or at what level of sleep you might be.
But with every word I have written,
I better envision you, my reader,
with your closed eyes
and tilted head. If you allow me the license
to imagine what I hear as well,
I can also hear scholarly indifference
escaping through your snore.

I will name this position "the sleeping position."
Let me be clear: you are not permitted to sleep
while reading this essay or to assume
the sleeping position.
If I imagine you sleeping
over the next half hour or so
or assuming the sleeping position,
I will transmit vibes that will interrupt your dream
of running wild and free
and probably naked at the beach
and tell you to silence your snore.

You will not receive credit
for reading this essay
and the next time I write an essay
you might read
I will try not to imagine
your response to it
as I write.

I used a variation of this poem in my "Pedagogy of Creative Writing" course this term in lieu of a traditional directive forbidding students from assuming the sleeping position in my class. As an experiment, this poem only begins to accomplish what I'd like my syllabus to get done (collaborative poems with my students focusing on various policies we would all eventually have to abide by might better establish mutuality on these points); it reminds me nonetheless that I'd much prefer to give a poetry reading on the first day of my creative writing class than a syllabus reading. But the way something as simple-minded as this poem reconfigures social relations in the classroom reflects just one concern I have when I think of ways creative writing might be taught as a critical pedagogy. My point, of course, is not that we should turn our syllabi into long poems, but that we should interrupt the usual rhetorical strategies we employ in writing our syllabi and do so specifically to involve our students in the making of language that influences our relationship with each other. My poem is a step in that direction.

In spite of its flaws and its author's obvious lack of ambition, in its own way this poem introduces the notion that we might experiment with the speech genres we use in our syllabi and, by doing so, rearticulate our discourse relations with our students. Granted, this poem is better suited to the mature than to those who are propped up in their chairs and with eyes taped open, as they read; I use it here, at this point in this essay, because it opens a way of discussing how creative writing and mutuality might work together, in fact have long worked together as partners in language use. So, think of the poem as an opportunity to consider the way we use language in addressing our students as well as how teachers of composition might benefit from paying attention to how creative writing teachers have long engaged their students.

I want to conclude much as I started but in the context of what I've said so far. We need to think about the language we use when we introduce ourselves and our courses to our students, when we assign writing, and when we respond to that writing. Here's one statement on texting from a colleague's syllabus, very different from my poem on the same topic that follows:

> Technology: Please turn off all cell phones, blackberries, laptops, beepers, and other devices before class and put them away. None are permitted without prior authorization. Students using electronic devices without prior authorization will be assessed "electronic absences," which will count against the total number of absences described in the attendance policy above. Exceptions to this policy will be considered on a case-by-case basis.

There's much more we can do as creative writing teachers to employ speech genres typically unused in our syllabi. The poem that follows, like the one I started with, doesn't aspire to be a great poem. But it is a start for me in my current project of writing a series of policy poems for use in the syllabus for my creative writing class.

Texting while reading "Mutuality and the Teaching of the Introductory Creative Writing Course" for my friends, readers who have not yet fallen asleep

You are not permitted
to text while reading this essay.
I cannot tell what your hands are pressing
there, between your thighs
and under your desk. I will assume
if your hands are between your thighs

you are doing something that will distract you
from reading my essay. I will call it texting.

If I notice anyone's hands engaged
in any stage of texting,
I will politely ask that person
to concentrate on one thing or the other.
And I mean you, my friend,
yes, especially you over there
with the smile on your face.

I would want this poem to simply remind all of us who want to teach differently and for social equity that language is always the problem—but it is also always the solution. We should experiment in an effort to share subject positions with our students in our classrooms. And sharing a poem in a creative writing class might be a very good way to go about changing our discourse relations with our students.

Notes

1. Nina Wallerstein defines Paulo Freire's method for transformation of society, what we will call *critical pedagogy* in this essay, in the following terms in her essay: ". . . the learner is not an empty vessel to be filled by the teacher nor an object of education. . . . Learners enter into the process of learning not by acquiring facts, but by constructing their reality in social exchange with others" (34).

2. Increasingly, the democratization of creative writing has brought to classes students who would not have taken such classes otherwise. They are as new to creative writing instructors as the new generation of students admitted to universities in the late sixties by means of open admissions must have seemed to writing teachers then. No doubt, the inclusion of these students will give us the opportunity to reconsider how we teach them. For a more in-depth treatment of this subject, please see my "The Future of Graduate Studies in Creative Writing."

3. The argument that Parallel Text Response is a natural outgrowth of reader-response criticism can be found in chapter 4 of *Responding to Student Poems: Applications of Critical Theory*. See also Ann Berthoff's description of a double-entry format for student journals in *The Making of Meaning*. Connors and Lunsford's "Teacher Rhetorical Comments on Student Papers" and Anson's *Writing and Response: Theory, Practice, and Research* may be profitably consulted for support of the belief that alternatives to traditional methods of response must be developed to keep up with what we currently understand to be true about the reading process.

Works Cited

Anson, Chris M., ed. *Writing and Response: Theory, Practice, and Research.* Urbana, IL: NCTE. 1989. Print.

Behn, Robin, and Chase Twitchell, eds. *The Practice of Poetry: Writing Exercises from Poets Who Teach.* New York: Harper Collins, 1992. Print.

Bizzaro, Patrick. *Responding to Student Poems: Applications of Critical Theory.* Urbana, IL: NCTE, 1993. Print.

———. "The Future of Graduate Studies in Creative Writing: Institutionalizing Literary Writing. *Key Issues in Creative Writing.* Ed. Dianne Donnelly and Graeme Harper. Bristol, UK: Multilingual Matters, 2013. 169–78. Print.

Bourdieu, Pierre. *Language and Symbolic Power.* Ed. John B. Thompson. Cambridge, MA: Harvard UP, 1984. Print.

Brannon, Lil, and C. H. Knoblauch. "On Students' Rights to Their Own Texts: A Model of Teacher Response." *A Sourcebook for Responding to Student Writing.* Ed. Richard Straub. Cresskill, NJ: Hampton, 1999. 117–28. Print.

Cain, Mary Ann. "'A Space of Radical Openness': Re-Visioning the Creative Writing Workshop." *Does the Writing Workshop Still Work?* Ed. Dianne Donnelly. Bristol, UK: Multilingual Matters, 2010. 216–29. Print.

Connors, Robert J., and Andrea Lunsford. "Teacher Rhetorical Comments on Student Papers." *College Composition and Communication* 44 (May 1993): 200–24. Print.

Delpit, Lisa. "Introduction." *Other People's Children: Cultural Conflict in the Classroom*. New York: The New Press, 2006. xxi–xxvii. Print.

Donnelly, Dianne. "Introduction: If It Ain't Broke Don't Fix It; Or, Change Is Inevitable Except from a Vending Machine." *Does the Writing Workshop Still Work?* Ed. Dianne Donnelly. Bristol, UK: Multilingual Matters, 2010. 1–27. Print.

Freire, Paulo. *Pedagogy of the Oppressed*. Trans. Myra Bergman Ramos. New York: Continuum, 1989. Print.

Giroux, Henry A. "Who Writes in a Cultural Studies Class? Where Is the Pedagogy?" *Left Margins: Cultural Studies and Composition Pedagogy*. Ed. Karen Fitts and Alan W. France. Albany, NY: SUNY Press, 1995. 3–16. Print.

Gorzelsky, Gwen. "Working Boundaries: From Student Resistance to Student Agency." *College Composition and Communication* 61.1 (Sept. 2009): 64–83. Print.

Hesse, Douglas. "The Place of Creative Writing in Composition Studies." *College Composition and Communication* 62.1 (Sept. 2010): 31–52. Print.

hooks, bell. *Talking Back: Thinking Feminist, Thinking Black*. Boston: South End, 1989. Print.

Horner, Bruce, and Min-Zhan Lu. "Working Rhetoric and Composition." *College English* 72.5 (May 2010): 470–94. Print.

Hugo, Richard. *The Triggering Town: Lectures and Essays on Poetry and Writing*. New York: Norton, 1979. Print.

Kopelson, Karen. "Of Ambiguity and Erasure: The Perils of Performative Pedagogy." *Relations, Locations, Positions: Composition Theory for Writing Teachers*. Urbana, IL: NCTE, 2006. 563–70. Print.

Lee, Amy. *Composing Critical Pedagogies: Teaching Writing as Revision*. Urbana, IL: NCTE, 2000.

Murray, Donald. "Unlearning to Write." *Creative Writing in America: Theory and Pedagogy*. Ed. Joseph M. Moxley. Urbana, IL: NCTE, 1989. 103–14.

Pough, Gwendolyn D. "Empowering Rhetoric: Black Students Writing Black Panthers." *College Composition and Communication* 53.3 (Feb. 2002): 466–86. Print.

Quintilian. "[F]rom *Institutes of Oratory*." *The Rhetorical Tradition: Readings from Classical Times to the Present*. 2nd ed. Ed. Patricia Bizzell and Bruce Herzberg. Boston: Bedford/St. Martin's, 2001. Print.

Recchio, Thomas. "A Bakhtinian Reading of Student Writing." *College Composition and Communication* 42 (1991): 446–54. Print.

Smith, Jeff. "Students' Goals, Gatekeeping, and Some Questions of Ethics." *College English* 59 (1997): 299–320. Print.

Shaul, Richard. "Foreword." *Pedagogy of the Oppressed.* 9–15. Print.

Shor, Ira, and Paulo Freire. *A Pedagogy for Liberation: Dialogues in Transforming Education.* Westport, CT: Bergin and Garvey, 1987. Print.

Tainor, Jennifer. "Critical Pedagogy's 'Other': Constructions of Whiteness in Education for Social Change." *College Composition and Communication* 53 (2002): 631–50. Print.

Wallace, David, and Helen Rothschild Ewald. *Mutuality in the Rhetoric and Composition Classroom.* Carbondale: Southern Illinois UP, 2000. Print.

Wardle, Elizabeth. "'Mutt Genres' and the Goal of FYC: Can We Help Students Write the Genres of the University?" *College Composition and Communication* 60 (June 2009): 765–89. Print.

Welch, Nancy. "Sideshadowing Teacher Response." *College English* 60 (Apr. 1998): 374–95. Print.

4

A Feminist Approach to Creative Writing Pedagogy

Pamela Annas and Joyce Peseroff

Once a woman poet begins telling the truth, there is no end of
possibilities.
                                                              —Judy Grahn

A FEMINIST APPROACH to teaching creative writing invites writers to
explore the raw material of their lives in the context of their experiences
as parents or on the battlefield, their historically specific memories of the
racial or ethnic, working-class or professional-class neighborhood(s) in
which they grew up, their gender socialization and choices, their cultural
and religious traditions, the food they eat, the Internet sites they visit, the
ways they have been and are situated in a multilayered and socially complex
world—and of course, their intimate relation with language, perhaps with
more than one. Gender itself has become more complicated and multi-
faceted or, alternatively, more fluid, in the twenty-first century. How does
this situation interweave with the multiplicity of formal options in both
writing and teaching for the poets, fiction writers, and nonfiction writers
that we are and with whom we work in our classes?

The feminist approach to teaching composition—centered on empowerment, process, and voice—developed in the 1980s is now one of the bases
of contemporary writing pedagogy. Central to an emerging creative writing
pedagogy as well is helping students to locate their material, empowering

78

them to write it in their own voice(s), giving them a safe place in which to take creative risks, providing experienced teacher/writers to mentor them, introducing them to the tools of their craft, and guiding them through prompts, sequenced assignments, and revision strategies to explore the wild country of their own writing terrain.

Quite happily with students in courses I (Pam) teach in the three divisions of English departments (literary studies, composition studies, creative writing), I've included creative prose and poetry assignments in every literature course, analytical essays in every creative writing course, and a mix of creative and analytical writing in every composition course—and have encouraged student writers to mix creative and rhetorical strategies. Inviting one's students and oneself to cross borders, whether cultural, social, intellectual, linguistic, or aesthetic, can initially be disorienting, even vertiginous. It pulls us out of the comfort zone of what we know or think we know. A range of writing assignments, writing and revision strategies, a focus on the writing process, nontraditional exemplary texts, and a relatively nonhierarchical classroom environment that invites students to take risks and be messy as well as to take responsibility for helping to shape the class, have been characteristic of my own feminist approach to teaching literary studies and writing since I began experimenting in the 1970s. Since I am a woman from a working-class background, the first in my family to go to college, and luckily settled in at an urban commuter public university in Boston that serves a multiethnic working-class student population, it has never been possible to separate my feminist, social-class, antiracist, antihomophobic, antiageist politics from my awareness of the complicated selves each student brings to the classroom and to the blank page.

Writing as Women

Writing as Women, a course in English and women's studies I developed in the early 1980s, was designed to provide a noncompetitive, nonhierarchical writing community where students from working-class and middle-class backgrounds, from a range of ethnic and racial backgrounds, from ages 18 to 80, could find a women's space where the exemplary texts had been written by women from a similar multiplicity of backgrounds and perspectives and were focused on issues women considered primary. We looked at silences and the assumptions underlying the language with which we had to work that, as language tends to do, expressed the perspective of a ruling class. We looked at the ways in which women had been and were silenced or muted in their gender socialization, in their workplaces, and in classrooms, given subtle or brutal reminders that what they had to say was of little interest and how they said it was silly, sentimental, incomprehensible, and thoroughly uncompelling. That their very speech rhythms were wrong, their images baffling and not powerful, not excellent, certainly unlikely to attract the attention of an editor considering their work. Lest we think this is no longer a problem, see a recent statistical updating of relative publication by gender in a number of major journals, including the *Atlantic, Harper's,* and the *Times Literary Supplement.* In 2010, the *New York Review of Books* published 39 book reviews by women and 200 by men; 59 books by women were reviewed and 306 by men (VIDA, the "count"). *Poetry* magazine did better, publishing 165 pieces by women and 246 by men that same year. Obviously, there are questions that can be asked about any such study, for example, how many women and men submitted work from which to choose. Nevertheless, the statistics are suggestive, and imply why in the 1990s *The Women's Review of Books* was established to make sure women writers and academics received visibility for their work. Wendy Bishop points out that "voice is not always defined for women as it is for men." And she offers this simple example:

> [T]he older I get the more interested I am in the "sentimental" poem. The poem that expresses my experiences, full of sentiment, experiences of generation, childbirth, child raising. What could be more powerful than exploring the opportunity the child gives us to one last time see our younger self? Why am I wary of this risky writing? Why was my naturally unconservative voice so channeled? (2)

In the competitive kick-ass arena of the writing workshop or in the typical college classroom, women had the choice of being good girls (Griseldas), angry hysterical witches, or silent (Bolker, 906–8). Their experience of writing coming into the *Writing as Women* course was often good-girl bland or ragged rant or they were so blocked they couldn't write at all.

In Writing as Women, a title carefully chosen for this course cross-listed in English and Women's Studies, the first exercise asked the students to describe either a positive or a negative incident in their relation to language. The second assignment asked them to write about their relation to language and to writing in the context of their background, considering factors such as age, social class, race, ethnic group, sexual politics and identity, region or country, religion and whatever else seemed relevant in addition to gender. Next, the class collectively compiled a list of writing blocks, which included perfectionism, fear of criticism or judgment, depression, numbness or blankness, fear of taking risks, fear of success, coping with an alien subject matter, fear of one's own power or anger, worry that one has nothing to say, writing for an audience indifferent or hostile to what one wants to say, fear of knowing oneself, getting stuck between objectivity and subjectivity, fear of being trivialized or conforming to what's expected, private vs. public writing, talking vs. writing, having the right to one's opinions, discomfort with the mechanics of writing and organizing a paper, and fear of being boring, dumb, insignificant, or ridiculous (Annas, WSQ, 38–39). We considered the historic role of consciousness-raising groups, the hidden genres of journals and diaries, the small press women's publishing movement beginning in the late 1960s and poet Judy Grahn's comment at that time that self-publishing isn't vanity; it's an act of revolution.

Blocks to writing were followed by the writing process assignment in which women kept a journal that followed their intellectual, psychological, and material process from the initial self or other assigned project minutely through the stages of writing day by day as the writing emerged from and took place within the rest of their lives. They detailed the modes of procrastination, the initial forays into the writing, the need to go to a job to pay rent, the emotions and doubts, the physical space in which to write (the kitchen table, a room of one's own, a local coffee shop), the initial rough draft or promising fragments, the distractions from children, friends, mates, and the voices inside one's head that say there is no talent and nothing to say that anyone would care about, the moments of joy when the writing starts to come together. I ask them to chart their process with vivid everyday details and also to consider some images for their writing process—one student imaged her process as putting a jigsaw puzzle together, another saw it as finding an old chair on a sidewalk and slowly and lovingly refinishing it. Another wrote despairingly early in her process paper, "My ideas are as profound and original as Ronald Reagan's press conferences." Later, when she found her rhythm, she added,

> It's the words that I love. . . . They congregate, like old Southern ladies at church, into sentences and paragraphs. The rise and fall of their cadences is punctuated by exclamations (Yes, Jesus!) and commas (MmmmHmmm) and question marks (Ain't it so?). In their silences, their hushed pauses, a quiet hymn as soft as magnolias rises from their lips.

We considered the nature of language, words we use, words we avoid, words we can't find to express our particular experiences, whether we feel we own the language we learned at our mother's knee—and considered June Jordan's comment: "the white child is rewarded for mastery of his standard, white English: the language he learned at his mother's white and standard knee. But the Black child is punished for mastery of his non-standard Black English: for the ruling elite of America have decided that non-standard is sub-standard, and even dangerous, and must be eradicated" (*Civil Wars*, 70). Whatever their race or class or age or country of origin, the women in my course talked about how many fewer ways there are to express female perceptions. How much energy does it take to constantly have to translate your own perceptions, images, narratives into terms your male colleagues can understand and value?

We looked at several areas of research: feminist linguistics, feminist literary criticism, the French feminists' writing about language, creativity and the body, and women writers in the United States writing about their writing process, for example, Mary Daly, Susan Griffin, Adrienne Rich, Audre Lorde, Gloria Anzaldua, Judy Grahn, Alice Walker. The French feminists ground creativity and the enormous potential of women's writing in the sensual and cyclical rhythms of the female body. Marguerite Duras writes about women's creativity as a shutting off of analytical and linear thinking and "returning to a wild country" (Marks and de Courtivron, 174–75). Similarly, Audre Lorde's groundbreaking essay "Uses of the Erotic: The Erotic as Power" locates creativity in the body and defines it as the "capacity for joy." Lorde writes: "In touch with the erotic, I become less willing to accept powerlessness, or those other supplied states of being which are not native to me, such as resignation, despair, self-effacement, depression, self-denial" (7).

Adrienne Rich writes: "Nothing can be too sacred for the imagination to turn into its opposite or to call experimentally by another name. For writing is re-naming" (43). One of the more challenging assignments in Writing as Women is to make up a new word that expresses a female experience for which there are currently no words, and to write this in the form of an extended OED-style definition with history and examples. Creating genuine new words based on newly recovered perceptions is a tough job. I had created a definition in that form, "radicalteacher," which lived on the back cover of the pedagogy journal *The Radical Teacher* for a number of years. Probably the best example produced in the class was "motherfail," written by a woman who had raised six children, including one who had taken the course two years before and recommended it to her mother. Her definition contained a number of ironic and moving examples of how as a mother, no matter what you do, it isn't good enough. This assignment brought us face to face with the difficulty of imagining the things for which we don't have a linguistic framework, and with how completely and unconsciously we live inside the bell jar of the language we inherit. The course also includes forays into poetry and prose fiction or creative nonfiction, including in-class assignments where we collectively write poems or flash fiction, each person starting a poem or story and passing it on, the next person taking a minute to add a line or a sentence and passing it on again until each person has had a chance to conclude one of the circulating poems or stories, and the last person gets to create a title. For another assignment, students each went to some live event—a play, concert, restaurant, or reading—and wrote a review in the mode of a personal essay. Toward the end of the semester, each wrote a position paper—a nontraditionally sequenced version of the argument/analysis assignment.[1]

The last two weeks of the semester we reformed into an editorial collective and put together an anthology of class work. Each person submitted two pieces from which one would be chosen, and each joined a working group: editorial, layout, graphic design, and those who had volunteered to write the preface to the anthology and submit possible titles to be voted on by the whole collective. One year we were able to have the entire anthology included as an insert in the university's literary magazine; in other semesters we assembled the work into a manuscript that was printed and bound at the copy shop.

A Feminist Approach to Writing in Literature Courses

Writing as Women was my experimental lab for feminist approaches to teaching writing. In mixed-gender literature courses like Working-Class Literature, I found that what I had discovered about women's relation to language, creativity, and expression and women's history of being silenced or muted had significant parallels in the experience of working-class men and women.[2] Since *Working-Class Literature* included exemplary texts by African American, Italian, Latino, Asian, Native American, Jewish, Southern, gay and straight, urban and rural working-class writers both male and female, we noted the struggle of writers defined by the dominant group in this country (white, male, middle to upper class) to get past self-censorship, find their own voice, mine their own material, and then try to gain access to an audience for their work.[3]

In addition to reading nontraditional exemplary texts, the writing assignments in *Working-Class Literature* included forays into poetry and prose about working-class experience or cross-class encounters, for example, write a page in the mode of a working-class writer whose work is teaching you something about style, or write a short scene of a cross-class encounter. The analytical writing for the course consisted not of the usual formal papers but rather three pages per week of a critical reading journal, based on my theory that understanding is not necessarily best achieved within the parameters of a traditional narrowly focused explication or research paper but through a less formal, cumulative, and constantly circling back approach of building connections between the texts and between the texts and the students' own lives, which they were invited to interpolate into their analyses. In the graduate seminar version of the course, the agenda of a number of participants was figuring out how to insert working-class texts into the American literature courses they were teaching in high school. We collectively co-taught Sandra Cisneros's *The House on Mango Street* (an excellent exemplary text for beginning fiction writers); each seminar participant chose a chapter and made a fifteen-minute presentation on how s/he would teach it, complete with in-class writing exercises.

Contemporary Women Poets, like Working-Class Literature offered on both the graduate and undergraduate levels, led with Alicia Ostriker's proposal that women poets are the "thieves of language." The course focused on poetry from 1960 on and considered whether there is a tradition of American women poets into which these contemporary poets fit, the relation between poetics, politics, and gender, and the ways in which contemporary women poets have created new forms and new content and changed our sense of the nature of poetry. We begin with a palette of contemporary poems by Tess Gallagher, Sharon Olds, Susan Griffin, June Jordan, Sylvia Plath, Anne Sexton, Audre Lorde, Adrienne Rich, and others that raise issues central to women as well as the struggle to write one's own experience, and I introduce them to a way of reading poetry that places the poet in her social context as well as considering the craft of the poem (Annas and Rosen, 1510–11). For the remainder of the semester, we focus on the work of six or seven poets, studying a stage in the work of each; in one version of the course we read exemplary texts by Gwendolyn Brooks, *The Bean Eaters*; Judy Grahn, *The Common Woman Poems* and *A Woman is Talking to Death*; Joy Harjo, *In Mad Love and War*; Muriel Rukeyser, poems from *The Speed of Darkness* and *Breaking Open*; Mary Oliver, *American Primitive*; and Patricia Smith, *Close to Death*. We do short in-class writing exercises, some analytical and some creative.

Each student memorizes a poem by a contemporary woman poet and recites/performs it in class. Each leads a discussion on a poem by one of the poets we are reading (undergraduates do so in pairs) formulating questions on poetics, politics, and connections to other poets we are reading and to the literary history and criticism assigned, which includes Ostriker's *Stealing the Language: The Emergence of Women's Poetry in America* and Kim Whitehead's *The Feminist Poetry Movement*. Each student attends a poetry reading in the Boston area and writes a review of the reading and her experience of the reading. Each gives a presentation on one volume of poems by a contemporary woman poet not on the syllabus, passing out three exemplary poems from that text to the class. Each student writes two original poems during the semester, accompanied by a paragraph on what they thought they were doing with sound, line, and image in their poem, what specifically they were most pleased about with the poem, and where they wanted some advice on how to improve it. Students then work on these poems in class, in groups of three. Graduate students have the option to write a pedagogy paper, or a lesson plan on how to work with a poem or group of poems with their middle-school, high-school, or college students and how to develop writing prompts from the assignment.

A Feminist Approach to Personal Narrative Writing

Contemporary Women Poets and Working Class-Literature are primarily literature courses in which nontraditional exemplary texts are central and analytical writing is expected, even if the form is untraditional. Life Writing, which I've taught both as a graduate and as an honors undergraduate course, is a course in personal narration—memoir, personal essay, lyric narrative poetry, and graphic memoir. While the center of this course is writing, and the final project twenty to thirty pages of personal narrative, students also write short analytical essays on aspects of craft in the traditional and non-traditional exemplary texts we read, such as Sonia Sanchez's "Dear Mama," Tommy Avocolli's "He Defies You Still: The Memoirs of a Sissy," Richard Wright's "The Man Who Went to Chicago," Dorothy Allison's "Gun Crazy," Tobias Wolff's *This Boy's Life*, Marjane Satrapi's graphic autobiography *Persepolis*, Riverbend's *Baghdad Burning: Girl Blog from Iraq*. The syllabus is expanded by the students, who each choose a personal narrative not on the syllabus for an independent project; they select a ten-page excerpt to assign to the class and are responsible for "teaching"/leading a discussion on the text. In-class writing exercises are offered each week, for example:

- Make a list of "characters" likely to appear in your personal narrative. Choose one of these and write down details that come to mind, quirks that characterize him or her, using the senses—sight, touch, smell, sound, taste, movement—and using vivid details.
- Choose a physical object that has resonance in your life. It could be a pair of shoes or favorite jacket, a porch swing or a baseball glove, a piece of sea-worn coral from a trip to the Virgin Islands, a button from an antiwar march, a picture you drew when you were seven. Let the physical object open up into a story from your life.
- Drawing from graphic memoir (and drawing if you can, though most of us will have to use words), visualize one *frame* of a scene from your personal narrative. Consider light and dark, placement of figures, the setting both background and foreground, how the figures are placed in relation to each other, what they are wearing, what their gestures are, what words if any are in the frame.
- Following up our examination of Barrington's diagram of concentric circles of the memoir from inner life all the way out to the world, and our examination of chapters from *This Boy's Life* to see how this works in practice, the in-class exercise today is: choose a time period from the personal narrative on which you have settled to write (Barrington, 141–50). In class, make a list of references to the cultural, historical, political, scientific context of your life during that time—technological advances, mass culture, for example, music, television, food fads, fashion, the arts, books, major events both natural and social. For homework, check your references for accuracy. Also, research five to ten more that you might not have immediately thought of but will remember when you read about them; these will provide more vivid historical texture to your personal story.

Since students are working sequentially on an extended project—whether personal essay(s), a chapter of an envisioned larger narrative, a connected series of shorter memoir pieces, a collection of lyric narrative poetry or some combination—and each week includes work in small groups of two to four depending on length of assignment that week—and since the groups rotate each week—all the writers in the class become familiar with each other's work and are invested in each other's progress and success.[4] The end of semester reading and class anthology confirm the collective and noncompetitive character of the process.[5] A number of students go on to extend their projects into senior honors or MA thesis projects.

Writing across the Writing Curriculum

One of the threads in discussion of creative writing pedagogy is the silo effect within English departments where specialists in literary scholarship, rhetoric and composition, and creative writing have, historically, eyed each other suspiciously across the barricades. I believe that students in literature courses learn about poetry, fiction, and other genres in part by writing them, struggling with issues of craft from the writer's perspective. Creative writers deepen and enrich their own imaginative writing through a careful study and analysis of literature, the literary tradition, and the social and historical context in which it is produced. The critical thinking and research skills we teach as our bread and butter, and as community and civic service to every student in the university in our composition courses, are equally necessary to the next generation of poets, playwrights, and fiction writers in our creative writing courses. In the second half of this chapter, Joyce Peseroff will discuss the traditional creative writing workshop model as limited, in ways connected to the discussion of feminist writing pedagogy in this section, in what it can provide for students.

It is important to keep in mind that what feminist and other radical approaches to teaching writing have at their center is a combination of inclusion and disruption—to *include* a multiplicity of ways of seeing and saying from a multiplicity of experiences and to *disrupt* a hegemonic, or prevailing systemic, ruling class discourse and world view. An early and very useful example in literary studies is Judith Fetterley's *The Resisting Reader*. By approaching the classic canon of male literary texts, for example, *The Great Gatsby*, "A Rose for Emily," *The Bostonians*, from a feminist perspective, Fetterley was able to explore and question the assumptions, narratives, images, and central archetypes of the patriarchal texts that constituted most of the canon of American literature that we were raised on and, if we were aspiring fiction writers or poets, were encouraged to emulate. To then go on and provide a different, more inclusive, set of texts to use as models was and is a disruption of literary business as usual. To provide a more inclusive, less hierarchal, and process- as well as product-oriented pedagogy in the writing classroom is another way of disrupting an almost entirely product-oriented and competitive creative writing classroom format that is actually less effective for the majority of students.

It goes without saying that high expectations, rigorous feedback, careful attention to training writers in the tools and materials of their craft, not accepting less than the best effort from students, and pushing them (and their instructor) to grow and change, are central to a feminist writing pedagogy. For example, students in Writing as Women were encouraged to be disruptive. It was a regular occurrence in my classes for working-class, Black, Hispanic, lesbian, etc., students to challenge white middle-class assumptions they saw in the texts or the pedagogy or the classroom process. Every day in the classroom brought new and surprising disruptions and inclusions. We rose to the challenge, learned from each other, and changed. "If theorizing and disruption are detached from lived experience and material history, they may remain irrelevant," write Joy Ritchie and Kathleen Boardman.

> And if disruption only fractures and doesn't again create connection, a sense of an even tentatively inclusive agenda, it will lack the vital energy and supportive alliances to sustain its own taxing work. Over the last 30 years, feminists have demonstrated that critique and disruption are never finished and that coalition-building and collaboration are vital for change. (602)

My twenty-one-year-old son said to me this morning during a kitchen-table discussion of economics and changing gender roles, while eating the breakfast he had prepared (I was going to wash the dishes), that he'd heard that "men are the new women." It may be that fifty years from now women will be in the ascendant position, socially, economically, and linguistically, that men have enjoyed for millennia. It may be, for example, that my constant substitution in academic discourse of the word "germinal" for the entrenched and patriarchal "seminal" will take hold. What a different worldview when "germinal" expresses the place where the creative and transformative begins. Committed to social justice as I am, I think that when words, images, rhythms, and syntax that thoroughly express women's experience become an integral part of our languages, our literatures, and our everyday discourse, that rather than create a new linguistic hierarchy it will expand and enrich language for all of us.

Pam has noted two issues common to literature, composition, and creative writing classrooms that feminist pedagogy can address directly. Women's fears about writing—worry that one has nothing to say, worry that what one does have to say will be trivialized or fail to conform to what's expected, worries about looking boring, dumb, insignificant, or ridiculous on the page—suffuse all three contexts (and are hardly limited to women). As our classrooms become more culturally diverse, the feminist practice of including a multiplicity of reading experiences that disrupt a hegemonic system becomes more necessary. In this section, I'll focus specifically on two aspects of the creative writing classroom that reflect these responses: the structure of the creative writing workshop and the uses of exemplary texts. Both employ techniques of feminist disruption whether introduced by actively feminist writers like Wendy Bishop and Katherine Haake, or adopted by men like Rob Pope and Ben Knights.

The Creative Writing Workshop

Since first developed by the MFA program at the University of Iowa, the creative writing workshop has been the signature practice of the discipline. In a traditional text-centered workshop, students bring their apprentice work to class and offer it for criticism to their fellow students under the direction of the professor, a distinguished writer and master craftsman. Students present their work to the full class without introduction and sit silently during class discussion, responding only when discussion ends. Focus remains on the work as product; the object is to probe the product's weaknesses and persuade the writer to fix them, much as a home inspector might point out the need to replace a sill or upgrade wiring. Though the master craftsman might propose exercises for students to follow, no writing happens in class. Suggestions for radical revision are rare; if so, they're a sign of a writer's failure rather than an invitation to go more deeply into the impulse from which the work first developed. Process remains a private matter, considered irrelevant to the appearance of the final product, which is judged by a literary verdict that, as D. G. Myers argues in *The Elephants Teach* (177), "is really the social campaign to assign dominant status to a particular perspective." Such a perspective, in practice, is as likely to exclude women now as it did when the Iowa workshop was first established in 1936; statistics published by VIDA: Women in Literary Arts still show an overwhelming bias toward male authors published and/or reviewed by the *London Review of Books*, *The Atlantic*, the *Paris Review*, *The Nation*, and other journals.

Feminist writers like Wendy Bishop, Mary Swander, and Katherine Haake were first to examine the drawbacks to the Iowa model. The mentor/apprentice relationship supported sex stereotyping since women rarely appeared in the role of master craftsman. It encouraged rivalry and competition for approval by the professor and fellow students, marginalizing voices that didn't conform to a preferred style and flattening writers' most original ideas. It trivialized subjects that constituted the experience of half the human race while enforcing silence and separation rather than dialogue and community. As Mary Swander has noted, this type of classroom was never intended for novices; rather, it was designed as a "boot camp" that would toughen and prepare practicing writers for criticism from the outside world (167–69). This militaristic model developed in a program that was mostly male, including many veterans on the GI Bill, and it intimidated and marginalized women as it sorted members into stars and drones, "real" writers and disappointed ones. Like canaries in a coal mine, women's experiences in the traditional workshop alerted instructors to practices that discourage all students from writing while failing to promote learning. In *What Our Speech Disrupts: Feminism and Creative Writing Studies*, Katherine Haake writes, "What I began to see was that what worked in teaching 'the best' writers was of little value to the rest" and that "the very way we conduct ourselves as a discipline is alienating and problematic for male students as well [as women]" (143).

Feminist thinking provides a framework for considering alternatives to the traditional workshop by (1) decentering authority and (2) focusing on questions of the excluded voice. By asking who gets silenced by traditional practices and by what authority the silencing occurs, instructors can foster workshops that respond to student needs rather than the master crafts-man's approval. The first way that instructors can decenter authority and invite student voices to participate is by asking students to frame work-shop guidelines. What do students want others to say about their work? What will they find helpful? How do they want to introduce a piece before discussion begins? How will the writer participate in discussion? Who will lead? Should there be page limits to submissions, or time limits? In my Intermediate Creative Writing Workshop, students decided that work would be discussed in the order students posted it on the class website, rewarding early posters who gave students more time to read the piece.

Since students get a chance to speak more often in a small group, switching from full-class to small-group workshops, as Pam did in her Life Writing class, makes it more likely students will be heard. It also disrupts the master/apprentice relationship since the master craftsman isn't in charge; the instructor can designate a group discussion leader that rotates from meeting to meeting. The instructor can also vary the make-up of the group, giving students a chance to hear from each member of the class while maintaining the benefits of small-group work. Within groups, substituting a vocabulary of descriptive terms for critical ones encourages expression rather than shutting it down. Instead of offering a critique, group members can

1. allow the writer to introduce the piece and set an agenda with an introduction
2. respond by giving a summary or précis of the work
3. read aloud examples of good writing, with the understanding that they must distinguish not just what they like, but why
4. read aloud each other's work, allowing the writer to hear what it sounds like, and if the reader has any difficulties
5. make suggestions for change in the form of questions, often beginning "What if?"
6. write letters, expressing what they might not have had time to say in group in a thoughtful and personal way

Some models for the creative writing workshop offer more radical change by borrowing structure from other disciplines. Justin Maxwell, in an AWP Pedagogy paper, describes the methodology of the lab report adapted for creative writing classes:

> The lab report lets students employ the strengths of the scientific method to lay out their agenda for a text, give them real ownership of their development process, and allow a new democratization of the creative writing classroom. From this, students can explore their own artistic agendas and better understand each other's approaches, allowing students to see their work individuated from the group and preventing mob aesthetics. (5)

In this model, the instructor and class together generate a series of prompts that students answer as they write "to get students to think about the artistic 'what,' 'why,' and 'how' of their writing; about its agenda" (6). This report is revised as the student revises, helping students articulate their work in the way a lab report helps other scientists understand the nature of the experiment. Maxwell suggests three core elements for the creative writing lab: a hypothesis or statement of agenda (I want to write a poem about my grandmother's death and how I felt sad but relieved); a discussion of methodologies or procedures (I made a list of things I remember about her organized by color; I wrote down words she forgot when she got sick); and a list of areas where the writer struggled (I couldn't decide whether the poem should begin at her funeral or when she first came to America; I had a hard time describing her at the end). The workshop then focuses on the question, "Does this text fulfill the criteria of the lab report?" Members avoid imposing their own subjective notions of a "successful" piece and instead "assess how well the text's agenda is laid out and how well the text fulfills its agenda" (5). Workshop members might discuss whether feelings of sadness and relief are expressed so a reader gets both; how the colors help readers understand the grandmother; whether the poem seems to begin or end at the right moment (if the goal is to express sadness and relief at her death).

Jenny Dunning offers an example of classroom structure borrowed from another artistic discipline. She points out that the original model for the creative writing workshop was the art studio (1). (Indeed, AWP classifies MFA curricula into three basic types: the Studio Program, the Studio/Research Program, and the Research/Theory/Studio Program). In the art studio, rather than critique finished products, artists practice creativity: "A recurring theme in the art department . . . is the exhortation to play, experiment, take risks . . ." while a traditional writing workshop encourages students "to stick to strategies that have met with group approval in the past or worked for them in an earlier piece of writing" (2). Dunning's curriculum calls for more in-class writing and response to "low-stakes" collaborative assignments that "spread risk around" and promote "a greater mix of strategies" in reply to a given prompt (2). Rather than discussing a polished product, Dunning's students report their progress in solving problems offered by a variety of assignments, whether begun in class or done at home. For instance, students might be asked to imagine a character and list what would be in the character's refrigerator, including one item that would surprise the character's best friend, then invent a dialogue between the two. The discussion process would involve suggestions for developing the story evoked by students' characters and their dialogue. While learning the importance of significant detail, surprise, and conflict in character development and story construction, students also engage in educating the imagination—the "creative" part of creative writing. "How much more relaxed might 'workshopping' be if rather than feeling like their classmates are critiquing a 'finished draft,' they feel like they're simply discussing, exploring, questioning, and brainstorming all of the different potential iterations of an 'unfinished final piece?'" wrote a student in my Teaching Creative Writing course (Van Hagel). Dunning's model foregrounds and examines the infinite variety of voices and choices available in creative work, as students' solutions inspire each other; peer discussion avoids the risk of becoming a forum for work to be judged as "successful" or "good," or for writers to be weighed and found wanting.

These alternatives emphasize process rather than product. They remove the master craftsman as the sole source of authority, and, shifting focus from ends to means, they acknowledge and value each student's expertise in the development of his or her voice. Each model encourages students to think like writers by doing what writers need to do—*write*—without alienation and anxiety generated through traditional workshop practices.

Exemplary Texts

Feminist pedagogy also challenges the use of exemplary texts in creative writing courses. Creative writing classes typically ask students to approach texts in a manner different from that of literature classes while including some of the tools and vocabulary of critical analysis—if "reading like a writer," as the phrase goes, asks less about what a text means and more about how meaning is made, it still requires some discussion of what "meaning" is. Most creative writing textbooks, such as Janet Burroway's *Imaginative Writing: The Elements of Craft*, use literary texts to name and model elements of good writing that create meaning. Students discuss exemplary texts in class with the goal of becoming more aware of these elements in their own work, then create new work modeled in one way or another on these pieces. In traditional exercises, students study sonnets or sestinas in order to learn how to write their own, or a story rich in dialogue to understand the "best practices" for using dialogue in their own work.

But, as Susan Hubbard quotes Elisabeth Daumer and Sandra Runzo in her essay "Gender and Authorship" (134): "How are we to reconcile the pervasive message in feminist theory that language oppresses women with the fact that it is exactly this language we are supposed to teach?" And, in "Valuing the Community of Undergraduate Writing" (1), Wendy Bishop argues that using anthologized texts can lead undergraduates "to value seemingly monolithic writing conventions, that lead them to overvalue the commercially printed text" and, feeling intimidated or marginalized, avoid risky writing by mimicking other voices and suppressing their own.

One solution, as Pam suggests, is to encourage students to invent and define new words based on newly recovered and recognized perceptions. An exercise based on Tillie Olsen's iconic short story "I Stand Here Ironing" can lead students to create words like the one Emily invents for comfort: "shoogily." A second approach is to incorporate a variety of texts with a diversity of language. These would embrace, along with race, gender, and ethnicity, a diversity of aesthetics that extends the notion of "good writing" beyond canonically approved work. Even this is problematical for Katherine Haake: ". . . to the extent that we continue to proceed by presenting unproblematized literary models in our classroom, we will work towards reinforcing already anachronistic twentieth century views of what counts as writing" (20). Or, as Robert Pinsky writes in *Slate*,

> Life is unpredictable, and that general truth has plenty of illustrations in the course of artistic reputations. The hack movie directors of one decade may be recognized as geniuses in the next, while those hailed as serious artists are revealed as pretentious phonies in the ascent (or spiraling Tilt-A-Whirl?) of time. In the 18th century, many esteemed Colley Cibber more highly than Alexander Pope. In living memory, John O'Hara was well-known and influential, and Frank O'Hara was not.

Another solution is to replace modeling with the practice of textual intervention, a term Rob Pope developed in 1995 with the publication of *Textual Intervention: Critical and Creative Strategies for Literary Studies*. Students interact with published writing by creating a conversation with an individual text that allows them to observe how a piece of literature operates without holding the text itself sacred. Although many writing prompts can be text based—Oulipo N+7, word bank, translating from unknown languages (homophonic), substitution, and reversal—they don't necessarily engage students with close reading and attention to craft that an intervention with the original requires.

Pope includes this exercise, "De-centering and Re-centering a Literary Classic" (14–29). He asks students to read Robert Browning's "My Last Duchess," then approach the text using these seven steps:

1. Translate the whole poem into a conversational idiom with which you are more familiar, presenting the results on the page or in live reading as you see fit.
2. Draw up a list of all the people actually presented or referred to in the text.
3. Go on to distinguish these "included participants" insofar as they are represented as "speaking," "spoken to," or "spoken about."
4. Now look again at the text and draw up a list of reference to all those artifacts and practices that must at some point have required human

labor—even though the laborers themselves are absent and their existence is merely assumed or ignored. (The "excluded participants.")

5. Go on to add the actual writer (here Robert Browning) and some actual readers (for example, you and me) to the picture. (The "extra-textual participants.")

6. Now reconsider what participants you personally would prefer at the center of a parallel, counter-, or alternative text. Go on to envision a new version of the poem with this participant at the center of the text.

7. Sketch and draft your refined or revised version now. Put a provisional title to it. Go on to add a commentary comparing your version with the base text, explaining your critical rationale and chronicling the decision-making process.

In order for students to complete this exercise, they must understand what's going on in the original text enough to paraphrase it (step 1). The exercise asks students to think about inclusion and exclusion, and writers' choices regarding whose voice is heard, while giving them an opportunity to give voice to an otherwise excluded character, including participating in the text themselves. In completing the exercise, they must use what they know from reading the poem to complete a character imaginatively, entering a conversation with Browning's work that educates them as readers as well as writers. The exercise teaches several craft elements at once—diction, character development, and plot (if by putting herself at the center of the text the student decides to push the Duke off his balcony)—without requiring the student to esteem the work in a personal way.

Another example of textual intervention involves rewriting something that students have heard before—a biblical story, myth, fairy tale, history, poem, or play—taking the point of view of a character with a limited role or perspective in the original. Making "Cinderella" into the stepsister's story, for instance, demonstrates to students how shifting the point-of-view character alters the plot. The climax of the story, if the story belongs to the stepsister, is not Cinderella's discovery by the prince but the stepsister's decision to carry out a crippling act of self-mutilation. This allows students to understand how "story" becomes "plot," and how plot is generated by character. We may discuss these craft issues in the classroom, but through writing, students experience them. This also brings up questions of ownership—who does the story belong to? Tales and poems about Eve, Penelope, Persephone, Lazarus, whaler's wives, and war wives interrogate assumptions made in both Testaments, Homer, Ovid, *Moby Dick*, "The Things They Carried." These creative readings and rewritings encourage students to take control of story from a perspective that resonates with them, giving them authority over the original text. They ask students to consider who *doesn't* get to speak in a given work; how who controls the discourse affects the story; and they demystify how writers make conscious decisions about these matters.

An example of textual intervention I've used in class involves the first section of T. S. Eliot's "Preludes," "The Winter Evening Settles Down." I use this poem as the basis for a lesson in imagery that includes close reading followed by a classroom reconstruction and finally a new work created by each student. The poem begins

> With smells of steaks in passageways.
> Six o'clock.
> The burnt-out ends of smoky days

and ends ". . . at the corner of the street / a lonely cab-horse steams and stamps." We list the poem's images, noting that some of them appeal to more than one of the senses: you'd smell as well as hear and see a stamping, steaming horse. I ask them, by looking at adjective and noun pairs, to explain the mood of the piece. A gloomy winter evening, the class agrees, naming the burnt-out ends, gusty shower, grimy scraps, withered leaves, vacant lots, broken blinds. They note the metaphor of cigarette butts in line 4, and the verbs: settles, wraps, beat. Although the traces of other people are evident, as in any urban setting, no character appears in the poem other than the "you" in line 7—no cabman, no lamplighter, not the worker coming home to a steak dinner. All in all, pretty grim, and all the grimness conveyed through imagery.

I ask about their individual experiences: Have you had a gloomy winter evening? A pleasant winter evening? What made your winter evening delightful? We start to list the images that would convey the details of an inviting winter night. I refer back to the Eliot poem. What images would need to change in order for the poem to reflect a different feeling about its subject? Line by line, we rewrite the poem. Gradually, the winter evening changes as the class replaces Eliot's language with their invention.

By asking students to take apart and rewrite a canonical work, I give them permission to foreground their language, feelings, and processes. By doing this in a group, I prepare them for the protocols of workshop. Suggestions for replacement lines and images are offered, debated, added to, edited down. As with the collectively written poems and flash fiction in Pam's Writing as Women class, no single writer "owns" the product, which allows them more freedom to improvise and take risks. Students must give a reason for any additions to or revision of the common text, which prepares them for discussion of each other's work while emphasizing the reflection necessary for revision. It also teaches them to read closely for detail, identifying parts of speech that create feeling—what happens, I ask, if we eliminate the adjective from those adjective-noun pairs we discussed? What are some synonyms for "smells" in line 2 that would make the steaks more appetizing? Finally, I ask them each to write a poem using their own observations after walking through campus, creating either a gloomy or joyful scene, beginning with a list of things they can see, smell, hear, taste, and touch. After they've worked on this prompt, students read their work aloud and we vote: pleasant or gloomy? Why do you say so? By first reading then intervening in Eliot's text, students learn the power of significant detail in their own work. It also gives them a kick to rewrite a "master" they've been taught to revere, if they've heard of him at all.

Ben Knights, director of the United Kingdom's English Studies Program, 2003–2011, developed an idea that he has termed "re-creative writing" with class activities that include "practices of imitation, re-centering, parody, shift of tense, focus or point of view, and the translation from one genre to another" (17–22). Some of the exercises that Knights has suggested include

1. rewriting a paragraph of a fiction text in a different genre (first person stream of consciousness into third person realist; fiction into radio play; poem of place into opening setting for a novel, romance into detective story, etc.)
2. lifting some "voices" from a modernist poem and writing their back story (considering Eliot, one could use Prufrock)
3. writing the first paragraphs of a sequel to a short story (what happens after the end of Raymond Carver's "Viewfinder"?)
4. inserting a moment of fantasy into an otherwise realistic text (perhaps Carver's character flies off the roof?)
5. selecting some key images from a novel or short story and arrange them into an imagist poem (the student must identify and thus understand what those images are before completing the exercise)

Through both literature and composition, feminist pedagogy has influenced and continues to influence the discipline of creative writing. Mindful of students' fears, histories, empowerment, and passions, we've used these techniques to encourage those in our classrooms to cultivate writing *as* a part of their reflective, intellectual, and emotional lives.

Appendix: The Workshop Format

- Give each person in your group a copy of your writing.
- Someone else in the group will be reading your piece of writing out loud. So, make those assignments, then take a few minutes to each read silently the piece you have volunteered to read aloud. The prereading is so that you can do the oral reading well, with expression and care (as you would hope your own piece will be read).
- Plan to spend about fifteen minutes listening to and discussing each person's work.
- First reader reads aloud to the group the assigned piece. Each person listens and can makes notes on her own copy. *This includes the writer*, who hopefully, through this approach, is experiencing enough of a separation from the writing to become a relatively objective reader/audience.
- As you listen and read along, note any places in the text where your attention is riveted. This usually means the writing is powerful and effective. In the discussion, you should talk about such passages and how and why they work (images, verbs, sound, rhythm).
- Similarly, note any places in the narrative where your attention wanders or where you are confused. In the discussion, you will want to explore what is not working here. What could the writer do (for example, add some detail, change the word choices) to bring this part up to the level of the most effective parts of the narrative?
- When the reading is finished, each person in the group, *including the writer*, will find at least one part of the narrative or poem that s/he thought was particularly good and talk about why. It is important that the writer also do this. What did you like most about your piece of writing when you heard it read? What were you most proud of when you had finished writing the piece? No need ever to apologize for or explain your writing in this class or in any workshop.
- Now go around the group again, and each person brings up at least one place in the narrative that could use some revising. It could be a confusing or dragging line or sentence that could be rewritten. Or it could be that it feels like there is something essential missing. Or it could be that the narrative feels too vague and talky and would benefit from more vivid detail. Or you name the specific issue. Again, it is important that the writer say what he notices. What part of the narrative did you still

not feel satisfied with when you had finished writing? Did you notice something when you were listening to it being read that nagged at you to fix it, or something that was missing and should be added, or some section that didn't seem to advance the meaning?

- Make some *specific* suggestions for revisions, for example, stop for a moment and collectively brainstorm some alternative word choices.
- Thank everyone.
- Go on to the second writer in the group and follow the same process.

Notes

1. For a complete discussion of the process and sequencing of this assignment, see Annas, "Positioning Oneself: A Feminist Approach to Argument" in *Argument Revisited, Argument Redefined.*

2. For a longer discussion of this course, see Pamela Annas, "Pass the Cake: The Politics of Gender, Class, and Text in the Academic Workplace," in *Working-Class Women in the Academy: Laborers in the Knowledge Factory,* eds. Michelle M. Tokarczyk and Elizabeth A. Fay (Amherst: University of Massachusetts Press, 1993), 165–78.

3. Frequently, in the first couple weeks of the semester, male students would come up to me at the end of class to complain that there were far more texts by women than by men on the syllabus. Their perception was significant, but in fact, the proportion of texts by gender was exactly equal.

4. See the appendix for one version of the workshop format I've developed.

5. Likewise in my freshman seminar on Writing about Food and in my graduate and honors courses in memoir (Engl. 618: Life Writing and Honors 290: Personal Narrative), we concluded the semester by producing a class anthology.

Works Cited

Annas, Pamela. "Pass the Cake: The Politics of Gender, Class, and Text in the Academic Workplace." *Working-Class Women in the Academy: Laborers in the Knowledge Factory.* Ed. Michelle M. Tokarczyk and Elizabeth A. Fay. Amherst: U of Massachusetts P, 1993. 165–78. Print.

———. "Positioning Oneself: A Feminist Approach to Argument." *Argument Revisited; Argument Redefined.* Ed. Barbara Emmel, Paula Resch, and Deborah Tenney. Thousand Oaks, CA: Sage Publications, 1996. 127–52. Print.

———. "Silences: Feminist Language Research and the Teaching of Writing." *Teaching Writing: Pedagogy, Gender, and Equity.* Ed. Cynthia L. Caywood and Gillian R. Overing. Albany, NY: SUNY Press, 1987. 3–17. Print.

——. "Style as Politics: A Feminist Approach to the Teaching of Writing." *College English* 47.4 (1985): 360–72. Reprinted in *Feminism and Composition: A Critical Sourcebook.* Ed. Gesa E. Kirsch, et al. Boston: St. Martin's, 2003. Print.

——. "Explicating a Poem." *Literature and Society.* 4th ed. Ed. Pamela Annas and Robert Rosen. Englewood, NJ: Pearson, 2007. 1510–11. Print.

——. "Writing as Women." *Women's Studies Quarterly,* 12.1 (Spring 1984): 38–39. Print.

Barrington, Judith. *Writing the Memoir.* Portland, OR: Eighth Mountain Press, 1987.

Bishop, Wendy. "Valuing the Community of Undergraduate Creative Writing." Oct.-Nov. 1989. Web. <http://elink.awpwriter.org/m/awpChron/articles/wbishop02.lasso>.

Bolker, Joan. "Teaching Griselda to Write." *College English* 40 (Apr. 1974), 906–8. Print.

Eliot, T. S. "Preludes." Web. 2 Nov. 2014. <http://www.poetryfoundation.org/poem/173478>.

Dunning, Jenny. "Toward a Pedagogy or Process in the Creative Writing Classroom." Web. 2010. <http://elink.awpwriter.org/m/awpPed/articles/jdunning01.lasso>.

Fetterley, Judith. *The Resisting Reader: A Feminist Approach to American Fiction.* Bloomington: Indiana UP, 1978. Print.

Haake, Katherine. "Against Reading." *Can It Really Be Taught?* Ed. Kelly Ritter and Stephanie Vanderslice. Portsmouth, NH: Boynton/Cook, 2007. Print.

——. *What Our Speech Disrupts: Feminism and Creative Writing Studies.* Urbana, IL: NCTE, 2000. Print.

Hubbard, Susan. "Gender and Authorship." *Power and Identity in the Creative Writing Classroom.* Ed. Anne Leahy. Clevedon, UK: Multilingual Matters, 2005. Print.

Jordan, June. "White English/Black English: The Politics of Translation." *Civil Wars.* Boston, MA: Beacon Press, 1981. Print.

Knights, Ben. "Reading, Writing, and 'Doing English': Creative-Critical Approaches to Literature." *English Drama Media.* 12 Oct. 2008. Print.

Lorde, Audre. *Uses of the Erotic: The Erotic as Power.* Trumansburg, NY: The Crossing Press, 1978. Reprinted in Audre Lorde. *Sister Outsider: Essays and Speeches.* Trumansburg, NY: The Crossing Press, 2007.

Marks, Elaine, and Isabella de Courtivron, eds. *New French Feminisms.* Amherst: U of Massachusetts P, 1980. Print.

Maxwell, Justin. "Transcending Talk: The Role of Discussion and Context in the Creative Writing Classroom." November 2009. Web. <http://elink.awpwriter.org./m/awpPed/articles/jmaxwell01.lasso>.

Myers, D. G. *The Elephants Teach: Creative Writing Since 1880.* Chicago: U of Chicago P, 1996.

Pinsky, Robert. "With a Little Help from My Friends." *Slate* (9 Apr. 2013). Web.

Pope, Rob. *Textual Intervention: Critical and Creative Strategies for Literary Studies.* London: Routledge, 1995. Print.

Rich, Adrienne. "When We Dead Awaken: Writing as Re-Vision." *On Lies, Secrets, and Silence.* New York: W. W. Norton, 1979. Print.

Ritchie, Joy, and Kathleen Boardman. "Feminism in Composition: Inclusion, Metonymy, and Disruption." *College Composition and Communication* 50.4 (June 1999). Print.

Swander, Mary. "Duck, Duck, Turkey: Using Encouragement to Structure Workshop Assignments." *Power and Identity in the Creative Writing Classroom.* Ed. Anne Leahy. Clevedon, UK: Multilingual Matters, 2005. Print.

Van Hagel, Lauren. "Disabusing the Muse: Writing Is Rewriting." Unpublished.

VIDA: Women in Literary Arts. "The Count." 24 Feb. 2014. Web. <http://www.vedon.UKvidaweb.org/the-count>.

Writers Inc.: Writing and Collaborative Practice

Jen Webb and Andrew Melrose

The Myth of Isolation

"Nobody sees my work until I'm ready to show it," said one student.

"I can't work with anyone else; my writing is so much about me," said another.

"I can't even *read* other writers while I'm working on a piece," said a third; "I have to protect my own voice."[1]

And, in perhaps the most persuasive of the complaints, a fourth student said, "Show me even one famous writer who writes collaboratively, and maybe I'll be convinced."[2]

THESE STUDENTS WERE all enrolled in a creative writing subject, and pretty annoyed about the prospect of group assessment. Their points of view are easily understood; creative writing is invariably treated as a private, even a secret act, though one that (ideally) ends up in the public domain. What's more, like many of us, they have bought into what Alex Pheby (2010) calls "myth of isolation," which holds that writers must preserve not just their independence but also their solitude if they are to be able to produce genuinely original works. Harold Bloom's *The Anxiety of Influence: A Theory of Poetry* (1997) treats this concern—that to be too closely associated with other writers is to risk one's writerly integrity. Pheby's and Bloom's accounts both exemplify the desire among so many writers to be *sui generis*; to be dependent on, and to collaborate with, no one; to see works emerge independent of other people.

Both the myth of isolation and the anxiety of influence contain a germ of truth. Most of us are anxious to develop our own voice rather than to mirror that of another author; and there is a notion that the writer needs to retain a distance from others so that the magic of inspiration can strike—the muse can visit. Perhaps as a corollary, most of us write alone, even when we are actually working collaboratively. It is remarkably rare, for example, that coauthors sit shoulder to shoulder, like pianists playing a duet. Instead one will write a section, then send it to a collaborator who reviews that section, and then adds another, and so the cycle goes.

The need for isolation is evidenced too in the fact that many writers find a need to be alone while working on a project. We take off from our families to spend a long weekend sequestered in a hotel somewhere, writing. We take time off to hide away in the study or the shed at the bottom of the garden and spend hours there, writing; at least, those of us who possess Virginia Woolf's ideal—"a room of one's own"—might do this. Or like Jane Austen, scribbling away while surrounded by her family, we remain physically present, in among our friends and family, while in fact we are far, far away, in the middle of the story world we are crafting in our heads, and keeping our stories secret.

It is not surprising that this is the case: it takes great tracts of time to write. Writing a novel is like running a marathon: you go on and on, alone, and often with little sense of how you manage to keep moving, or where the end might be. You go on and on with no rewards in sight; and by the time you are finished with the book, you are yourself "finished"—exhausted, drained, but—very often—burning to start on the next marathon. The writing of short stories and poems is less like a marathon than a series of sprints, but still demands of its writer endurance, and tracts of time alone to think, to write, to think some more, to rewrite, to end the work or just give up on it.

Does this suggest that writers are social isolates, or solipsists, or egoists? Some commentators suggest that this is so: Joan Didion, for example, writes,

> In many ways writing is the act of saying I, of imposing oneself
> upon other people, of saying listen to me, see it my way, change
> your mind. It's an aggressive, even a hostile act . . . there's no

getting around the fact that setting words on paper is the tac-
tic of a secret bully, an invasion, an imposition of the writer's
sensibility on the reader's most private space. (Didion 224)

The writer who is a *secret* bully; the reader who needs a *private* space. Both reader and writer are presented here as isolates—and yet at the same time, as engaged in a relationship of sorts. In Didion's essay about the self-identity of the author, the interaction between writer and reader is made visible. We are independent, and yet always connected.

Writers are not alone in this. This apparently contradictory practice has a history in that many religious and cultural groups practice periods of isolation as a way of tamping down the noisy demands of the world, re-engaging with the divine, or the inner self, or the natural environment, and returning later, refreshed and with new insights. Many writers too are eager to leave their familiar environment for a month, three months, six months, and retreat to a conventual space—such as a writer's residence—where the writing is all. Like Saint Simeon up on his sixty-foot pillar, we remove ourselves from the world. But attractive and, often, productive as this might be, sustained isolation is not a good idea. Even in the religious tradition that valued the practice of solitary retreat, the permanent hermit was often viewed not as a holy person, but as "ignorant," "dissolute," or "idle" (see Georgianna 45). We must have periods alone; we must engage with others.

In this chapter, while acknowledging the need for and the value of isolation in writing, we reject the myth of isolation that is so thoroughly entrenched in the writing world. We explicate the ways in which this myth has emerged, and how it interacts with the actual collaborative practices that characterize the field of writing. Our focus is on ways in which teachers of creative writing can build students' knowledge of their field of practice, and in particular how they can introduce skills in collaborative knowledge and practice that support intelligent, reflective, and creative writing.

The Problem of Solitude

Why has the myth of the solitary author been so enduring? What do we gain, by buying into it, and what do we lose? What we gain is, of course, validation for the periods of great selfishness that are in fact required to complete the enormous task that is the writing of a major work. Let someone else worry about paying the bills on time, or ensuring that the kids have clean clothes to wear to school: I have serious work to do! What we gain too is a sense of "specialness"; the solitary writer is an immensely romantic—and Romantic—ideal, because withdrawing from the crowd means you stand out from the crowd.

But what we lose is much greater than what we gain. Because though we are all individuals, we are born into, live as a part of, and die within, a social arrangement. As John Donne pointed out,

> No man is an island,
> Entire of itself.
> Each is a piece of the continent,
> A part of the main.

To ignore our embeddedness in a greater whole is thus to ignore a vital part of ourselves.

Donne here avers the central importance of connectedness, and he is not alone in this. Walter Benjamin identifies in the solitary nature of the author "evidence of the profound perplexity of the living," because the writer "is no longer able to express himself by giving examples of his most important concerns, is himself uncounseled, and cannot counsel others" (87); a good writer, we might conclude, is a connected writer. And Virginia Woolf, in her paean to privacy, *A Room of One's Own*, muses, "would *Pride And Prejudice* have been a better novel if Jane Austen had not thought it necessary to hide her manuscript from visitors? I read a page or two to see; but I could not find any signs that her circumstances had harmed her work in the slightest" (67). Which implies that the myth of isolation does not necessarily serve the interests of good writing.

Each of these specialists points to the need for community and the collaborations that flow from interconnection; and each speaks from a position of personal (bitter) experience. Donne suffered from crippling despair and suicidal ideation; both Benjamin and Woolf suffered from chronic depression and did in fact commit suicide. Psychiatric research into the connections between mental health and art consistently shows that writers are more likely than are the general population to suffer from an affective disorder (see, e.g., Crisp, or Jamison). It is feasible to suggest that if isolation is not a necessary and sufficient cause, it may still be an important contributor to mental illness; and, as Erikson points out, to acknowledge that the capacity to achieve intimacy is an important marker of adult development. (Interestingly, the same psychiatric research that showed high levels of psychological disorder among novelists and poets suggested much lower incidences among scriptwriters; is there a connection between willed isolation and ill health, and between collaborative writing and positive affect?)

To counter both the problem and the myth of isolation, it is important to begin from Donne's understanding that individuals are "part of the main," simultaneously independent and interdependent. Walter Benjamin expands this notion in his writing about translation, where he observes that "fragments of a vessel which are to be glued together must match one another in the smallest details, although they need not be like one another"; they are individual pieces, each with their own ontology and identity, but they are parts of a greater whole (78). Homi Bhabha reads this notion of discrete fragments as a metaphor for the postcolonial nation (170)[3]— dissimilar fragments, connected only at the interstices. We take this metaphor a step further, suggesting that just as text is comprised of lexical fragments collated bit by bit into a whole; just as a nation is comprised of cultural fragments collated into a community; so too writing depends on a practice conducted by an individual who may indeed be an isolated fragment, but who is necessarily connected, however metonymically, to others in a reciprocal arrangement.

So, when students insist on knowing why they should have to work with others we can respond: because we are human beings, and humans are necessarily social. Because it is good for our mental health. Because the work of writing often is, in Orwell's terms, a "horrible, exhausting struggle" (316), and connecting with others can reduce the exhaustion and the loneliness. Because almost all writers are, in fact, writing about society and the people who comprise that society—and how can we do this if we are apart from it? And because, if we hope to do more than just fill 220 pages with story, or provide more than a few hours of entertainment—if we want to influence others or inform the discourse—we need to connect with others.

The Community of Writers

The representation of the author as an isolate is a fairly recent one and perhaps should be seen in this context. Historically a community of writers was a collaborative norm, embedded in a community of practice, and connected to others in their social world. During the Middle Ages, practitioners in any art form were members of collectives, or guilds: skilled workers, or artisans, rather than the alienated artists of later periods (Williams 59). During the Renaissance they began to seek out points of distinction from artisans or manual workers and, by attaching their practice to scholarly and philosophical knowledges, distanced themselves from the guild system (Zolberg 10). The story of the solitary genius reached its apogee during the Romantic period (Howard 55) and has remained attractive; but in fact writers are not solitary at all. They are attached to each other by skeins of influence and patterns of friendship, critique and review. They are attached, too, to the industry that is the field of literary production—agents, editors, publishers, designers, printers, distributors, reviewers, booksellers, and readers. And they are attached to society more broadly, having been made human beings within their particular culture and time, and with their tastes, knowledges, and predilections established by their personal and communal history.

We rehearse this history of writing and the myth of isolation because our students, and we ourselves, occupy positions within the field of creative production. If we are to be reflexive, informed, and productive members of that field, it is vital that we know the discourses that shape writing, and the values that underpin our practices and hence our identities; and that we equip our students with that knowledge. Education, write social philosophers such as Michel Foucault (2005) and Pierre Bourdieu (1977), comprises the work of constituting the subject as well as that of training the individual, and we consider it important to ensure that our students graduate from their studies with high-level conceptual skills as well as technical capacity. Part of that skill base is a sophisticated knowledge of the field, one grounded on professional skills, aptitudes, and ways of thinking. Among these are the capacity to examine evidence, and apply objective reason to a context. This involves reflective thinking and practice, as well as skills in writing alone and in collaboration, and in knowing when solitary or communal practice is most appropriate.

Whether an author is writing in isolation, or in a close collaboration, she or he is always a member of a community of practice: the community of other writers. This is not a homogeneous community; some individuals adopt a highly experimental mode, writing works that are read only by a few patient friends. Others write comfort-food novels that sell in the millions. Most of us occupy a position somewhere on the continuum between these two extremes. And all of us both collaborate with others to varying degrees, and benefit from this collaboration.

Students begin to take up a position in this community of practice, and in collaborative work, from their first creative writing class, if not before. Creative writing programs in tertiary institutions in many ways have stepped into the space that editors used to occupy. In times past when a writer would be nurtured by a publisher and an appointed editor, the collaborative process was much in evidence: we have written a great number of books between us and not one of them escaped the editor's blue pencil contribution. Now the nurturing role of a publisher has been replaced by teachers and mentors. Indeed, in our experience, publishers are inclined to "expect" a polished first draft that has gone through this kind of collaborative process; one that can occur only when a student or other writer is connected to others, an individual fragment of the whole community. As Milan Kundera writes, "the novelist has available a whole *apparatus for fabricating the illusion of reality,*" (154, italics in original) and, we suggest, there is little use in closing some of them off for the misplaced appearance of isolation.

The "communities of practice" approach to learning is embedded in a pedagogical approach that values the idea of collaboration, of co-learning, and of the possibility of transformation of individuals and the community itself. Associated closely with the early work of cognitive anthropologists Jean Lave and Etienne Wenger, it involves a democracy of membership among people involved in the same general field of practice. There is no room for the top dog in this logic, and also no peripheral position where individuals can lurk (Lave and Wenger 36): everyone participates fully in learning, teaching, leading, making, critiquing, and so on. And no community of practice is independent of the world, in this formation: "their members and their artifacts are not theirs alone. Their histories are not just internal; they are histories of articulation with the rest of the world" (Wenger 103).

This is important for teachers of writing, because we need to remember that, however experienced and skilled we might be, we remain members of the community, and not "top dogs." We are learning in our participatory classroom practice as much as the students are learning; and we need the community as much as they do. Andrew Cowan, an award-winning novelist and director of the MA in Creative Writing at the University of East Anglia, writes in this regard: "I think the truest thing I can say about my own experience of writing is that I don't know what I am doing. Writing is the activity where I feel most adrift, least competent, most uncertain, least aware. I stumble along. And of course I'm not the only one." Paul Auster, holder of many honors and awards for his prose, writes similarly:

> I sometimes feel that I am wandering in a haze of things
> that cannot be articulated and the struggle to put things

down clearly is so enormous that I think at times my brain is damaged. I do not think as clearly as other people. The words don't come when I want them. I can spend fifteen or twenty minutes trying to decide between prepositions and then I have no idea which is right any more; absolutely stupid basic stuff, basic grammatical questions. It is just a tremendous puzzle for me all the time. (20–21)

This very common experience of uncertainty can be ameliorated by practice, training in techniques, the use of a good style manual, the application of reflective skills, and perhaps of cognitive behavioral thinking. But while these may all be necessary at different times, in our experience as writers and teachers of writers what is always necessary is a productive connection with other members of the community of practice, whose input through commentary, editorial corrections, or simple affirmation can help wandering, stumbling authors to find a way through.

This raises several interesting elements for consideration, for those of us who are teaching student writers ways of becoming professional writers. One point is the democratic construct of a community of practice, which can be challenging for a teacher. We are usually more accustomed to being in control—to being the single core or center of the group—and to being responsible for students' learning and their experience. It can be a risky, but a salutary, approach to identify ourselves as co-members and co-learners, rather than as directors of a course of study.

There is also something very ethical about this; ethical first in that it is a point of acknowledging that, as teachers, we in fact learn a great deal; and ethical for the other members of the community of practice, who must participate and engage, who cannot sit back and leave it to everyone else. And third, it is an important reminder that the classroom is not actually a sterile cell, where writers can practice a sort of extended isolation, connecting only with other "isolated" writers. D. G. Myers may feel able to insist that "A work of literary art seeks only to express itself—not the clash of living discourses in society" (172), but this does not mean the writer lives in isolation of those living discourses. Instead, all members need to identify how their histories articulate with the history of the world as it touches them, and they it. As Woolf says in "Life and the Novelist" (131), "The novelist . . . is terribly exposed to life." It is a constant effort of give and take; which is just a way of saying we do not live, far less write, in isolation. We have to be aware of others and of the other.

To make this work, what is required is that all members are committed to moving beyond tacit practice to find ways of being "literate" not only in their writing but also in their thinking; and that they are committed to reflective practice, "the deliberate and purposeful act of thinking which centres on ways of responding to problem situations" (Loughran 14). This is integral to quality learning and thinking. And as we build our own skills in reflective practice, we are better able to support students as they develop the same ways of thinking.

There are several issues associated with reflective practice that spill over into teaching practices. One is that individual members of the community of practice need to take time, regularly, to reflect on what they are doing. A second point is that reflective practice is a conscious act—one that is "deliberate and purposeful." Reflective practice is, for Donald Schön, "one of the defining characteristics of professional practice" (104): professional practitioners must do it; amateurs need not. This is because an effective professional is not just a technical expert, but someone capable of innovation; and a creative writer who is working at a significant level must always be seeking innovation.

Further, a reflective practitioner must be able to recognize a problem—for which Schön uses the lovely phrase "stimulated by surprise" (50)—and then generate ways to approach it. This cannot be done on automatic pilot; they are highly conscious and aware practices. After all, no one can be stimulated by surprise while dozing off. One way to enable this, and encourage all members to make it second nature, is to require that all members—teaching staff and students—write weekly blogs that allow them to tease out and report on their practice that week. Some university programs ensure that these are confidential, read only by the author, or the student author and teacher. Others require that they are read by a small subgroup of that community; others again expect that all blogs will be available to all members.

The mention of small subgroups raises a further feature of communities of practice. While all writers are, effectively, part of the same community, being a part of "all" is not helpful or productive. Groups need to have boundaries that enclose everyone that is the case, if they are to afford points of identity. So, in teaching situations, the "community of practice" might be reduced to "all writers in this university." From this community, subgroups should be formed so that students have an immediate community of reference as well as one of practice. It is feasible that subgroups will be self-constituting, but it is usually necessary for a teacher to intervene. We have seen, and employed, several approaches, all of them productive. The loosest is simply to organize the teaching room into clusters of desks, and when, during the first class, the students have seated themselves, inform each cluster that they are a group for this semester or year (or longer), and that this group will be the first point for reference for each other for critique, evaluation, reflection, and support. Another approach is to arrange the students by some predetermined criteria—similarity of demographic features; month of birth; height; or other entirely arbitrary feature—and again require them to identify with each other for that semester or year. A more extreme form is to arrange small groups by difference: a colleague in another university program told us that there the teaching staff make a point of connecting students with (apparently) nothing in common but the fact that they are writers. The criteria are not really important; what matters is that students buy in to the subgroup relationship and develop the sort of confidence and trust to expose not only their own work to each other, but also their own ideas, in the interests of building knowledge, skills, and capacity for learning.

Collaborative Pedagogy

Is it necessary that students coauthor works in order to make this subgroup or community of practice relationship "real" to them? Not necessarily; but it helps. But there is not much point in simply directing students to collaborate: it is not a natural act, but a learned one. And in addition, if students are to graduate as informed and insightful practitioners, they need more than just practical experience; they need to understand theory and principles. We therefore need a pedagogy of collaboration so that we can teach students what is involved in this process, what collaborative models are available to them, and how to evaluate the best model for a specific context.

Up to this point, having used the term "collaboration" to signify its embeddedness in a community of practice, and connectedness of writers to others in their social world, we now narrow our definition somewhat, to describe collaboration as interactive and student-centered learning, focused on generic rather than specific or technical skills (Panitz 1996). And it is not confined to writing classes: collaborative pedagogy is a well-established practice in teaching right across the curriculum. The value of this approach is that it trains students to think creatively and generatively, and prepares them for a career that is likely to include the generation of new ways of thinking, doing, and knowing. It emphasizes "critical thinking, problem solving, personal transformation and the social construction of knowledge" (Tait and de Young 193), which is an exceptionally good foundation for writers who aspire to produce original creative works.

Rebecca Moore Howard's excellent account of collaborative pedagogy includes her suggestion that teachers apply a range of techniques in order to teach collaboration to composition students: these run from small-group discussion, through peer critique of drafts, to the actual coproduction of a piece of writing (55). She is, of course, focusing on composition broadly, and not simply on *creative* composition. However, the principles apply reliably, regardless of the mode of writing, because the aims of collaborative pedagogy are not necessarily to train students in the sort of writing they are likely to do, but to train them in a range of other skills and ways of knowing.

One important outcome is that students develop an understanding of the extent to which knowledge is, as Bourdieu (1991, 57) writes, "won, constructed, and confirmed" rather than given. Another is their having the opportunity to practice the art of negotiation: as Nietzsche pointed out, community is shot through with the "will to power," and even a group of students who are relatively homogeneous will not have equal social or intellectual standing. Meeker students will, in the best circumstances, learn how to engage with greater assertion to achieve an outcome that satisfies all in the group; more dominant students will, hopefully, develop the capacity to see an issue from someone else's perspective, and cooperate rather than simply compete.

Howard's paper explores ways of teaching collaboration, collaboratively, in any composition classroom. As such, it is able to offer something very valuable to teachers of creative writing, but a little more is needed to show how it is relevant to writers who are not interested in crafting a line of argument, or an expository account, but who are committed to the production of work that emerges from the imagination, and is directed toward the literary rather than the communicative domain. Something very different is at stake when writers—by which we mean literary writers—engage in their work, and that is to a considerable extent the production of a personal vision, the expression of personal individuality, and use of a personal diction, cadence, and accent. These have considerably more heft in the literary domain than in the world of professional or academic writing. We have never written a poem or story that was coauthored, though we have written a great many coauthored academic or professional works; there is a different intent, and a different investment of the self, in each mode of practice.

But that is of course an ambit claim, not far removed from the myth of isolation. Screenwriters invariably work collaboratively to produce the blueprint for the final film or television product (see, e.g., Sternberg). Theater writers may work in isolation, but like screenwriters, they rework in collaboration, holding read-throughs of their scripts, participating in workshops, rewriting as necessary to ensure that lines are sayable, directions can be followed, and the narrative structure produces the preferred effect. In 1989, novelist Ben Elton and screenwriter Richard Curtis wrote the final episode of the BBC period sitcom *Blackadder* by swapping computer disks and agreeing to a rule not to add back material the other had removed. But crucially too, additional material was provided by the cast members. And it didn't end there—the final sequence, which shows the main characters going "over the top," was filmed using slow motion because the directors were unhappy with the result of the scripted ending scene. Subsequently, this collaboration has been voted one of the greatest moments in television, and is critically acclaimed.

Benefits of Collaboration

The decision to incorporate a conscious and deliberate element of collaborative practice into the writing class is on solid ground, because it aims at developing students' capacity, imbuing them with graduate attributes, and ensuring that they are better positioned to practice effectively after they leave the university. It is worth noting, though, that most of the benefits of collaboration seem directed to professional, rather than creative, practice. Philosopher Paul Thagard, in a paper designed to explore how collaboration enhances knowledge-generation in the sciences (and hence could benefit philosophers), identifies a number of advantages. Thagard's vision of the benefits of collaboration are drawn from work by Alvin Goldman on measures to evaluate epistemic practices. These are; the reliability of the practice (does it produce good outputs?); its power (is it effective as a way of achieving interesting answers?); its fecundity (does it deliver many outcomes for many people?); its speed (does it quickly produce results?); and its efficiency (does it provide value for money/inputs?). These are not necessarily directly appropriate to creative work, but they can be translated from the scientific domain to the creative.

Reliability, for example: Thagard observes, perhaps dryly, "it is easier to identify blunders in others than in oneself." This is perhaps even more the case for creative writers. During much of the process of making a work, we hold that work in our minds, and what is down on paper is still rough or underdigested. But because in our imaginations it is whole and perfect, a sole author can find it difficult to see its blunders. If a work is shared, group members will talk it through more frequently, clarify their own images of the work, observe holes in plots, clumsy characterization, cliché, and all the flaws that damage a perfect idea. So, just as a group of scientists examining a collaborative project are better positioned than is a lone practitioner to spot flaws and weaknesses in a work, so too a group of writers will be better able to critique and interrogate potential weaknesses than a sole author, utterly invested in the work, would be.

This is largely because a group of people introduces the possibility of variation to a project. Each person in the group brings her or his own tastes, preferences, knowledges, and skills, contributing something that is qualitatively significant. For scientists, this might allow the use of several research methods, and thus the ability to triangulate results and validate the outcomes. For writers, it allows the combination not only of different ways of seeing and knowing, but different uses of written language. A poet collaborating with a screenwriter, for example, is likely to contribute a sense of tact in their use of language, and a sense of rhythm and image; while the screenwriter is likely to contribute a strong sense of story, and a good understanding of readers and their needs and expectations.

Power and fecundity are related benefits that are as suitable for writers as for scientists. While scientists might read this as the capacity to achieve answers and deliver outcomes, for writers it might be the capacity to deliver lines of thought, of possible story, and do it in a fresh and engaging way. Innovation, spurred by lateral thinking, imagination, and exploration, is an important product of such fecundity. Energy, productivity, and positive competition are also relevant here. The latter especially can drive members of a group to come up with more, wilder, and perhaps better ideas, and in the process galvanize an ordinary work. This process too can help when a story, script, or poem has run aground, lost its way, or fallen into the *déjà lu*: the cliché, the already read. At such points, the fecund capacity of several creative imaginations and technical competences can offer remarkable advantage, finding fresh ways to shape a scene, construct a character, or craft a metaphor.

Which leads to a fourth benefit: synergy. The whole can often be greater than the sum of its parts, a popular quote often attributed to Aristotle or to the nineteenth-century German Gestalts. This is in fact a misquote: Aristotle's point was that the whole is prior to, and different from, its parts; the Gestaltists argued that the whole determines the nature of the parts (Shane and Jordan 263). But both the idiom and the actual origins of that idiom offer useful ways of thinking about how collaboration can add benefits associated with synergy. The "parts" in this case include each writer involved in the project, all their individual qualities and properties; the ideas and narrative elements brought together; and the artisanal work involved in its completion. The sum of these individual parts ideally will add up to a greater whole, through the magic of synergy that masks the labor of thinking, making, correcting, and refining, leaving visible a seamless and coherent story or poem or play. The idea that the whole precedes the parts, or determines the parts, is particularly interesting, because it suggests that in some way the ideal possible end is held by each collaborator, who starts with the ideal and works backward, gathering the parts that are needed to make the whole—this gathering involves not only thinking, observation, and research, but possibly also the gathering in of new personnel who bring skills not otherwise available to the project.

Models of Collaboration

Howard warns that collaborative writing is the most difficult of all collaborative pedagogies (62), and for that she blames the enduring myth of authorial isolation. But she suggests that the difficulties can be ameliorated if we train students in how to think and work collaboratively before asking them to tackle a cowriting task. One approach is to begin with the philosophy of collaborative practice; and a useful, if somewhat impenetrable text is Deleuze and Guattari's *A Thousand Plateaus*. In the early pages of this book, they describe issues related to collaborative practice, to the process of making, and to the models of collaboration. The first model they identify, the "root-book," is an arbitrary and bureaucratic form, one designed to reproduce "truth" and knowledge rather than to encourage experimentation and innovation. Visualized as the single root and trunk of a tree, it describes a process and a product that is grounded in realism in both form and content. It is hierarchical and linear, with little if any allowance made for difference or risk. Start at the bottom, this model implies, go on until you reach the top, and then stop. As collaborative process, this seems to permit little space for independent thinking, for negotiation or flexibility—in fact, it seems more committed to the idea of "getting the job done" than to putting collaboration to work in order to achieve the best, and possibly not-yet-imagined, results.

Set against this is their notion of the "rhizome." This model lacks the order of the root-book, lacks the beginning-middle-end pattern, lacks the uniformity and focus of its alternative. But what it offers is very attractive because its untidy, nonlinear, relatively unfocused shape allows the flow of thought, difference, and potential, allows room for serendipity, allows points of connection that are quick light touches rather than legally binding associations, ways of coming together and apart. This is a promiscuous vision of production and practice, but a potentially rich one. It is not tightly controlled, of course, which can be alarming for students seeking a comfort zone or the assurance of a good grade. Nor will it necessarily result in a professional quality work: a rhizomatic structure may manifest as a beautiful lawn or field of flowers, or as a tangled mess of weeds. But the benefits outweigh the risks when attempting to train students in collaborative pedagogy—because the rhizome model of collaboration provides the sort of open space, and space for "breathing," that helps group members avoid feeling divorced from the group or project, avoid feeling overwhelmed or helpless. It lets each member follow her or his own path, get on with each one's part of the work, and then brings everyone together at appropriate moments to advance it.

Something messy may emerge; something extraordinary and unexpected may emerge; but whatever the quality of literary product, the learning outcome is likely to be of high quality. Oldfield and MacAlpine write, "One of the indicators of quality in undergraduate education is the extent to which self-learning ability is nurtured in the participants" (125); and the rhizome model, in its combination of fecund thinking, innovative and lateral approaches, independent and mutual connection, provides students with every opportunity to build this capacity. In more pragmatic terms, Australian writing academics Donna Lee Brien and Tess Brady— who completed several collaborative writing projects together—provide a summary of some technical and practical aspects of collaboration, and list models of collaboration in a very useful article.

Of these, the contribution model is the most common approach. This is the situation where a number of people work on the same project, and make discrete contributions to it: for example, a director, scriptwriter, camera operator, and sound engineer all working on the same movie, with occasional group discussion. The contribution model is attractive because by and large the members can work on their own, without interference; but at first glance it seems less easy to apply it to a creative writing project than to another professional/creative practice: for writing, the same skills are deployed by each contributor, and the same types of inputs are required. What does work effectively is for the group to spend time collaborating intensively in the early part of the project—setting the parameters, discussing narrative arcs, developing characters and so on—and then separate, returning to the writer's "necessary isolation" to write a part of the work. They then exchange drafts, and each writer edits and reworks the other's part, before meeting again to workshop progress and approach. This process can continue through to the final read-through when the script is read out loud by the contributing team, timed, and checked for consistence and inconsistencies. This is a slow, iterative process, but can result in a strong coherent manuscript. A good example of this is *Caverns: A Novel by OU Levon*,[4] which was actually written by Ken Kesey and his graduate workshop students at the University of Oregon (see Mark McGurl's discussion, McGurl 212).

Related to this is the cooperative model. Here one team member begins a task, and circulates it among others for their contribution. Again, the film world provides an example: one person crafts the script treatment, the next fleshes it out, and it goes on through many hands to end up as a film. Often there is little discussion between team members in this model, but the director has the overall vision and is the point of contact for all the other members. A group of writers may find it less easy than a team of filmmakers to nominate one person as director; after all, they all have, and need to use, similar skills, and will all want to "own" the overall vision of the work. To produce a finished manuscript in this way requires immense trust in the others, and a willingness to let go of your work at a particular point. It also requires great integrity of writers later in the process, to ensure that the earlier content and form are preserved in the finished work. A common exercise that uses this model of collaboration is where, after discussion about the overall shape of a possible work, each member of a group writes a paragraph, and then attempts to link it into a whole. What tends to happen here is that a "director" will emerge from the group, the most assertive member or the one best able to see possible links and flows, and to convince the group of this vision. The outcome tends to be less coherent than in the contribution model, but can offer a sort of dada charm.

The synchronous, or mutual model, also known as joint collaboration, is another model of collaboration that is difficult for a writing project. Here group members work closely side by side on each aspect of their project, and the finished project belongs to them all. It can work very effectively when different skillsets are required; there are good examples of, say, a poet and a media artist spending time shoulder to shoulder in front of a monitor, producing a new work step by step; but because their skills and art forms are different, there is less need to preserve the individual ego, and the collaborative process flows more smoothly. But set a group of writing students in front of a monitor to write a short imaginative piece, and there is a risk it will end in blows or in tears, with arguments over each choice of word, the placement of each comma.

While the synchronous, or mutual model allows the group members to work closely side by side on each aspect of their project, and the finished project belongs to them all, a further model is in secondary collaboration. This is where one person makes a product, and the next finishes it. It might be the collaboration between the author who writes the manuscript, and the editor who reworks it so that it is ready for publication. It can be an effective class exercise where, for example, each student writes a short piece, and then they exchange these pieces for editing by their peers. Provided this is followed by open discussion and reflection, it can be a valuable way of understanding both collaboration in writing, and the extent to which one has or has not achieved readability. A version of this is where again each student writes a short piece, and then exchanges this piece with her or his peer. The next part of the exercise is to read the new work, and then write another piece that emerges out of the first—a creative response, a different "take." Though this process may not necessarily result in a publishable work, if it is followed by peer discussion and reflection, the learning outcomes can be profound.

It is acknowledged that the secondary collaboration relationship relies on a great deal of trust and empathy between the collaborators, such as that which a writer and editor may have in a rewriting process. Creative apprehension in this practice could be addressed by a more discrete (or compartmentalized) collaboration. In this approach, each member completes a discrete element of the task independently, with occasional group discussion. These parts are then combined to render the final product. A common example of this is the annual anthology of student writing produced by many universities. Of course, it is valuable for students to write and polish a work to publishable standard, and to engage with and respond to editorial comment. And it is delightful to see what is often their very first publication emerge; so there are pedagogical and professional benefits from this. But they are not the benefits we expect of collaboration; they do not gain, from this, the sorts of skills—negotiation, lateral thinking, organizational capacity, communication—that true collaborative pedagogy provides.

It is useful for creative writing academics to be alert to the ways in which the word *collaboration* is used, and to evaluate the extent to which each model actually delivers the values we expect. Discrete collaboration is unlikely to do so, although it is otherwise a productive element in a writing program. The counterintuitively named "dictator collaboration," where one person is in charge, or takes charge, of the project, making all the decisions while the other members carry out their designated tasks, is another that will not deliver the graduate attributes that should come from collaboration. Students involved in this model may gain immensely from the mentoring they receive from their "dictator," but they will not learn the self-management and other-oriented thinking and practice that are required. There is also what is sometimes called hidden collaboration, where one member takes all the credit although others have made enormous contributions. This is of no value to anyone (except, perhaps, the person named publicly as the producer; Brien and Brady point to the relationship between T. S. Eliot and his first wife, Vivienne Haigh-Wood Eliot, as an example of hidden collaboration. Interestingly, this is subject to dispute, as opposed to Eliot's acknowledgement of Ezra Pound's contribution to his work. In fact, he referred to Pound, in the dedication in *The Wasteland*, as *il miglior fabbro*—loosely translated as "the better maker."[5]

It is feasible that a form of hidden collaboration occurs in group assessments, since it is a commonplace that in any group work, some students will do nothing, some will contribute useful bits, and one or two others will do nearly all the work. But the most common approach in assessing group work, according to Michael Sergi, is to distribute a group mark equally across all group members (107). This can be a source of anger and resentment for many students, because members receive equal marks for unequal input. The issue of group assessment is a fraught one, and has become a topic of ongoing discussions at education conferences.

Finally, when teaching the various models of collaboration, how they work in practice, which one is most appropriate for particular tasks, and how to organize and evaluate the process, it is useful to remind students of two key issues. One is that this taxonomy of collaborative models is not "real"; it is the effect of decisions made by a number of scholars over a number of years to obey the nominative and taxonomical impulses that seem to drive human beings. This naming and organizing of types is only one possible approach; coming from a different perspective, a different set of names and categories might have occurred. The point then is not to fetishize the model, but to pay attention to the principles at its heart, and also to remember that the barriers between each model are made only out of words, and hence are both permeable and temporary. And this is the second point: it is rare, Brady and Brien write, for a collaborative project to fit just one model, and remain in that form for the duration of the project. At different stages in a project, the members are likely to move in or out, take more or less responsibility. The work being undertaken, the processes followed, and the composition of the group all have an effect on what is required and expected of each member at various points along the way. Reminding students of this, when they are preparing for a major collaborative task, allows them to think reflectively at various stages of the project about how it is processed; helps them expect, and plan for, changing practice and changing levels of input; and may avoid tears toward the end, because they are more likely to be transparent and communicative about how the collaboration is actually going. Indeed, it is rare, for example, that a PhD in creative writing ever fails to go through a collaborative process. The supervisor of such a venture inevitably suggests edits and corrections as well as commenting on the direction of the narrative, whether poetry, prose, or script, as the student/researcher writes.

The myth of the solitary writer is comparatively recent, but it has endured in the face of all the evidence of its absence. We suggest that it is time to detach ourselves from it, and take a more scholarly approach, if only in our teaching. Encouraging students to see themselves as isolates, as solipsists, or on the other hand, as somehow less adequate if they find they need the presence and support of others, does them no favors. Imbuing them instead with the sort of professional, creative and artisanal practices that set them up to be capable, inventive, resilient, and connected to others and to themselves seems a much more appropriate outcome. Because after all, they are not alone, and cannot be, if they are to engage in quality practice. Deleuze and Guattari point out when describing their own collaborative writing, "Since each of us was several, there was already quite a crowd" (3). And the work of writing requires a "crowd." Scriptwriter Matt Marshall, in his doctoral thesis on the work of authorship in screenwriting, observed,

> The template nature of the film script, since it is designed for adaptation into another textual form, the film, introduces two elements that lead to these modifications. The first element is the implied reader, which in this textual form, operates as an implied director. At the same time, placed within the text

as part of the construction process is an implied author that operates as a hidden director. These implied constructs operate to foreshadow potential power relations in the adaptation of film script to film. Simultaneously, the writing self acts in opposition to the mechanistic, industrial, commercial forces also present in the film script in the form of the template format itself. This oppositional relationship leads to the writing self masking the traces of its presence to the extent that it becomes a haunting figure.

So perhaps, in the end, there *is* after all a true solitary author; but that "author" is just one element of the whole writing subject. We are large; we contain multitudes (to paraphrase Walt Whitman, badly); we contain the reader, the director/editor, the presence of the industrial machine that is the field of literary production. We contain the householder and the employee, the parent and the child. We contain the writer; and, though it is masked by the complexities of this "crowd," we also contain the "writing self," the secret me that comes and goes in the crowd, that drives me from my work and family to lock myself away, writing. Would that writing self be as effective if it were all I did—or does it need the mess, the complexity, the *society* of the me, and the community in which that *me* lives, to function?

Appendix: Classroom Applications

Short and simple exercises

1. Tandem writing (variant of Dadaist Exquisite Corpse game): in order to produce a lighthearted mood, and willingness to interact with each other, provide groups of three to five students with the starting point for a story, and then have them take turns to write the story, sentence by sentence.
2. The Eliot/Pound exercise: students work independently on a short prose piece or poem. Then, working in pairs, each edits the other's work. Finally, they discuss their approach and its logic with one another.

Slightly longer exercises

1. Multiple voices: organize students in groups of three; each writes half a page, and then passes the work to one of the group. At this first exchange, each student completely rewrites the piece, retaining

the integrity of the topic and content but using her or his own voice and style. They then exchange the works once again, and now each student edits the work received. Students then workshop the approach at both the rewriting and editing stages.

2. The *Magnetic Fields* exercise: following the example of André Breton and Philippe Soupault, pairs of students commit to work together over the course of a week, exchanging drafts each evening. One student writes until s/he dries or loses interest, and then passes it across to the second student. The partner continues—beginning her or his section either as a segue from the final paragraph, or from some entirely random point—and writes until giving up as well. After several days, they then take turns editing the work.

Longer term exercises

1. Group production: this works effectively in a group where students have a range of creative skills—for example, poetry and music, screenwriting and filmmaking, storytelling and graphic art. . . . It results in a collaborative project that takes a full semester's work. Early in the semester, the students pitch their skills and interests to the class as a whole. Those with relevant skills and similar interests organize themselves into groups with the aim of producing a substantial group work. They then work according to negotiated roles and practices, and also demonstrate an understanding of the various collaborative models and justify their choice of model/s. During the course of the semester, students independently produce a production diary or blog that explicates their reflective practice during the course of the semester; and collectively present work-in-process demonstrations. By semester's end, the group should have a reasonably polished piece of work to display or perform.

2. Critical friends: this begins in the very first weeks of students' initial enrolment, and involves their agreeing to a lifetime's collaborative work. The classroom teacher needs to spend the initial weeks building some understandings of the students' interests, tastes and demographic location, and then will pair students according to their differences. Throughout their degree, those students will exchange work for editing, critique and other feedback. The logic of difference ensures that each student in a dyad can offer the other a truly arm's-length reading of the work.

Notes

1. An instance, it seems, of the "anxiety of influence" described by Harold Bloom: "Influence is *Influenza*" (95).

2. Though clearly this student had not yet come across André Breton and Philippe Soupault; Paul Eluard and Max Ernst; Robert Bly and Marion Woodman; Flora Eldershaw and Marjorie Barnard; Frank O'Hara and Bill Berkson; Denise Duhamel and Maureen Seaton; James McAuley and Harold Stewart; Julianna Baggott and Steve Almond; T. S. Eliot and Ezra Pound; Dymphna Cusack with Florence James and Miles Franklin; Jack Kerouac and William Burroughs; Neil Gaiman and Terry Pratchett; Nicci Gerrard and Sean French; Lyn Hejinian and Emilie Clark; Ted Kooser and Jon Klassen; Ken Kesey and his students; and many others.

3. We found Homi Bhabha's work on Walter Benjamin's ideas on translation, especially the essay "How Newness Enters the World" in *The Location of Culture* (212–35) extremely useful here.

4. *Caverns: A Novel by OU Levon* (New York: Penguin Books, 2009).

5. Carole Seymour-Jones makes a strong case for Vivienne's influence on Eliot's development as a poet, and particularly for the production of his 1922 masterpiece, "The Waste Land." See her 2001 work *Painted Shadow: A Life of Vivienne Eliot* (New York: Random House).

Works Cited

Benjamin, Walter. *Illuminations: Essays and Reflections*. New York: Random House, 1968. Print.

Bhabha, Homi. *The Location of Culture*. London: Routledge, 2004. Print.

Bloom, Harold. *The Anxiety of Influence: A Theory of Poetry*. 2nd ed. New York: Oxford UP, 1997. Print.

Bourdieu, Pierre, with Jean-Claude Chamboredon and Jean-Claude Passeron. *The Craft of Sociology: Epistemological Preliminaries*. Trans. Richard Nice. New York: Walter de Guyter, 1991. Print.

Bourdieu, Pierre, and Jean-Claude Passeron. *Reproduction in Education, Society and Culture*. London: Sage, 1977. Print.

Brien, Donna Lee, and Tess Brady. "Collaborative Practice: Categorising Forms of Collaboration for Practitioners." *TEXT* 7.2 (Oct. 2003). Web. 12 Feb. 2014. <http://www.textjournal.com.au/oct03/brienbrady.htm>.

Cowan, Andrew. "Blind Spots: What Creative Writing Doesn't Know." *TEXT* 15.1 (Apr. 2011). Web. 12 Feb. 2014. <http://www.textjournal.com.au/april11/content.htm>.

Crisp, Arthur H., ed. *Every Family in the Land: Understanding Prejudice and Discrimination against People with Mental Illness*. Rev. ed. London: Royal Society of Medicine Press, 2004. Print.

Blackadder. Writ. Richard Curtis and Ben Elton. Dir. Richard Boden. Prod. John Lloyd. BBC. 1983–89. Television.

Deleuze, Gilles, and Felix Guattari. *A Thousand Plateaus: Capitalism and Schizophrenia*. Trans. Brian Massumi. London: Continuum, 1988. Print.

Didion, Joan. "Why I Write." 1976. *Major Modern Essayists*. 2nd ed. Ed. G. H. Muller with A. F. Crooks. Englewood Cliffs, NJ: Prentice Hall, 1994. 224–28. Print.

Eliot, T. S. *The Waste Land*. London: Faber and Faber, 1922. Print.

Erikson, Erik H. *Identity and the Life Cycle*. London: W. W. Norton, 1980. Print.

Foucault, Michel. *The Hermeneutics of the Subject: Lectures at the College De France 1982–93*. Trans. G. Burchell. New York: Picador, 2005. Print.

Georgianna, Linda. *The Solitary Self: Individuality in the Ancrene Wisse*. Cambridge, MA: Harvard UP, 1981. Print.

Howard, Rebecca Moore. "Collaborative Pedagogy." *A Guide to Composition Pedagogies*. Ed. G. Tate, A. Rupiper, and K. Schick. New York: Oxford UP, 2001. 54–70. Print.

Jamison, Kay Redfield. *Touched with Fire: Manic-depressive Illness and the Artistic Temperament*. New York: Free Press, 1994. Print.

Kundera, Milan. *Testaments Betrayed*. London: Faber, 1995. Print.

Lave, J., and E. Wenger. *Situated Learning: Legitimate Peripheral Participation*. Cambridge, UK: Cambridge UP, 1991. Print.

Loughran, John H. *Developing Reflective Practice: Learning about Teaching and Learning through Modeling*. London: Falmer Press, 1996. Print.

McGurl, Mark. *The Program Era: Postwar Fiction and the Rise of Creative Writing*. Cambridge, MA: Harvard UP, 2011. Print.

Marshall, Matt. *Ghost Stories without Ghosts: A Study of Authorship in the Film Script 'The Seaborne.'* PhD thesis. University of Canberra, Australia, 2008. Print.

Myers, D. G. *The Elephants Teach: Creative Writing Since 1880*. Chicago: U of Chicago P, 2006. Print.

Nietzsche, Friedrich. *The Will to Power*. Trans. W. Kaufmann and R. J. Hollingdale. New York: Vintage Books, 1968. Print.

Oldfield, K. A., and J. M. K. MacAlpine. "Peer and Self-Assessment at Tertiary Level—An Experiential Report." *Assessment and Evaluation in Higher Education* 20.1 (1995): 125–32. Print.

Orwell, George. *A Collection of Essays.* 1946. Orlando, FL: Harcourt Books, 1981. Print.

Panitz, Ted. "A Definition of Collaborative Vs Cooperative Learning." *Deliberations* (1996). Web. 2 June 2002. <www.lgu.ac.uk/deliberations/collab.learning/panitz2.html>.

Pheby, Alex. "The Myth of Isolation: Its Effect on Literary Culture and Creative Writing as a Discipline." *Creative Writing: Teaching Theory and Practice* 2.1 (Feb. 2010): 51–58. Print.

Roberts, J. F. *The True History of the Blackadder: The Unadulterated Tale of the Creation of a Comedy Legend.* London: Preface Publishing, 2012. Print.

Schön, D. A. *The Reflective Practitioner: How Professionals Think in Action.* New York: Basic Books, 1983. Print.

Sergi, Michael. "Using Long-Term Peer Assessment to Derive Individual Marks from Group Work." *Tertiary Teaching.* Ed. A. Arnott, J. Cameron, and G. Shaw. Darwin, Australia: NTU Press, 2002. 105–18. Print.

Shane, Paul, and Karin Jordan. "Two Forms of Gestalt Family Therapy." *The Quick Theory Reference Guide: A Resource of Expert and Novice Mental Health Professionals.* Ed. K. Jordan. New York: Nova Science Publishers, 2008. 263–84. Print.

Sternberg, Claudia. *Written for the Screen: The American Motion-Picture Screenplay as Text.* Tübingen, Germany: Stauffenberg-Verlag, 1997. Print.

Tait, David, and Robert de Young. "Displaying the Law: A Cross-Disciplinary Learning Experiment Using the Internet and Multimedia Technology." *International Review of Law Computers and Technology* 14.2 (2000): 191–204. Print.

Thagard, Paul. "Collaborative Knowledge." University of Waterloo, Ontario. 1997. Web. 27 Sept. 2002. <cogsci.uwaterloo.ca/Articles/Pages/Collab.html>.

Wenger, Etienne. *Communities of Practice: Learning, Meaning, and Identity.* Cambridge, UK: Cambridge UP, 1998. Print.

Williams, Raymond. *Culture.* Glasgow: Fontana Books, 1981. Print.

Woolf, Virginia. "Life and the Novelist." *The Essays of Virginia Woolf.* Vol. 4. Ed. A. McNeillie. London: Hogarth Press, 1994. 400–06. Print.

———. *A Room of One's Own.* Orlando, FL: Harcourt, 1957. Print.

Zolberg, Vera. *Constructing a Sociology of the Arts.* Cambridge, UK: Cambridge UP, 1990. Print.

Writing Center Theory and Pedagogy in the Undergraduate Creative Writing Classroom

Kate Kostelnik

> Nearly everyone who writes likes—and needs—to talk about
> his or her writing, preferably to someone who will really
> listen, who knows how to listen, and knows how to talk about
> writing too. Maybe in a perfect world, all writers would have
> their own ready auditor—a teacher, a classmate, a roommate,
> and editor—who would not only listen but draw them out, ask
> them questions they would not think to ask themselves.
> —Stephen M. North, "The Idea of a Writing Center"

AS NORTH SAYS, we all need to talk about our work with someone. I've
found that person who will really listen in Claire, a fellow graduate student
at the University of Nebraska, Lincoln. We exchange story drafts, e-mail
one another notes, and meet to discuss everything over a beer. And by
everything I mean that these conversations go far beyond revisions of texts
at hand. We discuss what we want our work to do, who we're reading, and
why writing is important to us.

The last time Claire and I met, we talked about her draft in which a
college co-ed falls in love with a single mother. When I asked her why the
scenes of the lesbian relationship remained underdeveloped, I wasn't just
talking about her text; I was speaking to Claire as a writer and a person.
I was asking her to be braver and flesh out those missing scenes. Claire is

a proud member of the LGBT community, but doesn't writing reveal our fears as much as our hearts? And doesn't writing about what's important to us as well as what we try to avoid make us stronger writers?

Claire and I know how to ask questions of writers and prompt them to continue because we've studied writing center pedagogy and have experience working as writing center tutors. This training enables us to work collaboratively through our drafts, but more importantly, writing center pedagogy has taught us how to help one another become better writers. Many of our discussions move toward teaching our students to listen and speak to one another as writers, just as we do. From my experience, these kinds of relationships are not fostered in undergraduate classes that emphasize the traditional workshop model.[1] The workshop—a methodology designed for experienced writers—trains students to evaluate texts and perform their knowledge for an instructor. Beginning writers are not necessarily taught to listen and respond to one another in ways that support their development as writers. In this chapter, I propose frameworks and practices from writing center pedagogy that can replace text-centered workshops, emphasize writing as a process, and give developing writers the opportunity to dialogue about texts in progress. The incorporation of writing center pedagogy enables creative writing instructors to facilitate the growth of writers and support their engagement with one another, communication skills that serve students in the university and beyond.

The basic methodology of writing center pedagogy is conversation between peers. Through dialogue, a tutor helps a writer work into drafts as well as reflect on writing processes and goals. Above all, writing center pedagogy aims to make writers more independent (Harris 28); a tutor doesn't simply edit a text but facilitates a writer's attempt to revise his or her own work. Tutors listen, ask questions, and offer revision strategies. Rather than authority figures who act as gatekeepers or evaluators, tutors are supportive collaborators who entrust writers to continue writing and learning beyond the tutorial time. To promote self-motivated, student-centered learning that will continue beyond the duration of courses, creative writing instructors can train students to function like writing center tutors. Translating writing center pedagogy into undergraduate creative writing classrooms means that instructors work to support the development of writers, prioritizing writers over their texts.

I acknowledge the claim that, in order for students to understand writing as a serious craft, creative writing courses should be about writing rather than writers and their feelings (Kuhl 5). However, the development of writers and student-centeredness don't mean that courses will devolve into therapy sessions in which writing is seen primarily as a means of exploring one's psyche. Student-centeredness in the creative writing classroom means that writers are active, responsible participants in their own learning. I don't believe that focusing on writers will diminish the importance of craft; rather, instructors can teach craft *and* support writers. In fact, teaching craft (e.g., characterization, figurative language, setting, etc.) and form (e.g., short stories, nonfiction essays, various types of poems, hybrid genres, etc.) would be essential components of the creative writing classroom informed by writing center pedagogy. Before instructors could entrust students to work in pairs to critically read and discuss texts in progress, they would need to explain how to read analytically for elements of craft and form. The traditional workshop—the dominant pedagogy (Donnelly 3) and, in many classrooms, the sole methodology practiced—presumes that students already know both form and craft.[2] While some instructors do teach the aspects of form and elements of craft, imparting crucial content is usually in service of preparing students to evaluate texts in workshop.

Instead of training students to merely assess drafts, instructors can use activities informed by writing center tutorials in which pairs of writers take turns acting the roles of writer and tutor in order to discuss texts at hand and, more importantly, converse about processes, goals, and plans for continuing the work of being writers. Not only does this approach provide students with skills that will serve them beyond the classroom, it allows them to use a system of exchanging feedback similar to conversations by actual working writers. The traditional workshop has no real-world equivalent outside of the academy. How often does a writer present copies of a draft in progress to twenty-some colleagues who meet at the same time every week? Although undergraduate workshops do provide practice for students going on to MFA, not all of our students who continue writing will do so in graduate schools. Even MFA programs, with enrollment caps of twelve to fifteen writers with somewhat common goals and levels of experience, aren't sustainable. It's unlikely that a group so large will meet regularly and put forth serious effort if it's not in exchange for degree/course credit.

Undergraduate students should engage in classroom activities that are similar to the ways working writers progress through drafts. Writers doing labor-intensive revisions don't resemble the modernist myth[3] of the lone genius in the garret. Although many writers draft in seclusion, we all seek support and feedback from one another. And, as illustrated in my work with Claire, working with a peer goes far beyond just exchanging comments;

collaboration enables the reflexive work of discussing our poetics, or why we write how we write. In dialogic engagement, we compare and exchange craft and revision ideas. These discussions sustain writing lives, and they are what instructors should be facilitating in undergraduate classrooms.

The discipline of writing center studies, with its emphases on writing processes and the development of writers, offers a wealth of frameworks and approaches that support undergraduate creative writers. Training students to work like tutors scaffolds effective communication, critical thinking, reflection, and revision. Certainly, it's been argued that creative writing benefits from incorporating theory and practice from composition studies,[4] but writing center pedagogy in particular is rich because it brings a combination of various composition pedagogies into conversation. Process pedagogy, rhetorical pedagogy, collaborative pedagogy, feminist pedagogy,[5] and post-process theory[6] all influence both the training of peer tutors and the practice of tutoring writers.

What Are Writing Centers, and How Do They Foster a Writer's Independence as Well as Effective Communication?

By definition, writing centers—with their attendant policies, hiring, staff education, and mission statements—respond to the needs of the communities they serve, and no two writing centers are alike (Hobson 166). Nonetheless, the basic tenets of writing center theory define writing centers as places where a diverse body of writers can learn collaboratively and benefit from individualized instruction. Writing center historian, Elizabeth Boquet, traces the inception of writing center methodology back to the turn of the last century (466); however, collaborative tutorials between peers, as they are generally practiced today, came about around the time of open admissions (472–75). Although writing centers began and continue to be misconceived as places where writing can be "fixed" and remedial writers can practice basic skills, they are in truth sites of a distinct pedagogy in which writers have one-to-one conversations with peers about their writing goals, processes, and specific assignments at all stages of writing processes. Resisting common misconceptions of the writing center as a grammar fix-it shop, Stephen M. North famously summarizes: "in axiom form it goes like this: Our [writing centers'] job is to produce better writers, not better writing" (38).

Five years ago, as a doctoral student and first-year writing instructor, I was simultaneously attracted to and leery of this central concept that prioritizes writers over their texts. My very basic goal for first-year writing courses—that my students build on writing skills introduced in my classroom and find ways to apply these skills to their chosen disciplines—lined up with North's axiom. Yet as a creative writer, schooled in New Critical, Iowa workshop pedagogy, I'd been taught that when it came to imaginative, artistic writing, it was best to focus on the text at hand: talking about the writer who produced it was unfair and, in all too many workshops, similar to personal attack.

As I understood it, after years of being a student in various workshops, analyzing a text was *the work* of workshop. Francois Camoin explains how doing this work contradicts traditional, reverential literary study: "We [creative writers] are always inside the text, working feverishly to make it different, to make it more complex, to change it. Nothing in the workshop is *less* sacred than the text" (4). True, workshop participants work on texts, and these drafts are hardly sacred. However, as per New Critical frameworks, they *are* sacred in a different sense; they exist separately from their authors. This division struck me as false.

Yes, students learn to write by working on texts, but both writers and their texts need to be addressed in creative writing classes. In preparing to teach introductory fiction writing,[7] I looked to the work of creative writing theorist Katharine Haake, who reflects, "teaching [fiction] was simple. I had seen that [as a student]. How hard could it be to sit around in a circle and tell students how to make their stories better? I knew how to make their stories better" (43). Haake realized that if instructors want to support writers and help them keep them writing beyond courses, the teaching of creative writing should not be as simple as making stories better. Likewise, making students independent is exactly what writing center pedagogy emphasizes.

But creative writing courses can go beyond making writers more self-sufficient practitioners in their artistic endeavors. Creative writing students should learn, in addition to writing, skills that are applicable to other disciplines (Radavich 192) and life beyond the university.[8] Kenneth Bruffee has argued "the benefits of collaborative learning for all participants" (qtd. in Bouquet 474–75), in that writing center tutors, in the process of looking at their peer's work, learn to consider their own work objectively and in new contexts. In addition to writing skills, writing center pedagogy teaches students the art of effective communication. Reflecting on surveys from his "Situated in the Center: Peer Writing Tutor Alumni Research Project," Harvey Kail writes about what students take from their work as peer tutors:

> Peer tutoring helps individuals develop a deeper sense of their own competence, first as students and then, once they graduate, as individuals who can do the world's work, particularly the heavy lifting that has to do with language and writing. This increased sense of self-confidence that students acquire in the writing center and then take with them into their lives . . . is grounded in large measure by their proven ability to communicate effectively with others in complex and demanding circumstances. (n.p.)

These complex interactions prepare students for the workforce. A tutor at the Washington College Writing Center explains: "It [tutoring in the writing center] was so valuable to learn communication skills that translate into the working world after college. I learned how to advise peers in a positive way that they are receptive to, and how to elicit brilliant ideas from smart people who are unsure of how to word their thoughts" (n.p.). Like this consultant, students in creative writing classrooms informed by writing center theory and pedagogy would practice the work of questioning and supporting one another—tools that are applicable to a wide range of career pursuits as well as life in general.

Every semester, I ask my fiction students to consider how we might, as writers, replicate emotional experiences for our readers. I tell them that that's our job—to do something with words that readers can connect with and experience. And every semester I ask my students *why* this is such an important thing to do in this day and age. Students know that people in this technological era are disconnected from one another. Many are weary of being treated like consumers and realize that media depictions don't reflect complex realities. Even more of my students want to write because books have changed them; they hope to recreate their transformative experiences for readers of the future. As much as instructors are responsible for teaching students how to connect to their readers and tell their stories, we must also teach students how to listen and learn from one another; working one on one is ideal.

How Do Writing Center Tutorials Work, and How Are They Different from Traditional Workshop Pedagogy?

So, how do we prepare students to do the work of effective communication in writing center–style tutorials, especially since tutoring practices are as contextually specific as writing centers themselves? Despite the difficulty in naming general tutorial procedures, I will identify and explain the basic structure of tutorials as well as foundational practices, all of which are interconnected, in order to make the pedagogy concrete. To begin, writing center tutors "are educated, interested readers/writers who play the role of an engaged and supportive, yet simultaneously critical audience for texts in development. They provide tailored, one-to-one guidance to authors learning how to change their writing process with regard to specific rhetorical and/ or mechanical issues" (Hobson 166). In addition to establishing the claim that writing center tutors must see themselves as writers, I'd like to look closer at "one-to-one" conversation.

Clarifying the significance of conversation, the director of the writing center at the University of Notre Dame, Matthew Capdevielle, explains:

> The process of engaged dialogue is not just a means of attaining insight—it is actually its own end. Our primary purpose in the Writing Center is to engage writers in *conversation*. And this is not just a *means* of achieving something through the session—it is in fact the *goal*. More than anything else, the tutors are working to encourage writers to *talk* about their writing. (n.p.)

So, although talking through writing will improve texts, conversation itself is much more important. Kenneth Bruffee in "Collaborative Learning and the 'Conversation of Mankind'" argues that writing is internalized social talk made public again (641). Therefore, a conversation where a writer puts forth and explains her thinking is nearly the same thing as the composing process. Conversation is not *just* a means to an end; it's a means *to* writing itself.

But then how do tutors get writers to talk about their writing and engage in these conversations that are so closely aligned with writing processes? And what does it sound like? I can speak from my experience and say that conversations are improvisational; tutors respond to the specific needs of the writers with whom they work. As a tutor, I try to get writers talking about their work as well as themselves. Some writers clutch papers bleeding with red ink and need time to vent and explain. A great many writers have repeatedly heard that they're a "bad writer"; they "hate writing" because they believe they'll never improve. Others may feel confident about their writing but are unsure about how to get started on a specific assignment. Some identify themselves as great writers but want an extra set of eyes to look over a draft.

After writer and tutor get to know one another, most sessions then move to the consideration of goals and guidelines for the tutorial. Some tutors need to explain that their job is to facilitate learning, and they won't just fix things. Other tutors point out what the writer has done well, and then pick out a pattern of errors. When I'm tutoring, I tell writers why I'm doing what I'm doing. I'll say, "Here's why I'm asking you to tell me about the assignment: I want you to think about what the prompt is asking you to do and then consider if you've done it." But beyond transparency, the only similarity between all my past tutorials is that each one was distinct. In my capacity as a writing center administrator, working closely with tutors in staff education, I've learned that any kind of one-size-fits-all procedure a tutor develops will not last. But for the sake of being transparent, I can say that tutorial conversations generally entail higher order (or global) concerns of rhetorical awareness, organization, and the execution of literary/rhetorical devices. Given time constraints, the writer and tutor focus their discussion on whatever skill(s) they've prioritized.[9] The pair concludes the session with a recap of what has been discussed and comes up with a plan for the work the writer will do independently (Murphy and Sherwood 8). Feedback in writing center tutorials is geared toward giving writers options for revisions and teaching them skills they can practice on their own.

Traditional workshop pedagogy is quite the opposite. The writer leaves the classroom having listened to feedback and criticism but has not necessarily learned *how* to begin the crucial work of revision. Also, the writer hasn't played any kind of active role in this discussion, as she has likely been required to remain silent as her classmates talked about what didn't "work" or offered up prescriptive suggestions that threaten her authority over her own text. Particularly, then, the last step of the writing center–style tutorial—the discussion of what the writer will work on independently and how she can do this work—would benefit a creative writing student because she would leave a tutorial ready *to work* into her draft.

Creative writing scholars have addressed the issues of silencing and students' authority over their texts. Hal Blythe and Charlie Sweet, in "The Writing Community: A New Model for the Creative Writing Classroom," propose reform and describe a system of mentoring small groups, which eliminates the Iowa workshop edict of the silenced author as well as the problem that (especially large) workshops can become less about engaged conversation and more about "too much advice ('an avalanche of suggestions,' some of which is often contradictory)" (321). Their methodology emphasizes community and conversation—tenets of writing center theory, even if Blythe and Sweet don't name the pedagogy explicitly. In "Adapting Writing Center Pedagogy for the Undergraduate Workshop," Janelle Adsit applies writing center theory and pedagogy to address the problems of silencing and prescriptive suggestions when she asserts, "the workshop informed by writing center pedagogy is no longer a place where a writer goes to receive a revision to-do list. Rather the writer participates in the critical consideration of her own writing" (185). I agree with Adsit and Blythe and Sweet, and I want to build upon their ideas further by suggesting that writing center pedagogy need not be implemented into the workshop. Rather, instructors should incorporate tutor-training methods into undergraduate creative writing classrooms, and the workshop can be replaced altogether by one-to-one writing center–style tutorials.

How Are Tutors Trained, and Why Would Tutorials Work in the Creative Writing Classroom?

Despite the contextual nature of writing center pedagogy and tutor training, a series of frameworks from the field are translatable into a viable pedagogy for the creative writing classroom. Writing center theory and pedagogy provides approaches for engaging in conversation, fostering reflection, teaching students to respond to drafts in progress, and building a community of practice—in which all members are "learners on a common ground" (Geller et al. 7). Discussion of these approaches, as they apply to both tutorials and a tutor's individual growth, clarify why writing center pedagogy can be incorporated into the undergraduate creative writing classroom, as well as how these approaches remedy problems that arise in traditional workshops.

Contemporary writing center scholarship tends to avoid best practices in favor of narratives of actual tutorials and discussions of frameworks that support situated communities of tutors. In *The Everyday Writing Center*, Geller, Eodice, Condon, Carroll, and Boquet explain tutors' habits of mind:

> What we think is important is encouraging a community of practice that allows for change, mutability and learning. We recognize that although learning can be facilitated, as Wenger argues, it "cannot be designed. Ultimately it belongs to the realm of experience and practice. . . ." [I]n our work in our writing centers and at our respective institutions, we resist prescribing traveling practices. (12)

Geller et al. conceive of consulting as a process in which the tutor is always positioned as a learner, constantly reflecting and growing, rather than arriving at a level of mastery or performing codified procedures or "traveling practices." This concept of tutor as reflective learner also appears in Murphy and Sherwood's *The St. Martin's Sourcebook for Writing Tutors*: "This approach [tutoring as an informed practice] suggests reflective practice, one in which the tutor views rules as guidelines and avenues to further refinement of aptitude or 'know-how.' The 'know-how' of good tutors comes from a willingness to reflect on their efforts and to keep learning" (7).

"Efforts" here are two-fold: effective tutors reflect on both their work in tutorials with other writers and their growth as writers themselves. They consider their own recursive processes of drafting and revising. As mentioned earlier, learning to tutor other writers is as much a process as learning about oneself as a writer. In both processes, writers/tutors must allow for change. Murphy and Sherwood echo Geller et al.'s emphasis on the importance of flexibility when they state, "Ultimately, successful tutors are willing to modify their views and procedures as new insights emerge" (7). Basically, tutors grow and change in both their capacity as tutors and writers because they are constantly talking about writing: asking writers what works for them, listening to and learning from writers, and relating what they know about writing. The ability to think critically and objectively about one's own writing and convey this skill to other writers are certainly skills that would benefit creative writing students. Critical thinking is the first step in revision, and although this next tip is lore[10]: writing is *rewriting*. Also, discussing the creative process externalizes how the writer began the draft and makes her qualify which drafting strategies worked, so that these may be repeated.

Scholarship implies that undergraduate classrooms, in which the traditional workshop is practiced, don't necessarily foster community, dialogic engagement between peers, or reflection. In "Ethos Interrupted: Diffusing 'Star' Pedagogy in Creative Writing Programs," Kelly Ritter criticizes traditional workshop teaching that is an "individualized act reliant upon situated ethos, formulated on the basis of successful publication record and its accompanying public recognition, which creates a 'fan' base in the classroom and in the larger institution" (27). Ethos-based instruction can keep young writers from making connections with one another. Arguably, many students, at institutions that support the star system, are in classes to gain insight and feedback from their instructors. Undergraduate students aren't given in-class opportunities to dialogue with one another or form a community; they aren't necessarily practicing the conversations that working writers have when seeking feedback from peers.

Basically, an instructor won't be around to teach content or provide feedback when the fifteen-week course concludes. Practicing writing center–style tutorials provides a system that can be repeated beyond courses, without instructors. Additionally, training students to work like writing center tutors would effectively reform the creative writing classroom by changing the instructor's role to that of a collaborative mentor and inquiry leader, rather than a star to emulate. As opposed to rewarding students for replicating the aesthetics and writing practices of the master, instructors could invite students to discuss standards of "good" writing and how these do, or do not, "reflect universal and enduring aesthetic values that exist somehow outside of cultural construction" (Haake 45–46). Also, an instructor could share insights with students as to her specific processes and thinking as she works through drafts. However, she would also explain that her strategies are right for her; there isn't a general "right way" to write. Some of the work of the classroom could be exposing students to different revision and drafting strategies before having students reflect on which strategies worked for them.

This brings me back to writing center pedagogy's emphasis on reflection. Asking writers to consider their composing processes and goals for writing is not traditionally part of creative writing courses—especially those focused on workshopping. However, creative writing theorists have commented on how reflective writing would enrich our discipline. Stephanie Vanderslice asserts that "[the reinvented creative writing classroom] may include substantial reflection on individual process, so that students may discover the creative practices that most support and enhance their development as writers" ("Once More to the Workshop" 34). Putting Vanderslice's argument into practice, Katharine Haake employs lessons in critical theory to make students aware of "what we are doing when we write" (57). She states,

> Clearly, our first goal as teachers ought to be that writing should continue for our students. And if we are honest, we must also embrace the possibility that students' writing concerns may be different from our own, that their questions—even their desires—may not reflect ours. Doing so might well change the way our discipline conducts itself and lead to a true diversity of voices within it. (58)

Haake advocates for student writers to use reflection to create their own goals and aesthetics independent of instructors. Students wouldn't be writing for instructor approval. Therefore, promoting and assigning reflection contributes to the reform of traditional creative writing classrooms, in which "[c]reative writing teachers . . . position themselves to invert the pedagogical ethos of composition, to foreground their roles as the keepers of the castle rather than the openers of the castle gates" (Lardner 74). Also, reflection and student-designed goals allow writers to consider what they want to get out of their work in creative writing classrooms, and because not all students plan to continue on as professional writers, these goals are various.

In addition to reflection in writing center–style tutorials, specific reflective writing assignments in my classrooms have enabled my students to integrate diverse disciplines and design projects for themselves that are more creative and innovative than any I could conceive. In addition to meeting demanding course requirements and drafting creative works, my students in introductory creative writing courses have incorporated their knowledge of criminal justice into short stories, explored the psychological effects of poems, compared narratology to human genetics, and written lesson plans that use imaginative writing exercises in grade school classrooms. I believe that students have the right to engage with genres of their choosing and use imaginative writing however it best suits their specific learning goals and courses of study. Not all writers will decide to emulate standards of mainstream literary writing; some students may want to try genre or experimental fiction. Using reflective writing assignments, I ask my fiction students to articulate what they know about the conversations and genres they're entering (sci-fi, YA, experimental, graphic novels, etc.) and what their goals are in joining these conversations. I prompt them to consider what they want their writing to do and how they will achieve this.

In asking students to contemplate conventions of genres, undergraduate creative writing classrooms don't foster unchecked self-expression, as many who fear a move away from workshop-oriented pedagogy will spur. In fact, training creative writers to use writing center–style consultations would work against Romantic notions of art for art's sake and the overemphasis of self-expression—writing divorced from context and purpose.[11] Although Adsit primarily applies writing center theory to the workshop, she too sees the possibility for reflection when she writes:

> By asking writers to articulate how they perceive their own writing—how they see it communicatively operating—the

> workshop [informed by writing center pedagogy] moves away from the centrality of "self-expression." As students ask questions of each other they learn to ask the same questions of themselves as they write, leading to greater attention to the world in which their texts will circulate. (187)

Here we return to how questions posed in writing center–style tutorials ultimately benefit the tutor who can then consider "his or her own text and its methods of communicating to an audience" (Murphy and Sherwood 7).

Reflection is tied to questioning—another central tenet of writing center pedagogy that helps writers think critically about their texts as well as supporting them with inquiries that keep them writing. Capdevielle explains the prominence of questioning in writing center pedagogy and relates this to Socrates' "conversations with people about their ideas and [his] helping them to develop a clearer understanding of things by asking good questions" (n.p.). Questions posed by creative writers acting as tutors would draw writers out and give them immediate and early reader responses to characters and craft elements. However, questioning writers does not line up with traditional workshop pedagogy. In "Workshop: An Ontological Study," Patrick Bizzaro refers to the "work of the workshop," as "to interpret and evaluate" texts (40). I agree with Bizzaro's argument that instructors must teach students how to interpret and critically analyze texts (45), but a creative writing classroom informed by writing center pedagogy would shift work away from merely focusing on the evaluation of texts. Questioning would give undergraduates the opportunity to dialogue about their texts in progress and is a more appropriate means for considering early drafts than centrally focusing on interpretation and evaluation.

I realize it may seem superfluous to make the point that questioning strategies would benefit and change the dynamic of creative writing classrooms. But again, consider the traditional Iowa-model workshop. This method assumes that texts up for workshop are ready for interpretation and evaluation. Although undergraduates may present a second or third draft, for the most part, student work is in its very early stages and is not yet ready for multiple assessments. As I've said, in the traditional workshop, the writer remains silent while classmates discuss the draft; questioning strategies play no role. Certainly, the instructor can pose questions to steer the content of the workshop discussion, but the writer has no part in the dialogic engagement.

As established, in addition to listening to the evaluation and interpretation of one's early draft, the writer, in the traditional Iowa-model workshop, might also entertain prescriptive suggestions as to what should happen in a story. These types of suggestions begin with "what if this character were to . . ."; commenters project their own ideas onto texts. However, a question like, "what does this character want and how is he showing his desire in this scene?" opens writers to possibilities. Furthermore this latter type of question prevents others, whose vision and aesthetic might be quite different, from rewriting the text. Of course, peers who pose questions would need to understand craft; specifically that characterization is very much about manifesting intent through action. Questioning relies on a shared vocabulary that describes the global elements of creative writing. Just as writing center tutors focus their questions and comments on issues related to organization, rhetorical awareness, and clarity, creative writers learning to tutor would need to be taught to read for and discuss elements of craft, genre, and form.

In this section, I've been teasing out writing center theory's approaches and frameworks for application to the creative writing classroom, but I've already arrived at how instructors can begin to implement this pedagogy. Fostering writers' growth as reflective learners, members of a community of practice, and Socratic questioners are interrelated approaches, nearly as inseparable as writing center theory is from practice.

How Can Instructors Implement Writing Center Pedagogy into Creative Writing Classrooms?

When using writing center theory and pedagogy in undergraduate creative writing classrooms, instructors should explain that learning outcomes are quite different from those of the traditional workshop. Students need to know that the instructor will neither "fix" texts nor decide what's "good." Again, students will need to gain foundational understandings of literary forms, literary terms, drafting techniques, and commenting methods, as well as how the class will operate as a community of learners. In reference to how she begins her course informed by writing center pedagogy, Adsit writes, "Instructors should actively foster a sense among students that the course is about the communal exploration of textuality among writer-readers. This stance sharply contrasts the confrontational metaphors used for the traditional workshop (e.g., to submit a draft for workshop is to put it on the 'chopping block')" (186). I agree with Adsit that discussions about the importance of community would need to happen from day one, but how is this done?

In order to provide more concrete ways to lead a course informed by writing center pedagogy, I offer my experiences in fiction classrooms as a framework, not a prescriptive set of guidelines. I invite my readers to consider themselves as part of a larger community of practice, and like tutors in a community of practice, there is room for change, revisions, and diversity. Like Adsit, in the classroom I dispel metaphors of the traditional workshop and explain that our work together is about learning to do *the work* of being writers. I require a great deal of intellectually rigorous work as we investigate forms and define terminology. I incorporate community building into this work by having students team-teach lessons on elements of craft and form. Each week, in addition to class discussions and generative exercises, groups of four to six students present a chapter from Janet Burroway, Elizabeth Stuckey-French, and Ned Stucky-French's *Writing Fiction; A Guide to Narrative Craft*.[12] Each group offers an overview of their chapter and an activity that engages the class. Groups are free to add to or contest Burroway et al.'s content. Just as I want young writers to understand that the "rules" of form can be fluid, they need to feel that they are authorized to join in the larger conversations about craft and form. Above all, by giving students the opportunity to lead class and share what they understand about content, they recognize that their ideas and voices are valuable. For me, this activity builds a classroom community while simultaneously covering terminology, the common language that students will use in their writing center–style tutorials.[13]

Of course students also practice tutoring, and this begins with teaching students how to use their critical language in commenting. I've found that even students who are quite comfortable with critically analyzing a published text have trouble commenting on a peer's text in progress. Often, a student's initial response to a creative text is to "like" it. I explain that it's fine to be supportive, but I ask, "What can a writer *do* to a text that someone likes?" This kind of feedback, or lack thereof, gives no specifics for *how* to work further into a text or *how* a text is working, so that successful techniques can be repeated in future drafts. I remind students that the ultimate goal of writing center–style tutorials, as well as our class in general, is to give writers methods for continued work into texts and growth beyond the course. We talk about the kinds of feedback that encourage revision and keep writers writing. Peggy Woods, in "Moving beyond 'This Is Good' in Peer Response," details an exercise in which composition students list and discuss the different kinds of comments they've received on writing and rank them in terms of their effectiveness for revision. In discussion, students see that praise, if unconnected to specifics, is of no use to a writer working to improve. I build on Woods's exercise on effective feedback by incorporating the skill of Socratic questioning.

In class, I employ a tutor-training exercise in which the trainee acting as tutor can only ask questions of the trainee acting as writer; all interpretation must be phrased as a question.[14] For example, a commenter who rightly explains why and how she's responding might say, "This line, 'he was smart as a whip' is a cliché; it doesn't tell me anything fresh or specific about your character." But phrasing this comment as a question to engage conversation might sound like this: "Do you know what a cliché is and why this kind of language dulls your voice?" Or: "In order to make sure my language isn't cliché, I check my figurative language against an online list of clichés. What do *you* do to ensure that your descriptions are original?" Even though the tutor knows what a cliché is and how to avoid them, she positions herself to listen and learn from a writer. Both writer and tutor consider the term and exchange strategies for keeping language fresh. Furthermore, conversations can engage a text but also move toward larger questions that sustain writing for both writer and tutor. For example a tutor might ask, "How might a character show his intelligence rather than you, the writer, telling the reader about it?" In this way both participants think about how to show intelligence on the page, a productive inquiry with which all writers must grapple.

These writing center–style conversations based on questioning and other consultation strategies (see "Strategies for Consulting" in ancillaries) should be practiced throughout a semester-long course. In this way creative writers engaging in tutorials work up to having conversations about more developed creative projects. Just as writers learn isolated craft techniques and practice these in brief generative exercises, students can practice acting as tutors in short tutorials over these same lower-stakes exercises. In my classes, critical commenting on the work of a peer is part of every creative assignment. For example, I use a generative exercise that asks student to choose an abstraction, like "love" or "jealousy," and make it concrete with specific, significant, sensory details (Bernays and Painter 177). Students must show a character manifesting love or jealousy through action in a scene. I have students post their creative work on an online forum the night before our class meeting. I randomly assign partners and require students to comment on one another's work in a post below creative exercises. Then, in another post, I provide my comments on their creative work as well as comments on *their* comments. Half of their grade is based on the effort they've put into the creative exercise as well as, to an extent, their demonstrated understanding of the craft element. The other half of their grade is based on the quality and specificity of their analysis and comments to one another. Then, in class, students are given time to meet with their partners and discuss everything in greater detail. Often these smaller exercises and discussions spark work on larger projects.

Conversely, in traditional creative writing classrooms the instructor's evaluation of a creative text is often the only method of assessment. Again, some instructors may reward replication of their values and aesthetics, but I believe our job as teachers is to help students find their distinct voices and styles. Having students engage with one another collaboratively remedies the problem of students writing solely for an instructor's approval. Also, critical commentaries that students write to one another are measurable and provide instructors with a more objective means to gauge students' critical thinking and learning. Instructors can base final grades on a writer's intellectual growth, rather than just the success of her or his creative products. As posited earlier, I believe that reading critically as a writer, or considering the formal qualities of texts, is a crucial component of undergraduate creative writing classrooms. However, I don't penalize my students for not being able to incorporate lessons on literary techniques and forms into their own creative writing at the conclusion of a fifteen-week course. The ability to manifest learning into the crafting of creative texts can take much longer than a semester. And we must remember that learning is a long, often messy, process. It involves experimentation and failure. First attempts to write fiction and poetry rarely resemble polished pieces. I mean no disrespect to undergraduate work when I ask instructors, were *you* producing "good" writing when you were in introductory creative writing courses? I know I certainly wasn't.

So then what would instructors actually be doing at the end of semesters if they aren't presiding over large workshops or assessing stories, essays, or poems? And what would an instructor do after content has been imparted and students have learned how to read critically, reflect, and ask questions like tutors? When my students are working into their longer drafts in writing center–style consultations, I mentor consulting pairs, who, by this time, have self-selected each other after several opportunities to work with different partners. My work as a mentor in these moments entails overseeing the critical commentaries students write to one another as well as joining into conversations to pose questions and steer pairs through difficult spots. But mostly, when supervising, I watch and learn from my students.

I realize that while relinquishing authority may be difficult for some instructors, leaving students to learn from one another in pairs, mostly independent from instructors, may seem downright irresponsible or impossible. However, we can and should entrust our students to be responsible participants in their own learning as well as the learning of their peers. Consider how well one has to understand content in order to teach it. Training students to help "other writers to learn to handle concepts and skills more effectively creates an educational system built around a community of learners instead of single authority figures. Collaborative learning thus provides an educational environment in which students can engage in self-motivated learning" (Hobson 171). It's this self-motivated learning that will enable students to grow as writers beyond courses, and instructors need to let go so that students can practice it.

Again, to make everything transparent, I tell my students that my course is about teaching them to do what I do, as both instructor and writer. I teach how to read writing in progress and help writers revise and keep writing. For me it's less about relinquishing authority and more about sharing it. I ask more of students and get more. Sometimes *more* means particularly thorough, engaging critical analyses of texts. Other times I hear the beginnings of innovative voices. *More* always means students leave my class having learned critical content and what they need to do to continue writing. At the end of semesters, a great many of my students show their understandings of content in their creative work, and I have to admit, these are always students whom I initially hadn't expected would progress so quickly. But I love to be surprised.

Consider the lore: "No surprise for the writer, no surprise for the reader." Because writing and teaching lives are inextricably linked, this idea extends into our work with students. Creative writing instructors who can let themselves be surprised as they write and learn should likewise have faith in their students' writing and learning.

Although creative writing is its own distinct discipline (Bizzaro 49), we benefit from translating pedagogies and methods from composition studies. Specifically, writing center theory and pedagogy, in itself a hybrid of multiple composition pedagogies, enriches the creative writing classroom by providing a sound system of commenting and conversing that developing writers can use beyond courses. And it's this time, the years that follow our courses, when our students decide that it's worth it to do the work of drafting and revising, the recursive practices that make us writers. Of course, not all students who enter creative writing classrooms intend to be writers. These students will nonetheless learn communication skills that are applicable to many other disciplines and career pursuits. But if a student wants to write—to pursue the daily work of revision, rejection, discovery, and knowing that writing is her calling—we need to prepare that student to do the work of being a writer and engaging with other writers through conversations that not only address texts in progress, but also writing lives.

Recently, an undergraduate interested in taking my fiction class e-mailed me a question about "the product." He wanted to know what students produced in my classes. Other students have flat out asked me which agents I could introduce them to and how many of my former students have published novels begun in my classes. In my e-mail to this prospective student, I explained that students are the products and that I don't fix drafts in a workshop; I give students the tools to work into their drafts. I concluded my response by asking him what he hoped to gain out of a creative writing class, and I invited him to come to my office hours to talk in person. This student never got back to me, but I stand by my answer and understand that the reform of a discipline—to make creative writing about learning to work as writers—is no small task. Everything needs to be made transparent to students, who can be as resistant to new ideas as seasoned instructors. Had that student come in to have a conversation, I would have explained that becoming a writer is a long, difficult journey—one that I'm, in some ways, just beginning myself. I would have asked him what was important to him about writing and how he best learned. I would have told him a story about a girl who, despite garnering plenty of praise in undergraduate workshops and being called a "real writer" by her famous instructor, woke up one day and realized that she didn't know how to keep writing or what to do without workshop deadlines or feedback.

Today, my writing continues because of peers like Claire and students who challenge me as they grow as writers. Writing center theory and pedagogy in the creative writing classroom provide students with the tools to work with one another. Students are most important. They are the writers and thinkers of the future, and they will support one another on their journeys. We just need to give our students the time, space, and skills to begin.

Appendix A: Guidelines for Critical Commentaries and Suggestions for Starting Tutorial Conversations

Remember, we're working to analyze and discuss *how* a text is working as well as to support one another.

When drafting comments on a peer's work in progress please:

1. Address your feedback in the form of a letter to the writer. The point of feedback is not just to show me that you've read and considered how a piece is working but that you can translate your understanding into critical analysis or questions that will help the writer into the next draft. You should use terminology and refer to the discussion of craft and form from the textbook.

2. Consider your experience of the piece as a reader. Some examples: What is it about? What is the tone? How do you respond to the characters? Please also be thorough and specific. For example, if the central character comes across as unlikeable and unworthy of following through a story, why do you feel this way? Can you point to specific textual evidence or literary techniques?

3. Provide a synopsis of how the piece is "working" in formal terms. In this class, we will discuss what makes a story a story, a poem a poem, and an essay an essay. You might decide to break with traditional forms, but you need to know what they are before you do that. In your comments you should consider the specific form in which the writer is working. Address the conflict, stakes, and change.

4. Be specific and point to specific places in the text. Use evidence from the text to support your claims. Rather than saying the characterization is unbelievable, point out specifically where you see this and why you think this is happening. Look for patterns instead of nitpicking, and translate these patterns into the terminology of craft we learned from the textbook. If you don't feel engaged in the plot, consider where you get lost. Are there scenes missing? If the poem isn't comprehensible, where do you get lost?

5. Avoid "I like it." Comments such as "I like" are only helpful if you can articulate why you like a specific text or technique. Likewise for not seeing merit in a piece of writing—you need to say why and how the piece is failing. While commenting can articulate our experience of the text (see point 2), we're not going to appreciate or "like" all texts. Often being objective and commenting on *how* a piece is working (rather than *if* it is working) is most helpful.

6. Remember, we're not here to merely praise one another; we're working together as a class to investigate forms, try new ones, become stronger readers, and work further into our own texts—the work of being a writer. Consider what will help writers continue writing.

Even solid praise can stop the writing process; if your reader loves something and thinks it's done, how does that help you work into a text, or the next text? Consider asking questions.

7. Avoid comments that only address grammatical/mechanical issues. We're not here to be the grammar police. While everyone is expected to invest effort and to revise his/her texts, remember that these are drafts. Perfecting grammar in a draft in progress is akin to polishing gravel. Focus your comments that consider the global elements of imaginative writing: image, voice, character, setting, and story.

8. If you're lost, let the global elements guide you. Consider how the writer uses imagery, can you assess and explain the voice of the piece, how does the writer build character, how does the writer evoke setting, and if the writer set out to write a story, is the text a story as per qualities of the form?

After you've drafted your written feedback you will meet to discuss your partner's work. You should bring two copies of your comments: one for me and one for your partner. Class time will be spent discussing feedback. Take turns playing the role of writer and tutor. I will be around to listen in and join your conversations. You may or may not get to all aspects of your written comments, and you may find your conversations straying away from the text at hand. Let conversations go where they need to go. Here are some suggestions for getting conversations started.

The tutor can ask:

1. Who is the writer's primary influence or is there a specific text that inspired the one at hand?

2. What are the writer's eventual goals for the project? To which journals might she submit it? Is it a chapter of a novel? How long will it be?

3. In what genre is the writing working and why? Who is the writer's implied reader?

4. How did the writer compose the draft? What was the inspiration? Is it a continuation of an older piece?

5. What are the writer's working habits, and specifically what are successful processes that can be identified and repeated?

6. Why is writing important to the writer, and what does she need to do in order to continue with this piece and others in the future?

Appendix B: One-to-One Project Guidelines

How you assign work and allot class time is up to you; I certainly trust everyone to be fair and productive. But because writing is so important in terms of formulating and organizing what we think about drafts in progress (both our own and our peers'), there will be a written requirement in the form of comments/memos back and forth to one another. Copies of these will go into your final portfolio (factored into critical writing grade, 25 percent of final portfolio). In order to consider and organize what you will cover in class discussion, you will write memos to your partner prior to each meeting. You can e-mail them to one another, but I will need copies.

Please also, at the conclusion of the meetings, write a reflection (written collaboratively or different authors for each part) about the process you went through. What you write is up to you, but here are some questions you can consider:

- How did you work as a pair? What were each of your commenting styles? What do you need to work on in tutorials, both as a pair and as individuals?
- What kinds of revisions were suggested?
- What kinds of changes were made and how many drafts did each of you bring to tutorials? Technically, you could each have three new drafts, one for each day of class—or you could have more if you work outside of class time. Having someone read so many drafts is a real luxury. Enjoy it and work on supporting one another.
- What kind of writing did you do back and forth to one another in the memos? Do you feel that the memos you wrote and received were effective? What do you need to work on? What do your partners need to work on?
- How useful was this project? Do you feel you could continue with tutorials in the future? Why or why not?

Memos and the group reflection are due in class. Each of you should turn in a packet containing your memos and a copy of your group reflection.

Kate will also be observing and checking in with groups, and her observations will factor into your participation/attendance/commitment/professionalization grade (30 percent of your total grade). She'll pass around a sign-up sheet to meet with you as well. There will be times to meet both in and outside of class.

Notes

1. Vanderslice concisely summarizes the Iowa workshop model; she writes

> [t]he workshop method of teaching writing arose in the states, in Iowa, in the 1930s–1950s. . . . As conceived and implemented at the University of Iowa through the vision of Norman Forester and later Paul Engle, its primary intention was to provide a post baccalaureate incubator where "young polished writers come for a year or two and have their work critiqued." (Swander quoted in Vanderslice "Once More to the Workshop," 31)

Throughout this chapter, I am referring to this model of the workshop, where experienced writers bring their work for critique, when I say "traditional" or "Iowa method."

2. Swander comments on the absence of content in traditional workshop-centered classrooms.

> "Write a story for next week," the instructor told us. But isn't she going to show us *how* to write a short story? There must be parts, components to a short story, different styles and structures. Is she even going to explain the choices we could make? We had no text to illuminate these concepts. We were to learn through trial by fire, through negativity, through humiliation, through hearing what we and others had done wrong. In any other skill-building class, from foreign language to driver's education, students were asked to practice the basic steps of craft, carefully mastering one chunk of knowledge before adding another. Why was the teaching of creative writing so different? (167)

3. See Brodkey's "Modernism and the Scene of Writing."

4. See Bishop's "Crossing the Lines: On Creative Composition and Composing Creative Writing."

5. See Tate, Rupiper, and Schick's *A Guide to Composition Pedagogies.*

6. The basic premise of post-process theory posits that writing, for various reasons, is a radically situational process that can't be generalized.

7. I have taught and used writing center pedagogy in Introduction to Fiction, Advanced Fiction, and Introduction to Creative Writing (fiction, nonfiction, and poetry courses), but because I have more experience teaching

fiction, most of my examples pertain to my experiences in fiction courses.

8. For a thorough discussion of broader learning outcomes in creative writing, see *Rethinking Creative Writing*. Vanderslice calls for full-scale transformation at both the graduate and undergraduate levels; she recommends that programs offer "more thoughtful, outcomes-oriented curricula" (4)—with skills applicable to life beyond the ivory tower—and build "more resilient, environmentally responsive space[s] for the development and sustenance of young writers and literary culture" (16).

9. For a more detailed discussion of stages of writing center tutorials see Harris's "Elements of a Conference," *Teaching One-to-One: The Writing Conference*.

10. See Ritter and Vanderslice's, "Teaching Lore: Creative Writers and the University" for a foundational discussion of how the perpetuation of lore diminishes both the teaching of creative writing and creative writing's disciplinarity.

11. See Green's "Materializing the Sublime Reader: Cultural Studies, Reader Response, and Community Service in the Creative Writing Workshop."

12. In Introduction to Creative Writing, I have done this as well; students have team-taught chapters from Burroway's *Imaginative Writing: The Elements of Craft*.

13. In addition to the team-teaching activity, I put students in writing center–style tutorial pairs when exploring literary forms. In conversation, students can reflect on why it is, or is not, important to uphold elements of form in the context of their texts. For example, I consider change to be a global tenet of fiction: stories must show characters in moments of great change. I've worked with a number of students who, in early drafts, resist employing characters who change; characters remain stolid or unaffected by the world around them. These writers have explained that their character's inability to change is a comment on human isolation and a more authentic portrayal of the way people really are. I explain that writers can push on the form or break "rules," but it's risky. A more experimental writer in conversation with a tutor/reader will consider if such a risk pays off. She'll see if her reader/tutor can stay engaged in a text in which very little happens. In this way, writers aren't adhering to rules and lore; they learn craft and form through conversation. Much in the way that Bruffee explains in "Collaborative Learning and the 'Conversation of Mankind,'" students can be part of this conversation where knowledge is constructed rather than imparted from an instructor.

14. This exercise comes from prominent writing center scholar Dr. Frankie Condon but is not published.

Works Cited

Adsit, Janelle. "Adapting Writing Center Pedagogy for the Undergraduate Workshop." *Dispatches from the Classroom: Graduate Students on Creative Writing Pedagogy*. Ed. Chris Drew, Joseph Rein, and David Yost. New York: Continuum, 2012. 175–89. Print.

Bernays, Anne, and Pamela Painter. *What If?* New York: Harper Collins, 1990. Print.

Bishop, Wendy. "Crossing the Lines: On Creative Composition and Composing Creative Writing." *Colors of a Different Horse*. Ed. Wendy Bishop and Hans Ostrom. Urbana, IL: NCTE, 1994. 181–97. Print.

———. "Valuing the Community of Undergraduate Creative Writing." *AWP Chronicle* 22.2 (1989): 5–6. Print.

Bizzaro, Patrick. "Workshop: An Ontological Study." *Does the Workshop Still Work?* Ed. Dianne Donnelly. Bristol, UK: Multilingual Matters, 2010. 36–51. Print.

Blythe, Hal, and Charlie Sweet. "The Writing Community: A New Model for the Creative Writing Classroom." *Pedagogy* 8.2 (2008): 305–25. Print.

Boquet, Elizabeth H. "'Our Little Secret': A History of Writing Centers, Pre- to Post-Open Admissions." *College Composition and Communication* 50.3 (1999): 463–82. Print.

Brodkey, Linda. "Modernism and the Scene(s) of Writing." *College English* 49 (1987): 396–418. Print.

Bruffee, Kenneth. "Peer Tutoring and the Conversation of Mankind." *College English* 56 (1984): 635–52. Print.

Burroway, Janet. *Imaginative Writing: The Elements of Craft*. 3rd ed. Boston: Longman, 2011. Print.

Burroway, Janet, Elizabeth Stuckey-French, and Ned Stuckey-French. *Writing Fiction*. 8th ed. Boston: Longman, 2009. Print.

Camoin, Francois. "The Workshop and Its Discontents." *Colors of a Different Horse*. Ed. Wendy Bishop and Hans Ostrom. Urbana, IL: NCTE, 1994. 3–7. Print.

Capdevielle, Matthew. "Why Do You Ask? Questioning the Question in the Writing Center." *Another Word from the UW-Madison Writing Center*. 26 Mar. 2012. Web. 22 Apr. 2013.

Donnelly, Dianne. "If It Ain't Broke, Don't Fix It." *Does the Workshop Still Work?* Ed. Dianne Donnelly. Bristol, UK: Multilingual Matters, 2010. 1–27. Print.

Geller, Anne Ellen, Michele Eodice, Frankie Condon, Meg Carroll, and Elizabeth Boquet. *The Everyday Writing Center: A Community of Practice.* Logan: Utah State UP, 2007. Print.

Green, Chris. "Materializing the Sublime Reader: Cultural Studies, Reader Response, and Community Service in the Creative Writing Workshop." *College English* 64.2 (2001): 153–74. Print.

Haake, Katharine. *What Our Speech Disrupts: Feminism and Creative Writing Studies.* Urbana, IL: NCTE, 2000. Print.

Harris, Muriel. *Teaching One-to-One: The Writing Conference.* Urbana, IL: NCTE, 1986. Print.

Hobson, Eric H. "Writing Center Pedagogy." *A Guide to Composition Pedagogies.* Ed. Gary Tate, Amy Rupiper, Kurt Schick. New York: Oxford. 2001. 165–82. Print.

Kail, Harvey. "Situated in the Center: The Peer Writing Tutor Alumni Research Project." *The Peer Writing Tutor Alumni Project.* n.d. Web. 21 May 2013.

Kuhl, Nancy. "Personal Therapeutic Writing vs. Literary Writing." *Power and Identity in the Creative Writing Classroom: The Authority Project.* Ed. Anna Leahy. Clevedon, UK: Multilingual Matters, 2005. 3–12. Print.

Lardner, Ted. "Locating the Boundaries of Composition and Creative Writing." *College Composition and Communication* 51.1 (1999): 72–77. Print.

Murphy, Christina, and Steve Sherwood. *The St. Martin's Sourcebook for Writing Tutors.* Boston: Bedford, 2008. Print.

North, Stephen M. "The Idea of a Writing Center." Murphy and Sherwood 32–46.

Radavich, David. "Creative Writing in the Academy." *Profession* (1999): 106–12. Print.

Ritter, Kelly. "Ethos Interrupted: Diffusing 'Star' Pedagogy in Creative Writing Programs." *College English* 69.3 (2007): 283–92. Print.

Ritter, Kelly, and Stephanie Vanderslice. "Teaching Lore: Creative Writers and the University." *Profession* (2005): 102–12. Print.

———. Introduction. "What's Lore Got to Do with It?" *Can It Really Be Taught? Resisting Lore in Creative Writing Pedagogy.* Ed. Kelly Ritter and Stephanie Vanderslice. Portsmouth, NH: Heinemann, 2007. xi–xix. Print.

Siegel, Ben, ed. *The American Writer and the University.* Newark: U of Delaware P, 1989. Print.

Swander, Mary. "Duck, Duck, Turkey: Using Encouragement to Structure Workshop Assignments." *Power and Identity in the Creative Writing Classroom: The Authority Project.* Ed. Anna Leahy. Clevedon, UK: Multilingual Matters, 2005. 167–79. Print.

Tate, Gary, Amy Rupiper, and Kurt Schick, eds. *A Guide to Composition Pedagogies*. New York: Oxford, 2001. Print.

Vanderslice, Stephanie. "Once More to the Workshop: A Myth Caught in Time." *Does the Workshop Still Work?* Ed. Dianne Donnelly. 30–35. Bristol, UK: Multilingual Matters, 2010. Print.

——. *Rethinking Creative Writing*. Wicken, UK: Creative Writing Studies, 2011. Print.

Washington College Writing Center. English Dept. Washington College. 18 Oct. 2012. Web. 22 Apr. 2013.

Woods, Peggy M. "Moving Beyond 'This Is Good' in Peer Response." *Practice in Context*. Ed. Cindy Moore and Peggy O'Neill. Urbana, IL: NCTE, 2002. 187–95. Print.

Service Learning, Literary Citizenship, and the Creative Writing Classroom

Carey E. Smitherman and Stephanie Vanderslice

A series of concrete, known needs and goals runs counter
to the creative writing tradition. We may resist rules, resist
authority, and, at times, even resist working with others. We
may even resist the idea that creative writing can be taught
or that students without talent should be in our classrooms.
How can we, then, consider our classrooms as spaces in which
students can do work meaningful not only to themselves as
writers and learners but also to the surrounding community?
How can we encourage beginning students to share their work
with people outside the classroom when we also tell them that
publication is earned only after years of practice, feedback and
revision?   —Argie Manolis, "Writing the Community:
Service Learning in Creative Writing"

ALTHOUGH SOME STUDENTS may have participated in volunteer work in
the past, service learning meaningfully connects the classroom to the
world just as Manolis and others advocate. According to the *National Service-Learning Clearing House*, service learning is "a teaching and learning
strategy that integrates meaningful community service with instruction
and reflection to enrich the learning experience, teach civic responsibility,
and strengthen communities." Students are often able to move beyond the

traditional classroom space and interact with the community around them. Service-learning courses, then, provide a natural opportunity for students to gain a richer experience in the classroom.

But how do students in a creative writing classroom find meaningful service-learning experiences? What should these experiences look like? Transcribing the thoughts of dementia-stricken nursing home patients? Founding a reading series for at-risk youth? Administering a campus literary event? Reviving a defunct regional literary magazine? Actively promoting the work of other authors via social media?

The truth is, service learning in the creative writing classroom can take on all these visages and more. As instructors of college writing, we are continually reflecting on writing theory and classroom pedagogy that will support that theory, and we are increasingly, as Manolis points out, searching for a way for our creative writing students to reach beyond the self and into meaningful contact in the community. Instructors at campuses across the country have enacted a wide range of service-learning experiences in their classrooms, as we will enumerate below. Hopefully, these examples will encourage others to design similarly rich experiences that will help their own students engage with *their* communities.

As we continue to move through our careers, we are often serving as, in Donald A. Schön's words, "reflective practitioners" (Schön 295). We strive to keep writing in the academy both engaging and relevant for each new generation of college student. To reach that goal, then, we continually reflect on every aspect of our teaching pedagogies. And our assignments are a substantial part of this reflection. While a disconnect often exists between the writing projects students are assigned in college and the actual writing students most likely do postgraduation, we believe that experience through service-learning projects can provide authentic writing situations for students.

Students rarely have a reason to feel genuinely responsible for portraying their subject matter in an ethical way, no matter how much their instructors work to convince them of the importance of doing so. In traditional courses, the assignments students complete usually have little or nothing to do with their actual experiences. Although they may devote time to reading, researching, and drafting papers or projects, they may feel that they are not truly invested in the assignments they are completing for a course. Giving students the opportunity to participate in authentic learning can enable these students to more completely engage in the educational process. In "Authentic Learning for the 21st Century: An Overview,"

Marilyn M. Lombardi reports that "Students say they are motivated by solving real-world problems" and that "they often express an interest in *doing* rather than *listening*" (2). Service learning in writing classrooms, then, can provide that authentic learning opportunity and extra inspiration for students to become connected with the work they are doing. They will have the chance not only to read about the topics they are interested in, but students will also be able to conduct primary research (i.e., observations, interviews, etc.), and, through these experiences, will become experts in their own right and have their own ideas to share. Being given the chance to go through a service-learning experience can create a greater interest and responsibility for the coursework students do.

Service learning is becoming a strong element in many different writing courses because scholars and practitioners both have begun to see a need for this type of experience. This sort of work has been the answer to many issues surrounding authenticity of the writing situations into which faculty ask student to enter. Current issues and primary research speak to students' ideas about society; therefore, they can feel connected to course materials and see relevance in the rhetoric of what they're learning. By incorporating this type of learning into our writing courses, we are setting the tone for the type of critical thinking and social responsibility our students can continue to develop throughout both their college careers and into their working lives.

As service-learning courses continue to appear and flourish on college campuses, however, considerations must be made about how to create courses that will both teach students and inspire them. Choosing sites and/or partnerships for learning based on students' interests and concerns (or at least curiosity) has proven time and again to be a useful strategy in formulating innovative, interesting, and dynamic classroom environments where students can strive to be connected to course content and course requirements. Matching course goals with community partners who can further those goals is also crucial to the success of a course of this nature.

Service Learning in the College Classroom: History and Practice

Most students are used to sitting in a class, reading and discussing texts and completing assignments for an audience that usually consists of their professor and fellow classmates. The outside world has little to do with this process except for the possible real-world issues covered in readings and lectures. This can be especially true of a creative writing course, in which students are often accused of "navel gazing." Unfortunately, while a traditional course can help students learn the expected material and learn to write for an academic audience, it provides little opportunity to move beyond the classroom walls and integrate them into communities beyond their college or university.

In *Serving to Learn, Learning to Serve: Civics and Service from A to Z*, Cynthia Parsons warns that "[j]ust doing some service in the community doesn't automatically enhance academic course work . . . [w]e teachers have to work at making the positive connection between civic service and the study of civics" (vii). This assertion is true for the incorporation of service learning in any discipline. In these courses, students must be challenged to move beyond their comfort zone, beyond the familiar classroom practices. They are asked to build on traditional learning and accept a stronger responsibility for their learning experiences. In the creative writing classroom, moreover, service learning projects may also ask them to become more involved in their local, regional or national creative writing community, involvement that is critical to success in the literary arts.

Finally, as students become involved with a specific service project— helping at-risk students become writers and readers, helping veterans to tell their stories, highlighting the literary arts in their communities—they gain valuable insight into the world around them and their influence on it. They begin to feel strongly about their experience and will want to share it with others; therefore, a college classroom can be the perfect place for service learning if faculty is prepared.

To help faculty in their preparation, scholars have produced resources from which we can learn. In *Service-Learning: A Movement's Pioneers Reflect on Its Origins, Practice, and Future*, Timothy K. Stanton, Dwight E. Giles Jr., and Nadinne I. Cruz reflect on the history of the field of service learning. They point to both an increased number of campus- and community-minded individuals as well as an increased awareness of social problems in the country during the 1960s and 1970s that led some educators to look for ways to change the traditional structures of academia to better serve a more diverse population of students. Although this work began as a marginalized form of instruction, Stanton, Giles, and Cruz note that these individuals originally drew on concepts from the discipline of philosophy and extension education programs, as well as other social programs and movements to construct what is now considered the theory and pedagogy of the widely known concept of service learning (1–2).

The *National Service-Learning Clearinghouse* further adds to the discussion of the incorporation of service in higher education, describing the civil rights movement and the founding of the Peace Corps as some of the instigations for the service-learning movement. On their website, under "History of Service-Learning in Higher Education," it states, "It was during this time period that the early pioneers of the service-learning movement began to emerge and attempted to combine 'service' to 'learning' in a direct and powerful way" (1). These historical events helped to place civic responsibility in education in a stronger light.

Additionally, Stanton, Giles, and Cruz discuss early service-learning practitioners' questions about what needs to be included in the formation of community consciousness for students. They assert that a combination of service and structured education in which students have the opportunity for guidance and reflection on the issues surrounding their service lead to a deeper connection between the student and service (3). If students are given not only the opportunity to work toward a cause in their community but also a structure in which to work, faculty are creating unique "spaces" for a deeper connection between the work and the issues that create the need for that work. "Service-learning advocates differentiate their practice from volunteer service by evoking the concept of reciprocity between server and served . . ." (3).

Suzanne W. Morse frames this movement in her discussion of civic responsibility in American higher education. She states that there is a "rebirth of the civic purposes of education" (33) and that

> . . . this theme has had a long shelf life and has found its way into conversations about cultural foundations, general education, liberal arts, professional education, community or public service, citizenship education, service or experiential learning, or what, in [Hannah] Arendt's definition, might be termed political or civic education. (33)

Educators understand more than ever the importance of including civic themes in our classrooms and finding ways to incorporate them to enrich the integrity of our existing courses. We are becoming more convinced that combining service and learning can lead to civic-minded students who become more educated citizens.

Janet Eyler and Dwight E. Giles Jr. add to this conversation in *Where's the Learning in Service-Learning?* as they relate their experiences in observing a multitude of "service-learning programs" around the country. They state that a vast difference exists in what academic institutions consider "service learning" with some valuing the service over the learning and others emphasizing the learning over the service. Eyler and Giles respond to this chasm in their own description, which is drawn from Honnet and Poulsen's *Principles of Good Practice in Combining Service and Learning*: ". . . we have embraced the position that service-learning should include a balance between service to the community and academic learning and that the hyphen in the phrase symbolizes the central role of reflection as the vital link between service and learning" (4).

Although there is no "correct" model for civic education in higher learning, the "long shelf life" to which Morse alludes shows the continuous momentum of service learning. She points out that students are not born citizens; rather, citizenship is something that is learned. The assumption that citizenship naturally tied to education is widely argued; however, we contend that it must be a conscious connection. That is, faculty must knowingly include civic education in their course curricula if they hope to educate their students about civic responsibility (34).

It is apparent, then, that we should continue to search for new and unique approaches to incorporate the notion of civic responsibility across the university. Although there are no set rules about how civic engagement should be incorporated into a college education, there is clearly an emphasis on issues of social responsibility across the disciplines.

Before searching for compatible community connections, however, faculty must be aware of the multiple options for incorporating service learning. In "Building and Maintaining Community Partnerships," Vicki L. Reitenauer et al. discuss the differences in learning environments. They outline two basic types of service for students: direct-service and project-based opportunities. While direct-service means just that—working directly with partners in the community, project-based service takes an indirect approach. In a direct-service environment, students may be collaborating and working side by side with members of a particular organization as well as working directly with the community being served by the organization. They may be serving food, interviewing community members, tutoring library patrons, or any of a plethora of other direct work (19).

Project-based service, in contrast, asks students to focus on particular projects that will help the community partner achieve their goals. This type of work may include grant writing, social media and public relations, or a variety of other advocacy (19). Faculty, then, must consider the goals and objectives of a particular course in deciding what style of service will be most appropriate. Creative writing classrooms, of course, have their own goals and objectives and faculty who want to incorporate them need to keep these in mind when developing service-learning projects and initiatives not as "add-ons" but as meaningful elements of the course.

Another important factor to consider is the faculty who will teach this type of course. Not all of our colleagues will be interested in breaking from the traditional classroom instruction to incorporate civic and service learning. Finding faculty who are primed to take on this task is key to a successful program.

In "Teachers of Service-Learning," Rahima C. Wade discusses her research into the motivations of teachers who are drawn to service education. She conducted a study of eighty-four teachers with a range of teaching experience. As she begins to identify reasons behind teacher interest, she looks at different factors including their beliefs about teaching, their personal experience with community service, and their own rewards and problems related to service learning (77). Wade cites teacher motivation ranging from an obligation to instill social responsibility and self-esteem in their students to a personal interest in serving their community (80). She also points out that over three-fourths of the teachers in her study indicate that they have participated in some sort of community work in their lives (81).

We can see through this research that some faculty are more predisposed to incorporating service learning into the classroom than others, and while it comes naturally to them, many of our colleagues need assistance in learning to teach these courses. Many of them may have a desire to either participate in service themselves, and still others may see the need to help their students become more experienced citizens. But without proper guidance, faculty may be at a loss about how to successfully merge service and learning together.

These colleagues may also need to be made aware of the many benefits to service-learning courses. Besides the obvious reward of knowing both faculty and students are making a difference in the community, the state, the country, or even the world, we as teachers can observe unexpected (or at least less expected) benefits from facilitating these courses. An increased connection and enthusiasm between student and course material, better student social skills and self-esteem, and recognition for both students and faculty throughout the academic institution and community are only a few of the added rewards (Wade 86).

As certain teachers are drawn to service learning, so are certain students. In "The Role of Student Characteristics in Service-Learning,"

Alan S. Waterman contends that two personality psychology hypotheses affect the ways in which students participate in service:

1. Students will differ in their motivation for participation in service-learning programs and these differences will [a]ffect both how students involve themselves in service activities and what they derive from such activities in terms of both affective changes and cognitive growth and learning.
2. Student development, in both the affective and cognitive realms will be enhanced when there is a good "fit" between student characteristics (including motivations) and the nature of the service experiences provided to the student. (95)

Students more apt to gravitate toward service learning usually have a history of volunteerism. Most of these students also possess a greater motivation toward their education as a whole than those who are uninterested or unengaged in service-learning assignments (98–99). It is important to note Waterman's second hypothesis, however, in that if faculty are informed about service-learning theory and best practice and prepared to offer these opportunities, they are more likely to choose partnerships that match student characteristics (or at least modify options to fit).

If faculty can navigate this process, they can see immediate results. In Carey's first-year writing course, for example, a student wrote a response to his service-learning experience: "I think the service learning is a great thing. It is different and more exciting than regular classes. I also feel it is a really effective way of researching first-hand on [my] topic. Overall I really enjoyed it. It felt good giving back to Arkansas where I have lived my whole life (Ly)."

Not only will service learning provide a unique opportunity for students in the classroom, but it will also influence their lives after a particular course is over, both throughout their college career and beyond. Participating in service-learning projects helps students to become involved in something, and whether or not they continue to serve in the initial capacity that came from their project, they will most likely be open to many other opportunities on and off campus. These opportunities range from student government to social clubs to journalistic or creative opportunities for students to share their experiences. Many campus leaders today have participated in some type of service learning throughout their academic careers, bringing outside experiences into their roles as students.

Beyond their college careers, service learning can shape our students' adult lives. In today's highly competitive job market, we as instructors realize that it is not always sufficient to make good grades or to obtain a college degree. Graduate schools, companies, and other work organizations often look for what sets someone apart from other applicants. Service learning (and the opportunities students seek from their initial service) is a great resume builder and is something unique. These projects say to potential employers or graduate programs that these students are aware of the world around them and are serious about being well-rounded, concerned citizens of this planet. They show that particular students are well informed about real-world issues, and the students may even find the field and/or organization they wish to work in through the particular service they provide. Also, the people in the community students meet while they are participating in service learning can become valuable contacts for them in their job search.

Service Learning and the Creative Writing Classroom: A More Recent History

Some of the earliest explorations of service learning in the creative writing classroom include Chris Green's 1999 *College English* article "Materializing the Sublime Reader: Cultural Studies, Reader Response, and Community Service in the Creative Writing Workshop" and Argie Manolis's essay "Writing the Community: Service Learning in Creative Writing," in Anna Leahy's 2005 collection, *Power and Identity in the Creative Writing Classroom: The Authority Project*. As its title indicates, Green's article considers several issues relevant to the creative writing classroom and only touches on service learning near the end of the piece. Nonetheless, what Green has to say is important, as he observes that "[c]reative writers can play a central role in closing the gap between universities and communities" (170). What's more, community service can help writers not only create local audiences, which can be difficult for authors to cultivate (170), but also become aware of a *diversity* of audiences since, as Green notes, "Giving a reading to a class of seventh graders in the Ohio River town of Owensboro, Kentucky is different from giving a reading at a four-year liberal arts college in the mountains" (170). He also points out that service learning in the creative writing classroom might not have been extensively written about but that didn't mean it wasn't happening; after all "the poets from June Jordan's *Poetry for the People* go into community venues such as schools and churches to share their gift of voice" (171). Communities, moreover, are not a place to just enact service: "we must also strive to engage people in conversation and be ready to learn something ourselves in the dialogue" (170).

At the same time, Manolis was a strongly service-oriented MFA student who wondered why, in creative writing classrooms, "we did not grapple with larger questions such as, 'What was our responsibility to our communities?' or 'What might our communities think of our work?'" (141). These questions vexed Manolis until she herself developed a plan for bringing writing into the community while she was a student, teaching poetry writing to nursing-home residents. Now that she is a professor in Minnesota, Manolis's introduction to creative writing course requires that the students plan and implement "weekly activities for residents of a nearby nursing home" (144). Most of these residents suffer from some form of dementia. Students record the residents' "conversations and write found poems from those conversations, which they read back to the residents and give to the residents' families" (144). Not surprisingly, through this practice, Manolis hopes to "create writers who are engaged with and feel responsible to their communities" (144). Along the way, they also gain critical thinking and "enhance interpersonal skills, consider their civic responsibilities and overcome negative stereotypes" (148).

Certainly, these are not isolated examples. Literacy programs such as *Writers in the Schools* have partnered with MFA programs for years. Other programs, such as those at the Virginia C. Piper Center for Creative Writing at Arizona State University have developed local, regional, national, and global programs that engage their students in literacy outreach. The MFA program at the University of Nevada–Las Vegas encourages students to serve in the Peace Corps by offering up to a semester's worth of course credit for those who do. And programs like the California Institute of the Arts have developed courses such as "Tiny Press Practices," for those who want to enhance their community engagement by participating in a "hands-on exploration of contemporary autonomous small and micropress practices as they relate to the poetics of community accountability." Courses such as these, which feature project-based service learning opportunities, pose and answer important questions, such as, "How might we participate in creating the literary and artistic world we wish to inhabit? What is our responsibility, as writers, readers and thinkers, to a larger literary-artistic culture?"[1]

In the field of creative writing, such sites and experiences are also vital to connecting students to the literary environment they must navigate when they graduate. Consequently, courses that introduce students to this environment via the idea of "literary citizenship" have become increasingly important to the creative writing curriculum.

Originating with writer-teachers such as Dinty W. Moore (who coined the term) and Cathy Day, the concept of "literary citizenship" arose when Day, in particular, noticed that, among her own students, "what brings most people to the creative writing classroom or the writing conference isn't simply the desire to "be a writer," but rather (or also) the desire to be a part of a literary community." Moreover, she also observed that her most successful students made significant efforts to become a part of that literary community:

> My students attend MFA programs, yes, and they publish, yes, but they aren't my only "success stories." Some are literary agents; in fact . . . agent, Michelle Brower, is a former student of mine. They subscribe to lots of literary magazines. They have *founded* and edit magazines, too. They're editors. They write for newspapers and work in arts administration. They maintain blogs. They review books. They volunteer at literary festivals. They participate in community theatre. They become teachers who teach creative writing. Most importantly, they are lifelong readers.[2]

Observing these successes, Day sought to explore and examine ways of formalizing literary citizenship in creative writing courses, ultimately teaching an entire undergraduate course on the topic at Ball State University in 2013 which we will describe in more detail later in this essay. At the same time, literary service-learning programs were emerging nationwide, some within writing programs, such as those at Arizona State University and many others, and some were popping up outside of them, such as writer Dave Eggers's 826 National literary centers staffed by volunteer writers across the United States. Cataloging the benefits of this kind of literary activism, Stephanie Vanderslice urges creative writing programs in "Where Are We Going Next: A Conversation about Creative Writing Pedagogy," "to connect with the community and form a sense of civic responsibility among the next generation of writers. These kinds of connections are mutually beneficial, for the community and for the writer." In the same essay, Cathy Day notes, "there are more than 800 degree-granting creative writing programs in this country—an amazing number!—so it's important to think about how we, as writers and teachers of creative writing in those hundreds of programs, can channel all that interest constructively."[3]

So, what does all of this mean for us as faculty? How can literary citizenship and service learning be incorporated into a creative writing classroom by teachers who are already overburdened with pedagogical and professional demands? By examining how literary citizenship manifests itself in creative writing courses, we seek to answer that question, encouraging the creative writing professor to reflect on her practice, on the ways in which she may incorporate service learning in her courses, and why it is important to do so.

Cathy Day and Literary Citizenship at Ball State

Fortunately, as Day began to conceive of a course centered on "Literary Citizenship," she documented each step along the way online so as to make her course easily replicable (thanks for the service, Cathy!). For example, here is the course description:

> A literary citizen is an aspiring writer who understands that you have to contribute *to*, not just expect things *from*, the publishing world. This course will teach you how to take advantage of the opportunities offered by your campus, regional and national literary communities and how you can contribute to those communities given your particular talents and interests. It will also help you begin to professionalize yourself as a writer. . . . Students who complete the course in an exemplary fashion will be eligible to apply for internship positions as Social Media Tutors at the Midwest Writers Workshop in Muncie July 25–27, 2013.[4]

Day's next step was to create an online presence for the course at Literarycitizenship.com where anyone interested could see the course syllabus, see what the students were talking about from week to week, and even see what the students were blogging about themselves. As the syllabus shows, keeping a relevant blog is a large part of the students' grade. To help them stay relevant and answer the enduring question, "But what do I blog about?" Day organizes the course blog[5] around the following "outward" concepts:

Actions
1. Online Community
2. Attend/Organize Literary Events
3. Interview Writers
4. Review Books
5. Other? Create a category

What is literary citizenship??
1. Definitions
2. Shining Examples

Importantly, Day also introduces students to the fact that they will be responsible for helping to organize a literary event:

> You're all required to interview, review, and develop an online community (they are required assignments). You're also required to *organize* (not just attend) a literary event. Here are three to choose from. You may also create a literary event on your own, if you wish.

- On March 14, I'm scheduled to talk to you about going to grad school. I'm going to open up this talk to all students. This group will help me organize and promote this event.
- On March 19 and 20, we host the In Print Festival of First Books. One of Prof. Mark Neely's goals this year is for more non-BSU faculty/students to attend In Print. This group will help him do that.
- In April, the Midwest Writers Workshop is sponsoring a poetry reading for National Poetry Month with Mark Neely and Karen Kovacik. This group will help MWW publicize this event at BSU and in Muncie.[6]

As you can see (and as the course blog enumerates in fascinating detail) Cathy Day's Literary Citizenship course immerses her students in literary service learning in hundreds of ways, large and small, from becoming involved in regional literary culture by organizing a literary event to being tirelessly interested in other writers and promoting their work. In addition, through the case study and the presentation (see the course syllabus on the blog) her students do a lot of the written reflection that represents good practice in the service-learning classroom. Finally, the hands-on service nature of a course like Literary Citizenship introduces students to the many careers available in the literary world beyond "writer" and "college writing professor," careers that undergraduate students might not even realize exist until they take the course. Regardless of their ultimate career goals, however, the value of courses like Literary Citizenship can best be summed up by a dialogue from one of her blog posts, a dialogue that redefines the term and introduces students to the utter necessity of literary service to the twenty-first-century aspiring writer:

> Q: Professor Day, how do I get published?
> A: Work to create a culture in which books can thrive.

Q: No, seriously. How do I get people to buy and read my work? How do I get discovered?

A: What did you do today to help get *someone else's work* discovered?

This is the essence of literary citizenship.[7]

In Stephanie Vanderslice's Writing for Children Workshop, students engaged in service learning and in supporting the regional artistic community by volunteering with the Arkansas Literary Festival as part of the course. Occurring each April in downtown Little Rock, the Arkansas Literary Festival is the central literary event of the state whose main goal is the "development of a more literate populace."[8] It includes readings, workshops and author appearances for every genre and age level but Vanderslice's students have largely worked as volunteers with the children's events, since this is the craft they are studying in the course. They have served such roles as "author escort" for children's authors at the events, performed as children's literary characters (e.g., Clifford the Big Red Dog), and helped set up and take down children's literacy events at which they were able to observe children reacting to texts and their writers. In each case, they provided an important service to the event and learned a great deal in the process. In one reflection, for example, a student wrote about how much she learned about the life of a children's author by escorting her author throughout the day and listening to her talk about her career and her writing. In another, the student who performed as Clifford the Big Red Dog reflected on what she learned about writing for young children from reading the guidelines for "character actors" at a literary festival. For example, she extrapolated from the guidelines' imperative that one was never under any circumstances to remove Clifford's costume head in front of the children, as it is upsetting and confusing for them. This reinforced a notion that the class had been teaching her all along: that young children are a unique audience and writing for them requires a special approach, just as performing for them does.

What are the values of introducing students to service learning and literary citizenship in the creative writing classroom? As a review of the literature and select service-learning courses at universities around the country demonstrate, the values are many, including enhancing students' critical thinking and interpersonal skills, enhancing their sense of responsibility to the many communities in which they live, and, especially in the case of literary citizenship, introducing students to the kind of professional ethic, awareness, and behavior that can help them gain a foothold in an increasingly competitive literary environment that is defined by change. It can definitely be an undertaking to change our existing pedagogy in order to incorporate service learning. But it is a worthwhile change, one that will open up for them a world of literary possibilities beyond the classroom. Our students deserve no less.

Notes

1. Description of Tiny Press Practices course in Calarts' fall 2014 catalog, accessed 11 Nov. 2014.

2. Found by searching "literary citizenship" at the Bird Sisters blog, the-birdsisters.blogspot.com, accessed 24 Nov. 2014.

3. Found by searching "Where are we going next?" at *Fiction Writer's Review*, http://fictionwritersreview.com, accessed 24 Nov. 2014.

4. Syllabus pdf under "Resources" at Literary Citizenship website, http://literarycitizenship.com, accessed 24 Nov. 2014.

5. Ibid.

6. Ibid.

7. Found under "Actions" at Literary Citizenship website, http://literary-citizenship.com, accessed 24 Nov. 2014.

8. Found under "About" at Arkansas Literary Festival website, http://www.arkansasliteraryfestival.org, accessed 24 Nov. 2014.

Works Cited

About. *Arkansas Literary Festival*. 2013. Web.

Day, Cathy, Anna Leahy, and Stephanie Vanderslice. "Where Are We Going Next? A Conversation about Creative Writing Pedagogy, Part 2." *Fiction Writer's Review*. 2012. Web.

Day, Cathy. "My Next Big Thing: Literary Citizenship." Cathyday.com. 2012. Web.

———. Literary Citizenship Blog. Literarycitizenship.wordpress.com. 2013. Web.

———. "Literacy Citizenship." The Bird Sisters Blog. Thebirdsisters.blogspot.com. 2011. Web.

Eyler, Janet, and Dwight E. Giles Jr. *Where's the Learning in Service-Learning?* San Francisco: Jossey-Bass, 1999. Print.

Green, Chris. "Materializing the Sublime Reader: Cultural Studies, Reader Response, and Community Service in the Creative Writing Workshop." *College English* 64.2 (Nov. 2001): 153–74. Print.

Lombardi, Marilyn M. "Authentic Learning for the 21st Century: An Overview." Ed. Diana G. Oblinger. *Educause Learning Initiative*. Educause Learning Initiative. 2007. Web. 28 May 2013.

Ly, Stanley. "Class Reflection." Message to the author. 18 Dec. 2011. Email.

Manolis, Argie. "Writing the Community: Service Learning in Creative Writing." *Power and Identity in the Creative Writing Classroom: The Authority Project.* Ed. Anna Leahy, Clevedon, UK: Multilingual Matters, 2005. 141- 53. Print.

Morse, Suzanne W. *Renewing Civic Capacity: Preparing College Students for Service and Citizenship.* ASHE-ERIC Higher Education Report No. 8. Washington, DC: School of Education and Human Development, The George Washington University, 1989. Print.

National Service-Learning Clearinghouse. "History of Service-Learning in Higher Education." ETR Associates, 2012. Web.

———. ETR Associates. 2012. Web.

Parsons, Cynthia. *Serving to Learn, Learning to Serve: Civics and Service from A to Z.* Thousand Oaks, CA: Corwin Press, 1996. Print.

Reitenauer, Vicki L., et al. "Building and Maintaining Community Partnerships." *Learning through Service: A Student Guidebook for Service-Learning across the Disciplines.* Ed. Christine M. Cress, Peter J. Collier, Vicki L. Reitenauer, and Associates. Sterling, VA: Stylus, 2005. Print.

Schön, Donald A. *The Reflective Practitioner: How Professionals Think in Action.* New York: Basic Books, 1983. Print.

Stanton, Timothy K., Dwight E. Giles Jr., and Nadinne I. Cruz. *Service-Learning: A Movement's Pioneers Reflect on Its Origins, Practice, and Future.* San Francisco: Jossey-Bass, 1999. Print.

Tiny Press Practices. Courses, California Institute of the Arts. Web.

Wade, Rahima C. "Teachers of Service-Learning." *Service Learning: Applications from the Research.* Ed. Alan S. Waterman. Mahwah, NJ: Lawrence Erlbaum Associates, 1997. Print.

Waterman, Alan S. "The Role of Student Characteristics in Service-Learning." *Service Learning: Applications from the Research.* Ed. Alan S. Waterman. Mahwah, NJ: Lawrence Erlbaum Associates, 1997. Print.

Creative Literacy Pedagogy

Steve Healey

Teaching outside Genre

RECENTLY I TAUGHT several poetry workshops at a residential school for juvenile offenders in Minnesota. I don't have much experience teaching adolescent students, but over the years I've taught quite a few adult prisoners in various facilities. I've come to appreciate how these students can bring intense energy and honesty to the classroom, and I've also learned how challenging it can be to keep them focused on a single discussion or task. I knew that the teens had been learning some basics about poetry with their regular teacher, but beyond this, my guess was that many of them had very little experience reading or writing in this genre.

My goal was to guide these teens through a poetry-writing exercise and give them an opportunity to share what they wrote. But what kind of guidance would I offer? How would I create the conditions for them to begin appreciating poetry and to feel the creative freedom to write it, even for a few minutes? I have to ask these same questions when I teach creative writing on a college campus, and in recent years I've noticed that I increasingly look for answers outside the conventions of the literary genres we call poetry, fiction, and creative nonfiction. In other words, as I develop writing assignments and prompts, I encourage students to borrow familiar forms and techniques from the world around them. Rather than thinking of literary genres as closed systems with their own internal traditions and rules, we can find the literary in our everyday lives. We can write a poem in the form of a walk through a city neighborhood. We can write a short story in the form of a "things-to-do" list. We can write a piece of creative nonfiction in the form of a TV commercial. We can open the literary up to the extraliterary.

This approach to creative writing pedagogy is part of a larger effort to give my students an education in what I call "creative literacy"—a broad range of skills used not only in literary works or genres but in many other creative practices as well. Given that so few creative writing students actually go on to become published or professional writers, I want to offer students learning experiences that are more relevant, practical, and engaging. I also want to encourage the creative writing field to open up its boundaries and not cling so tightly to narrow definitions of the literary. In doing this I add to a small wave of recent scholarship that has examined the creative writing field's isolated position within the academy and proposed reforms for it, including the essay collection called *Can It Really Be Taught? Resisting Lore in Creative Writing Pedagogy*, a compendium that in various ways urges the field to embrace more critically aware methods and disciplinary identity rather than simply relying on informal and unquestioned teaching strategies passed along anecdotally. As the editors of the collection, Kelly Ritter and Stephanie Vanderslice, say in their introduction, "Indeed, the lore of teaching creative writing—that which positions the teaching of creative writing as a favorite hand-me-down in the clothes closet of academia—is systemic, pervasive, and rooted in creative writing's isolated academic status, at once frustrating and comforting to the writers and organizations who perpetuate it" (xiii). This kind of move to demystify the creative writing field has mostly focused on the necessary project of building more interdisciplinary bridges to the other major fields in English—composition and literary studies—and throughout the academy. In this way *Resisting Lore* furthers the work done in other important books that came before it, by people like Katherine Haake, Tim Mayers, and Paul Dawson.

My focus in this article is on opening up creative writing not so much *within* the academy but to practices *outside of* the academy. The concluding chapter in *Resisting Lore*, written by Peter Vandenberg, may actually point in this direction: "A more self-consciously critical discourse of creative writing will most certainly refuse to continue bracketing conventionally defined literary genres, instead pulling them into a theory of relation with other writing practices and decidedly *un*literary text types" (108). And for me, it's important to look for these extraliterary models in creative practices beyond the assumptions and limitations of our formal educational institutions. Teaching creative literacy means questioning what we call legitimate academic work and connecting literary practice to the lives students will actually live beyond the classroom.

In the workshops I conducted with the teens in the residential school, I was especially mindful of the need to make poetry more accessible and relevant, less intimidating and esoteric. I decided to build the writing prompt around a simple repetition technique. Here are the basic guidelines I came up with:

> Your poem should use some kind of repetition. You can repeat either a single word, a phrase, or a certain kind of sentence structure. The repetition should occur at least three times to establish a pattern of repeating. A repeated word or phrase can come at the start of each line or sentence (i.e., anaphora), or at the end, or anywhere that feels right.
>
> You can generate a word or phrase that you find inspiring, or you can use a generic word or phrase such as: *I remember; I see; I like; this place is; I don't know why; you forget; if we could; elsewhere; yes; maybe.* A repeated sentence structure could be a series of questions, commands, sentences starting with different names, sentences ending with different colors, etc.

As I presented this prompt, I asked the students to think about and name some other forms of communication that use repetition, such as songs, prayers, sermons, speeches, and lists. We discussed why repetition is used in these forms, and what effect it has: to build rhythm, emphasis, passion; to build a circular movement that's easy to follow.

Almost always after setting up a prompt and before asking students to begin writing, I offer them some specific examples of the technique in action. First, we listened to a song that uses frequent repetition: "True Blues" by the early 1970s proto-hip-hop group called the Last Poets. Then we watched a brief film adaptation of Bob Hicok's repetition-driven poem "Having Intended to Merely Pick on an Oil Company, the Poem Goes Awry." We read a few other poems using repetition on the page, by folks like Patricia Smith, Lawrence Ferlinghetti, Gwendolyn Brooks, and W. S. Merwin. I also read one of my own poems that repeats several key phrases throughout—I'd been commissioned to write this poem for a ceremony commemorating the fifth anniversary of the 35W bridge collapse in Minneapolis, and I talked to the students about how I wanted the repetition to have the quality of a prayer or sermon.

I could have limited the guidelines to this one cluster of techniques, but I wanted to give these less-experienced writers even more material to work with, and to help them avoid predictable, clichéd, beginner-poetry content. I also wanted to add more collaborative energy to the process, to build some community in the room. So I added another prewriting step to the process, asking them to generate spontaneously a specific item for each of the five following categories:

1. one color
2. one body part
3. one brand name (name of a consumer product or corporation such as Coke or Nike)
4. one specific, concrete image remembered from your life in recent days
5. one specific, concrete image remembered from your life years ago

I asked students to share some of the items in their list with the group, to help us see the variety within the task they had just performed collectively. Then I explained that their goal would be to include all their items in their poem, and since spring had just arrived in Minnesota, I gave them one final task: to make some reference to spring in the poem's first line.

By including these random elements, I said, they could invite the magic and chance of their imagination and not feel stuck in one subject that they think their poem *should* be about. Once again, I invoked other extraliterary forms to make the writing task feel more familiar. I invited them to think of what we were doing not only as making a poem but also as playing a game, or putting together a puzzle, or going on a scavenger hunt, or improvising a new recipe with whatever ingredients we find in the kitchen. So for both of the major components of this exercise, I tried to teach poetry writing in part by teaching outside the conventions of the poetry genre, by considering how repetition occurs in forms other than poetry, and by considering how including randomly generated elements occurs in activities other than writing poetry.

We wrote for about ten minutes, and in that time many of the students produced some really interesting writing. Most of the poems at least hinted at the challenge of their present situation—being confined to this facility by the legal system, feeling regret and anger, missing loved ones and their freedom—and the repetition gave these intense emotions some shape and rhythm, and the random ingredients often gave their poems a playful or unexpected quality, moving from images of feet walking under a pair of

Levi's to a bright red cardinal on a tree branch to parents yelling at each other in the kitchen. I never force students to read aloud what they write, but almost every student in these several workshops was not only willing but eager to do so for the group, and everyone received applause or finger-clicks in response.

Some Context for Creative Literacy

I've been teaching creative writing (along with other English courses) for more than two decades, and I've come to believe that, despite the popularity of creative writing courses, students often don't care much about the conventional forms, techniques, and traditions of creative writing genres. What they do care about is being creative, being expressive, using language in interesting ways, and they see poetry, fiction, and creative nonfiction as vehicles for these activities and experiences, not the goals themselves.

Many teachers and writers have bemoaned this state of affairs, accusing students of being self-absorbed and undisciplined, disrespecting the complex craft, rich history, and social power of literature, and even accusing the creative writing field of encouraging this casual, shallow approach to teaching. In his essay, "Poetry and Ambition," Donald Hall famously complained that the creative writing workshop is like an assembly line encouraging students to create McPoems—a fast-food poetry that shows little effort, little appreciation for the poetry canon, and even less artistic excellence. With dismissive authority he says, "We know that the poem, to satisfy ambition's goals, must not express mere personal feeling or opinion—as the moment's McPoem does" (sec. 16). Whether the critics are traditionalists like Hall, calling for a return to reverence for great literature and forms of the past, or champions of the avant-garde, calling for a revolution of language and society, they often agree that the great evil promoted by creative writing is some variation on "self-expression." As in: "Students these days don't really care about poetry, they just want to express themselves." With much fatigue and indignation, such statements are commonly tossed around the hallways of English departments all over America. The assumption is that merely writing about one's experiences or feelings lacks integrity, rigor, merit, and that students who want to do this are spoiled, self-centered, and lazy. And teachers who surrender to this "self-expression" mandate give students touchy-feely assignments like, "Write a poem about something that makes you feel sad."

I agree that students often don't care much about literary genres themselves, but I think the desire for self-expression is only part of a larger desire to learn creative skills and have the experience of being creative in a range of fields and forms. In other words, students want to develop their creative literacy, and creative literacy has gained enormous social and economic value in recent years. I've discussed this term at length in a couple of other articles (Healey), especially as a way to explain the enormous growth in creative writing as an academic field in recent decades despite an apparent decline in literary reading rates among Americans. I certainly don't celebrate this weakening enthusiasm for reading literature and studying the conventions of literary genres, but I do think we should be honest about why it's happening and allow this understanding to shape our creative writing pedagogies.

What's really at stake here can be framed as a question: who has access to creative writing, or who gets to be called a creative writer? Should we teach creative writing to juvenile offenders or any other disenfranchised populations, if what they produce might not be deemed "excellent" by critics? Should we teach creative writing to the vast majority of K-12, college, and even graduate-level creative writing students who will never go on to have a professional writing career or even publish a single piece of their writing? I think many creative writing teachers see their primary goal as producing writers of "great" literature, and when their students don't deliver, they feel frustrated. And critics of the creative writing field like Hall and Dana Gioia often say that it produces too much mediocre writing—it's harder to find the "great" literature in the ever-rising tide of competent but unremarkable, unoriginal self-expression. This line of thinking repeats the European Romantic view that real art is created by a few chosen geniuses; artists may speak for the people or to the people, and even encourage revolutions, but they are not the common people themselves.

The fear that real art might be mistaken for the personal outpourings of the masses is often complemented by another fear: that art might be mistaken for mere commerce. This is not simply anxiety about artists flirting with the marketplace, as when Warhol obsesses over product packaging or Nirvana's *Nevermind* goes number one with a bullet. Throughout the last century, and especially in recent years, "creativity" has become a buzzword in just about every area of our lives, from business to urban planning to parenting to cooking. We're encouraged to be innovative and think outside the box in both our work and play, in our professional and social lives, and much of our economy is focused on giving us tools, technologies, and knowledge to help us be creative, including the booming sectors of social media and digital technology. It has become commonplace for bestselling nonfiction to bow down to the god of creativity as the key to all good things. Often with flavors of self-help, business, science, and sociology—by authors like Richard Florida, Daniel H. Pink, Seth Godin, Thomas L. Friedman, and Jonah Lehrer—these books promote creativity not as a fringe activity but as the central path for a prosperous humanity in the twenty-first century.

What's so scary about all this creativity buzz? Well, if we can say that there's creativity everywhere from the boardroom to Facebook, what makes creativity special? In a recent article in *Harper's Magazine,* the unabashedly liberal Thomas Frank lambastes "the fantastic growth in our creativity-promoting sector" (7) and argues that it has "little to do with the downward-spiraling lives of actual creative workers" (9). This is an important point to make—plenty of impoverished artists don't share in the creative economy's bounty—but it's also a point that relies on a very tricky distinction between creativity that's "actual" and fake, authentic and inauthentic, good and bad. The notion that real creative work is only made by "starving artists" is a variation on that Romantic myth that talent and genius are possessed only by a few select outsiders.

As a creative writing teacher, I can't subscribe to this myth, but what's the purpose of teaching creative writing if the overwhelming majority of our students use the skills they learn not to write "great" literature but in all those other areas of their lives? If we give up the dream of producing only literary superstars, does this mean that the only alternative is to surrender the classroom to some squishy, amorphous idea of self-expression? I suggest that a pedagogical focus on creative literacy can avoid this false choice between two dead ends.

Three Ways That "Creative Literacy" Is Not Just a Fancy Way of Saying "Creativity"

1. Creative literacy is democratic. While the term "creativity" can often seem esoteric, mystical and mysterious, hard to access, a force we can't control, available only to those with special inspiration or talent, the term "creative literacy" tries to be more democratic, inclusive, concrete, a force that anyone can grasp and use, every day and everywhere. Instead of evaluating creativity on an aesthetic spectrum from bad to mediocre to good, creative literacy tries to suspend these judgments and embrace the possibility that anyone can be creative under the right conditions. I'm not

suggesting that all creative products are equally compelling and well made, but creative literacy postpones that critical evaluation so that everyone can access the experience of being creative.

2. Creative literacy can be learned and taught. It's a range of skills and techniques that can be studied, modeled, discussed, practiced. Practitioners can become more skilled the more they practice, the more they experience creative processes repeatedly over time, the more guidance they receive from teachers and other resources. Whether or not creativity comes from inspiration or magic or luck, whether or not creativity comes from a "natural talent" gifted to us at birth, creative literacy brackets these intangible possibilities and focuses on those tangible skills and techniques that anyone can learn, and that any teacher can teach.

Creative literacy very intentionally joins a range of other literacies, most notably "critical literacy," which is often promoted as the primary skill-set that students gain from liberal arts courses. These two literacies can and should complement each other, not only in creative writing courses but in any academic course or field. Creative literacy also joins an ever-evolving array of less formal, niche literacies, such as baseball literacy, punk rock literacy, nutrition literacy, or financial literacy. To use the term "literacy" in this way suggests that there's a legitimate body of knowledge and practices associated with the subject and that it can be learned and taught over time; in this context, "literacy" suggests an area of expertise or authority that can be accessed by immersing yourself in that subject.

3. Creative literacy is collaborative. Rather than framing the artist as the individual talent, the isolated genius with the private imagination who creates something completely "original," creative literacy encourages artists to collaborate, to participate in a creative community, to see language and other artistic materials as part of a larger public sphere that anyone can reference or appropriate (without actually plagiarizing or denying someone else's authorship). We often think of collaboration simply as people working together, but I also want to consider collaboration between the materials that those people work with—the working together of different texts, forms, genres, fields, traditions, and so on. So a writer can work alone on a piece of writing but still cultivate a collaborative attitude.

In the creative writing classroom, there are many ways to encourage people to work together directly and indirectly, for longer or shorter durations. Students can actually coauthor a piece of writing, collaborating for the entire process and developing guidelines for how to share that process. Students can also work together by generating material collectively and sharing it, by using the same techniques and devices, by responding creatively to each other's writing, and so on.

Students can nurture a collaborative spirit in less overt ways by creating a text that collaborates with another text. Instead of "inventing" a whole new text, students can do something with one that already exists, through various strategies such as erasure, creative translation, creative research or documentary techniques, epigraphs, collage, cut-up, sampling, remixing, along with many kinds of imitation that have differing levels of sincerity (from homage, pastiche, variation-on-a-theme-by, and allusion, to parody, spoof, caricature, and unauthorized sequels). The author of the other text certainly need not be present (or even alive), and the other text need not be literary—in fact, it's often more interesting to collaborate creatively with a text that doesn't call itself "creative." This kind of textual collaboration can open up new and exciting ways of working with language and ideas. It allows creative writing students to write a poem, for example, without feeling so stuck in its poem-ness, in the common assumption about what poems are supposed to do and sound like.

There may be even more opportunities in the classroom for collaborations between broader categories—forms, practices, genres, disciplines, fields, traditions. Creative literacy opens up to possibilities beyond and between these boundaries. It nurtures a generous spirit of interdisciplinarity and hybridization, crossover and cross-pollination, mixing and borrowing. Not simply ignoring the skills, techniques, and conventions that we associate with such categories, creative literacy expands the skills available to a given category, encouraging curiosity and continuous learning.

A class in poetry writing, for example, might include not only the study of conventions such as imagery, line breaks, and rhyme, but also explore the poetics of playgrounds, personal ads, and brain surgery. Although creative writing pedagogy often makes literary genres seem like museums of exclusive traditions and techniques, literary forms have always borrowed from the extraliterary. Think of a few Modernist poetry chestnuts, like Williams's "This is Just to Say," which takes the form of a kitchen note; or Hughes's "Theme for English B," which takes the form of a young person's school writing; or Stevens's "A Postcard from a Volcano," a poem announcing itself as a piece of mail from an improbable source; or Stein's larger work, *Tender Buttons*, which categorizes each of its prose-poems into sections called "Objects," "Food," and "Rooms." Part of literary tradition is the impulse to appropriate the traditions of other forms, and this impulse may be even more relevant and pervasive in our text-saturated twenty-first century.

As a creative writing teacher, I've been developing this more open spirit toward form for many years, although I've only recently begun to use the term "creative literacy" and see it in larger theoretical and pedagogical terms. I think a profound shift in my pedagogy occurred when I began to use Ron Padgett's wonderful *Handbook of Poetic Forms* in my poetry-writing courses. This book is remarkable for its plainspoken clarity and easy presentation of forms, techniques, and methods. Along with a solid overview of Western traditions, it also includes a sampling of the non-Western. Especially exciting for me as a teacher was how it mixes some nontraditional or uncommon forms with the traditional; alongside entries for "Haiku" and "Sonnet" are entries for "Alphabet Poem," "Event Poem," "Found Poem," "List Poem," "Performance Poem," "Ritual Poem," and my favorite, "Walk Poem," which is a poem that describes a real or imagined walk, or makes observations during a walk, or takes on the rhythm and shape of a walk, or explores the mental movements of the walker (200–01). Once you consider a "Walk Poem" as a legitimate poetic form, it's possible to begin seeing poetry in almost any activity. The spirit of Padgett's *Handbook* is not to define a firm boundary around poetry and present a definitive survey of forms; instead, it implies that forms and techniques are everywhere, and all poems have form even if those forms don't yet have a name.

In the rest of this chapter, I'd like to sketch out some more specific ways to bring creative literacy into creative writing pedagogy, using some of my own teaching experience and assignments as examples. I'll organize this material into three sections that address: (*1*) the creative process, (*2*) the creative product, and (*3*) the presentation (performance, publication, etc.). I don't want to suggest that it's always possible to draw strong lines between process, product, and presentation, but I find this distinction useful for the purpose of outlining this pedagogy.

Creative Literacy in the Writing Process

Teachers can bring a creative literacy approach to each stage of the writing process, from early generating to composing and drafting to later revising. Writing poetry, fiction, and creative nonfiction, sometimes even more than academic essays, can be intimidating and downright scary for students. Beginners who see these genres as containers of mysterious "meaning" may feel little power to get started beyond waiting for a muse to knock at the door and whisper those meaningful words into their ears. Creative literacy tries to make the stages of the writing process more familiar and approachable, and it tries to make students feel less isolated, more part of a community of writers, as they work through the stages.

Among my favorite generative writing exercises is one I call "Variations on a Theme by a Fellow Student," and the great energy of this activity comes from both collaborative and game-like elements. I usually do this exercise when teaching poetry, but I've also done it with creative nonfiction. On a day that students are submitting a final draft of an assignment, I collect all the printed copies and redistribute them randomly around the classroom so that all the students now hold someone else's writing. Then I ask everyone to read the fellow student's poem and extract from it the most interesting, inspiring, provocative passage they can find, about one to three lines in length. This passage then becomes an epigraph for a new poem that each student will now write spontaneously on a separate sheet of paper. Each new poem is titled "Variations on a Theme by . . ." followed by the name of the epigraph's author, and I encourage students to write somehow in response to the epigraph, perhaps borrowing some of its language, ideas, or tone.

To increase the collaborative and game-like intensity of this exercise, I've also had students write three lines in response to the epigraph in a timed, two-minute period, then pass the paper to another student who adds three more lines in another two minutes. This process continues for several rounds until the new poem is perhaps twelve or fifteen lines in length. This variation borrows from the well-known Surrealist parlor game called Exquisite Corpse, although the original game requires each writer to fold the paper to conceal the first two of their three lines, which adds even more chance energy to the composition.

After finishing the writing, I invite students to read the poems aloud, and this reading is often enormously entertaining and instructive—students love to hear which passages of theirs were chosen for epigraphs, and what kind of weird and wonderful serendipity unfolds in the new poems. Each student's authorship is affirmed by hearing a poem written in response to their own writing with their own name in the title; on the other hand, the traditional notion of authorship is destabilized because the new poem has multiple authors who have collaborated with each other and with an already existing text. The final product is almost irrelevant because what matters here is how the material was generated and how it was composed. Of course it would be inconvenient to do all our writing this way, but I hope that students let this experience inform their future writing processes. The next time they're staring at a blank page or screen, how can they recreate the generative energy of this exercise on their own?

Responding to an epigraph is a great way to get started in any writing process because you immediately have something to work with, and I find that other textual collaborations can serve this same purpose. Give students a copy of a news report and ask them to sample some of the language from it and mix this into a new writing. Give students a copy of a famous poem and ask them to begin writing a parody of it, then after a few lines, let go of the parody and let the new poem develop however it needs to.

There are many other ways to get students working together on activities that guide them through certain stages of the writing process. When writing fiction or creative nonfiction, you can have students generate a list of interesting opening sentences (with or without certain characteristics you've defined). Each student chooses her or his best opening sentence and writes it on the chalkboard; everyone then chooses one opening sentence written by someone else from the board and begins to write the story or essay spontaneously in ten to fifteen minutes. Or have students generate a list of interesting images, or pieces of dialogue, or shifts in action (e.g., "That's when the electricity went out"). They choose one of these items to write on the board, and from these, everyone chooses at least three items to include somewhere in a piece that they write spontaneously.

Teachers can invoke extraliterary forms in the writing process as well, as when I asked the teens in the residential facility to generate a list of items as if they were ingredients for a recipe, pieces to a puzzle, etc. Think of any activity or form, and you can have students appropriate that process for their creative writing process. For example, have students generate a list of five childhood memories and then compose them as if they were parts of a painted mural depicting key scenes from their lives, or as if they were snapshots arranged in a photo album, or tattoos inked on their bodies, or different kinds of make-up applied to their faces.

Many teachers know how mysterious and frustrating the revision stage of writing can be for students. They resist it, they see it as punishment, they say it takes the "life" out of their writing, and often they just don't do it, even if it's required. A creative literacy approach to revision can ask students to consider how revision occurs in a wide range of other forms and practices. For example, revise a story or essay as if it were a full-length film that needed to be edited into a film trailer. Or revise a poem by expanding it, as if it were a film trailer that needed to be developed into a full-length film. Or a strategy that focuses more on rearranging than adding or subtracting material: as if you were a sculptor or potter who uses the same clay but reshapes that clay into a completely new object, revise your poem by keeping most of the same language but rearranging it into a completely new pattern. This kind of pedagogical move has at least two important effects: (*1*) it helps students visualize or concretize the revision process via the analogy with another form, and (*2*) it helps students to destigmatize the revision process because they start to see it not as a sign of weakness but as a necessary part of any creative practice.

Creative Literacy in the Final Product

For years, one of my core assignments for creative nonfiction students has been to write a sectioned essay—an essay that somehow breaks up the text on the page into sections using blank space, numbering, subheadings, or other such devices. When I first developed this assignment, I vaguely sensed something timely and relevant about it, and with each passing semester I'd see more examples of sectioned writing out in the world. Especially with the rise of reading on screens, sectioning has become much more common in just about every form of written communication—in magazines and newspapers and books, in brochures and reports and product packaging, on websites and blogs and social media. We read constantly throughout the day, but for better or worse, that reading happens in smaller, bite-sized pieces, and "sectioning" is one way of conceptualizing many of these reading and writing strategies.

So as my assignment for the sectioned essay has evolved over time, I've increasingly presented sectioning as a strategy used not only in creative nonfiction but in a wide range of nonliterary written forms, including "top-ten" or "best-of" lists, how-to guides, instruction manuals, recipes, diaries, logbooks, indexes, outlines, glossaries, news headline streams, and so on. I prompt discussions with my students about why sectioning has become so pervasive, what effects it has on readers and writers, and what qualities they look for in effective sectioning. I encourage students to appropriate any of the nonliterary sectioning strategies suggested (or any others they can imagine), and we practice some of these strategies ourselves in class. Among the most popular of these exercises is one that combines the style of a how-to guide with some exploration of social identity. I suggest some example titles that are sincere and straightforward, such as "How I Survived High School as a Single Mom," but I also give them permission to be humorous, sarcastic, or absurd, with example titles like "How to Be a Target of Racial Profiling" or "How Not to Hook Up with Someone at a

Party." I give them time to brainstorm their own title and then write for ten to fifteen minutes from that title. Once students open up the door to all these sectioning models in the world, models that are waiting to be appropriated for creative writing, the possibilities for form begin to multiply rapidly. And I think most students are thrilled to be liberated from writing the single block of text in an academic setting.

Students often bring more rigid and misguided assumptions to poetry, I find, than other creative writing genres—they think it's supposed to use regular rhymes and flowery language, it's supposed to be "emotional," it's supposed to have a "meaning" but be elusive about it, etc. Creative literacy pedagogy is especially useful in unfixing these assumptions because it connects poetry to other forms that are more familiar and concrete.

When teaching poetry I often give an assignment I call "Journeys." Here are the main guidelines:

> Write a poem that resembles a journey in structure, always moving on to new territory, through time and space, rather than returning to the familiar (as we did in the repetition/ listing assignment). Your poem may or may not actually make reference to a journey (to travel, transportation, walking, etc.).
>
> Journeys can take on many shapes and patterns. A journey can look like a straight line between point A and point B, moving in a logical progression through time and space, like a conventional narrative. Many interesting journeys, however, keep digressing or taking detours away from their intended path, or they get lost entirely from their original destination. And many journeys, especially those that happen in the mind, move through time and space in unpredictable ways, making larger leaps, sometimes moving backward or sideways rather than always forward.
>
> Whether your journey poem is more linear or nonlinear or some combination of both, consider the multitude of forms that a journey can take.

I then suggest a number of more specific ways of defining a poem as a journey: as a form of transportation, as a walk, as a guided tour or travelogue, as the mind wandering, as a dream sequence, as a film trailer, as channel surfing, as a story, and so on.

I began developing this concept of a journey as a poetic form after feeling frustrated about how to help students access some more difficult contemporary poetry that tends to be digressive and doesn't follow an obvious, regular pattern or narrative. Upon first reading this kind of poetry, students often dismiss it as randomly arranged nonsense, but I think students begin to appreciate it when I frame some of these poems as a journey the speaker's mind takes as it moves through various observations, experiences, memories, judgments, and so on. I ask them to imagine transcribing what passed through their mind in the five minutes before they arrived at class today—what form would that writing take? It would almost certainly have a drifting, aimless movement, digressions leading to more digressions, but it would probably make some sense to the one whose mind went on that journey. One way to read digressive poetry, I suggest, is to see some of this poetry trying to represent that wandering energy of the mind without apologizing for it—although we often think that writing is supposed to overcome that chaos, this poetry can reclaim it and try to show the wisdom and beauty of it.

To practice this theory, I developed the following exercise prompt:

> Write a poem in which every sentence enacts a digression without calling attention to itself. In other words, keep swerving away from whatever language path you're on, but try not to announce that you're swerving: just do it, without apologies or excuses. Even though your content keeps morphing slightly, try to maintain a rhetorical flow and grace, so that readers keep feeling confidence in what you're saying.
>
> You might think of your voice as your mind telling a story about where it has been, or what has passed through it, in the recent past (or in the present). When or if you use "I" in the poem, think of it less as your body moving linearly through time or space, more as your consciousness encountering a nonlinear series of observations, impressions, images, sensations, thoughts, memories, dreams, desires, judgments, etc. Just as the mind usually processes all these disparate materials without an obvious organizing principle, let your voice accumulate materials by association, by digression.

This one simple exercise has perhaps been more successful than any others I've created, in that it inspires more students to write with more energy and enthusiasm, and it often seems to cause a fundamental shift in their attitude toward language and writing for the rest of the semester. I've developed plenty of exercises and assignments that have flopped, or more likely, just confused students with muddled directions. But this "digressions" prompt works well, I think, because it gives students a very simple, clear technique to create some interesting, complex effects on the page, and this is delivered largely by showing how the same kind of technique operates in a familiar, everyday activity or form (the mind on a wandering journey).

This kind of creative literacy approach informs many of my assignments and class activities. When we explore the traditional form of the epistolary poem, we consider not only letters in general but more specific kinds of nonliterary letters and other kinds of correspondence: a letter of complaint, a letter of recommendation, a generic year-end family newsletter, a postcard, an RSVP, a thank-you note, a greeting card expressing congratulations or condolences, an e-mail to a boss, a note confessing a crime, a suicide note, etc. When we explore a form I call "meta-poetry"—poetry that's self-referential, self-consciously discussing itself, its own making, its language or language in general—we spend some time considering where we can find these same "meta" techniques outside of literature. First I point to some TV shows, such as *The Office* and *Parks and Recreation*, that use a "mockumentary" style, with characters breaking through the action to speak directly at the camera as if being interviewed. This leads to other examples of creative works that are, to some degree, about themselves, such as TV commercials that cleverly call attention to their own selling strategy as a way to distance themselves from that selling, or cartoons that depict the cartoonist drawing the cartoon. Making a self-referential poem becomes a much less daunting task after seeing that task in relation to a world full of "meta" techniques that we encounter every day.

To encourage even more overt exploration of forms beyond the literary, I often give students the following assignment that's more analytical than creative:

> Choose one contemporary nonliterary artist and/or artwork that you find particularly compelling (interesting, thought-provoking, stimulating, pleasurable, innovative, excellent, awesome, etc.), and write a brief response describing the artist/artwork and explaining why you find the artist/artwork compelling.
>
> You can define the term "artist" and "artwork" loosely, but consider the following likely categories: music, film, TV, performance, comics, painting, photography, sculpture, architecture, etc. If you'd like to broaden the definition of an artist/artwork even further, that's fine.

Part of the purpose of this writing is to put our creative writing in the context of the larger art world. In this course we've been developing a vocabulary to discuss creative writing, using terms like "imagery," "layering," "sectioning," "character development," and I invite you to use some of these terms to discuss the artist/artwork you choose.

Many of my students love this opportunity to turn other members of the class on to an artist/artwork that they love, and it reaffirms that they're participating in a larger culture of creativity that thrives on healthy conversations and crossover between forms and genres. And it's a great lesson to discover creative writing skills at work in the extraliterary, because this can reveal a more general relevance and power for those skills.

Creative writing teachers can use more overt collaboration among students to lead to creative products. I've found that collaboration can be especially interesting when working with traditional forms. When teaching students to write sonnets, for example, you can arrange them into small groups to collectively generate a handful of interesting end-rhymes; then each group member writes his or her own sonnet using these common rhymes. Because traditional forms can be particularly intimidating for students, adding this collaborative, playful approach can be a good way to make the writing process more comfortable and accessible.

Usually late in the semester, after having guided students through so many assignments and prompts, I give them an opportunity to take on more teacherly authority with an assignment that first asks them to generate their own writing prompt that borrows a form from a nonliterary source. I then collect all the prompts and paste them into one document which I copy and distribute to everyone. Students then choose one writing prompt created by a fellow student and write based on those guidelines. This assignment can work with any genre, and here are some guidelines I give when presenting it for poetry:

> Many poems borrow their forms from outside of the literary world. Perhaps the most common way this happens is for a poem to take on characteristics of another kind of text that uses written language. For example, poems can look or sound like an advertisement, a corporate memo pitching a new product, a public service announcement, a menu, directions for a scavenger hunt, an alphabet book for children, an email,

a newspaper report, an encyclopedia entry, a dictionary definition, a movie review, etc.

Poems can also borrow from forms that are not obviously using written language. Imagine a poem in the form of a documentary film, a shoebox of old photographs, a board game or video game, a puzzle, a sport, any physical activity (such as swimming), a museum or art gallery, a face, an animal, a map.

Whether or not the students come up with inspiring or effective prompts, the process of surveying the world of forms beyond creative writing has great educational value, I think. This task takes them even deeper into creative literacy, showing them in an active, concrete way that the skills they're learning can be applied to a wide range of creative practices beyond poetry, fiction, and creative nonfiction. The collaborative element of sharing writing prompts also gives students the experience of being a teacher—someone who tries to create the conditions for learning—not only for fellow students, but also for themselves in the future.

Creative Literacy and Presentation

After a piece of creative writing is "finished," what do we do with it? Traditionally there are two options for presenting literary works to an audience: read or perform them aloud in a classroom or other literary venue, or publish them in a literary publication. But creative literacy pedagogy encourages us to think outside these typical modes. Because presentation can require substantial time and resources, it may not be practical to require students to set up a logistically complex public performance or to produce an expensive publication, but plenty of interesting possibilities can be pulled off efficiently and inexpensively, and more importantly, students can imagine *potential* presentation scenarios that can inform their writing without being required to actualize them. For example, write a short story as if it were a sermon being delivered by a preacher who is experiencing some personal troubles. Write a creative essay as if it were an improvised version of the president's State of the Union speech—the version that really tells the truth. Write a poem as if it were going to be published on the box of your favorite childhood cereal.

My regular teaching job is at a Minneapolis Community and Technical College in downtown Minneapolis, and our campus is just a short walk away from the Walker Art Center and its sculpture garden, through a city park and across a strange and beautiful pedestrian bridge. This bridge was designed by the artist/architect Siah Armajani, and as he's done with other works, he's included the text of a poem in the design. In this case, Armajani commissioned John Ashbery to write a poem specifically for this purpose—the text of the poem is etched twice across the bridge, on both its north and south lintels, so that pedestrians can read it in either direction. Although the poem doesn't make direct reference to the bridge, it does seem to be aware of the physical space it occupies and the surrounding environment, and reading it up there, above the traffic, closer to the sky, as you walk across this unusual-looking but very functional structure, is a really powerful experience, very different than reading a poem on the page.

I regularly take my students on a walk to this bridge, to have the experience of reading poetry that has been written to be presented in a public space. Back in the classroom, I give them the following task:

> Write a poem that you imagine will be presented or "published" in a nonliterary environment. Imagine poems with titles such as: "Poem to Be Spray Painted on the Side of a Taco Bell Restaurant," or "Poem to Be Used as Subtitles for a Video of Me on the Last Day of My Life," or "Poem to Be Read Aloud in the Mall of America," or "Poem to Be Sung on the First Day of Spring," or "Poem to be Inscribed on a Pedestrian Bridge in Minneapolis." In each of these cases, the poem would likely take some formal qualities from the context suggested by the title.

Of course I don't require that the poem actually fulfill the presentation its title suggests, but imagining such a presentation changes the way students write the poem, and it helps them to begin seeing literary form and language out in the world, off the page and off the screen. One of my students wrote a poem called "Poem Carved in the Wall of My Treehouse When I was Eleven Years Old," and it explored her childhood awareness of her transgender identity as if she could go back to that time and reclaim it. She could have just written about her personal experience however it came out of her, but the unique form she invented gave shape and rhetorical purpose to that experience, and it was a really powerful poem.

I've also assigned students to produce—collaboratively, in small groups of two to four members—an actual, tangible literary publication, except that I encourage them to be very loose and creative in their definition of the terms "literary" and "publication." Here are some of the specific guidelines I give:

Content: Among your first tasks as a publisher will be to decide what content to publish. You can publish original poetry, stories, creative nonfiction, plays, etc. written by yourself, or solicited from others. You're also welcome to expand your definition of what "literary" is, publishing graphic/comic work, an erasure, a list of imaginary poem titles abandoned by Sylvia Plath, or just about any other creative work that involves language. You can also publish anything that falls into the broad category of literary criticism: commentary, analysis, reviews, best-of lists, recommended-reading lists, etc. And you can go even further outside the box of original literature or criticism, generating some kind of oddball archival or information-gathering project. Ask yourself, what really needs to be published? What kind of content do you think will be particularly relevant and provocative to an audience?

Form/Design/Appearance: Your publication can take many different forms, and because you don't have the time or resources to use costly state-of-the-art printing services, you'll need to use your imagination. Your publication can be either in print or digital/online. It can take the form of a small book (e.g., a chapbook), a magazine (or "zine"), a pamphlet, a newsletter, a poster, a series of postcards, a website, a blog, an audio recording, or any other form that you can imagine actually producing. You don't even need to be able to name what the form is, as long as it can be defined loosely as a publication. If you really use your imagination, almost any physical object can become a publication. For example, you could remove the matches from a matchbook, replace them with tiny pages, and call it a published book. Perhaps you can recycle some discarded materials and turn them into an eco-friendly publication. Particularly in the midst of so much public discussion about the death of the book, making a totally unique-looking publication out of unlikely materials could be especially provocative. If possible, you should plan to make multiple copies of your publication to distribute to the entire class. I will also allow you to make a one-of-a-kind artist's book, however, if it is substantial and interesting enough to be "one-of-a-kind." And of course, a digital or online publication cannot be distributed as a physical object, but I'll expect you to present it to the class with whatever technology is required.

Once I open this door to thinking about the terms "literary" and "publication" in these new, more expansive ways, the students have gotten very excited about the project. Many of them tap into a playful energy, and the collaboration with other students adds to the pleasure because they can build ideas in a social, game-like way. Among the most memorable projects was a video publication produced by two students. First they collaborated on writing a poem together, then they attached lines of the poem to the sails of toy boats. They sailed the boats down a local creek and captured them on video with a camera. They edited the video so that the lines of the poem would read in sequence, and they added some voiceover to emphasize some of the lines, along with a subtle soundtrack of music. They posted the video-poem on YouTube, and then presented it in class with some discussion of their process.

Creative writing courses often side-step the issue of presentation altogether, but the open spirit of creative literacy can transform presentation into great opportunity. Perhaps the most important practice any writer can have is the practice of writing for an audience, understanding an audience's wants and needs, empathizing with an audience's attempts to make sense of your language and ideas. Thinking about presentation as teachers and students can add new depth to our relationships with audiences.

Start Seeing Creative Literacy

Creative literacy is collaborative in the strict sense of two or more people working together on a project, but also—more importantly—in a wider sense of texts, forms, genres, disciplines, fields working together. Collaboration is crossover and cross-pollination, hybridization and appropriation. It's creating community, sharing, empathizing. Poetry infused with film. Film infused with dance. Dance infused with cooking. Cooking infused with basketball. Basketball infused with meditation. Meditation infused with pyrotechnics. Pyrotechnics infused with gardening. And so on. The collaborative spirit is having permeable, flexible boundaries, being adaptable and willing to learn.

Creative literacy may seem like a threat to some folks in the creative writing field. It may be accused of "dumbing down" creative writing for the mainstream, promoting a creative writing "lite," encouraging students to further erode their commitment to poetry, fiction, and creative nonfiction. In response I would say that creative literacy pedagogy demands just as much or more technical, aesthetic rigor as any traditional creative writing pedagogy. Instead of rejecting or replacing the study of traditional literary form and technique, it adds to this a rigorous study of form and technique beyond the literary. Instead of settling into a vague, formless pedagogy emphasizing content or personal expression, creative literacy nurtures a deep and wide-ranging curiosity across the arts and throughout a world of creative activities.

As Ritter, Vanderslice, and other scholars have pointed out, creative writing as an academic field has tended to isolate itself from other academic fields. There has also been a steady din of criticism from those, like Hall, who position themselves outside creative writing and say that the field, despite its success in terms of enrollment, has become an insular system of insiders who support other insiders with publications, grants, and teaching jobs—insiders who have the privilege to promote esoteric aesthetics that are irrelevant to common people. Even defenders of creative writing, such as D. W. Fenza, longtime leader of the Association of Writers and Writing Programs (AWP), echo this isolation narrative with a positive spin, suggesting that the field needs to preserve a space for authentic literary appreciation and craft from the insidious forces of an overly intellectualized academy and a consumer culture that wants only sentimentality and predictability. The concept of creative literacy seeks a way out of these perceptions of isolation by exploring what literary production has in common with many other creative activities.

The "fine arts" in general are also often seen to be set apart from everyday life, either tragically unappreciated by the unsophisticated masses or selfishly resistant to communicating in real ways to real people. This isolation has a history, to which Ken Robinson has given much attention in his efforts to reform education and promote creativity. In his book, *Out of Our Minds: Learning to Be Creative*, he reminds us that the European Enlightenment's idealization of rationality, reason, logic, empirical observation, and linearity generated a profound schism with its supposedly opposing force, the arts and imagination. Romanticism is not just a collection of aesthetic tendencies—it defines itself in opposition to rationality, rebelling against the oppressive dominance of objectivity and scientific method. This schism still exists today, argues Robinson, and it is seen most profoundly and disturbingly in our educational systems, where we have seen a "narrowing of intelligence" to exclude creativity and confine the arts to a second-rate extracurricular status: "Making music, painting pictures, involvement with drama, and writing poetry are not associated with academic ability" (103). He goes on to argue that this bias is evident especially at the university level, where this narrow definition of legitimate academic work determines tenure, promotion, research funding, and so on.

I would add to this point, however, that the fine arts have not withered away in the academy; most fine arts disciplines have boomed in recent decades with growing enrollment, growing facilities, growing programs, including MFA and even PhD degrees. As with the creative writing boom, the rise in the academic value of the fine arts is explained more, I think, by a widespread desire for creative literacy skills than for professional training in a specific artistic form or field. Nonetheless, the split that Robinson identifies—or at least the perception of a split—between academic work and creative work, still persists. In most academic fields not associated with fine arts, some version of critical thinking is the dominant skill that students are supposed to learn. Many debates take place about what approach to take or what materials and texts to use, but the academic value of critical literacy usually goes unquestioned, as if it were self-evident. This leads many academics to see writing and reading only as vehicles for the ultimate goal of becoming good critical thinkers, not as having value on their own.

I promote creative literacy here not in opposition to critical literacy, not as a skill-set that should replace critical literacy, but as a complement, an ally. These two kinds of literacies can be in conversation throughout the academy, and I applaud efforts to promote creative writing in writing across the curriculum initiatives (as seen in this collection). My focus here has been what can happen in the creative writing course itself, and how we can see creative writing in collaborative relationships with all the arts and with creative practices in the world around us. And a crucial element of this pedagogy should be nurturing a critical awareness of how it operates in the world.

As teachers, we need to teach skills, techniques, and forms in their social and historical contexts. If it's true that the vast majority of students who take creative writing courses don't become published, professional creative writers, but they often do use their creative skills in all kinds of other vocations and activities, from marketing to child-care, then we should have honest discussions about this in our courses. We should encourage students to think and write and talk about why they take creative writing courses, what skills they hope to learn, and how they think these skills might be applied in their lives, in their future work and leisure. We should teach students that creative writing as an academic field has developed quite recently in the history of literary practice, and that this rise of creative writing coincides with major shifts in the United States from an industrial or manufacturing economy to a postindustrial economy that focuses on generating new ideas and adding value through creativity and innovation. We should talk about how the meaning of "creativity" continues to evolve and depend on the context in which it's used, and why CEOs of major corporations consider creativity just as valuable as creative writers do. We should talk about the relationship between creative writing and the dramatic increase in writing and reading used in new communications technologies, from blogs, wikis, and other online spaces, to e-mail and texting, to the endless stream of social media like Facebook and Twitter. We should certainly critique the commodification of creativity by the marketplace, but we should also be very cautious about claiming the status of an outsider rebel who uses creativity to fight against the marketplace.

What I'm proposing here is that the creative writing course should do much more than simply train students to become creative writers, and that creative literacy is one way to conceptualize the skills and awareness that creative writing students actually learn and use in their lives. I believe that most students take creative writing courses not as a step toward becoming published writers but as a way to develop their creative literacy. Even if students and teachers don't use this term, even if courses are still focused on teaching the craft of writing literature, creative literacy still has enormous power and helps to explain why creative writing has grown so successfully in recent decades despite declining literary reading rates. The teaching strategies that I've described in this chapter are a step toward giving creative literacy a stronger, more intentional theoretical framework and pedagogy. They're not a threat to the purity and rigor of literary craft but a way to put literary craft in conversation with other arts and creative activities, and a way to make creative writing classes more active, generative, engaging, communal, and relevant.

When I was a creative writing student taking courses based on the traditional workshop model of students evaluating each other's writing, this was central question: "How good is this piece of writing, and how can it be better?" As a teacher, I'd like to cultivate a learning environment that asks a different question: "How can we create a new piece of writing, and how can our creative process be shaped not only by ourselves, but by other people, other texts, other forms and genres?"

Works Cited

Dawson, Paul. *Creative Writing and the New Humanities*. London: Routledge, 2005. Print.

Florida, Richard L. *The Rise of the Creative Class: And How It's Transforming Work, Leisure, Community, and Everyday Life*. New York: Basic, 2002. Print.

Frank, Thomas. "Getting to Eureka." *Harper's Magazine* (June 2013): 7–9. Print.

Friedman, Thomas L. *The World Is Flat: A Brief History of the Twenty-first Century*. New York: Farrar, Straus and Giroux, 2005. Print.

Godin, Seth. *Linchpin: Are You Indispensable?* New York: Portfolio, 2010. Print.

Haake, Katharine. *What Our Speech Disrupts: Feminism and Creative Writing Studies*. Urbana, IL: NCTE, 2000. Print.

Hall, Donald. "Poetry and Ambition." *Kenyon Review* 4 (1983): n. pag. *Poets. org*. Academy of American Poets. Web. 27 May 2013.

Having Intended to Merely Pick on an Oil Company, the Poem Goes Awry. Dir. Joanna Kohler. *MotionPoems*. N.p., n.d. Web. 30 Apr. 2013.

Healey, Steve. "Beyond the Literary: Why Creative Literacy Matters." *Key Issues in Creative Writing*. Ed. Dianne Donnelly and Graeme Harper. Bristol, UK: Multilingual Matters, 2013. 61–78. Print.

———. "The Rise of Creative Writing and the New Value of Creativity." *The Writer's Chronicle* 41.4 (2009): 30–39. Print.

Last Poets. "True Blues." Rec. 1971. *This Is Madness*. Snapper UK, 1971. *YouTube*. Web. 30 Apr. 2013.

Lehrer, Jonah. *Imagine: How Creativity Works*. Boston: Houghton Mifflin Harcourt, 2012. Print.

Mayers, Tim. *(Re)Writing Craft: Composition, Creative Writing, and the Future of English Studies*. Pittsburgh: U of Pittsburgh P, 2005. Print.

Padgett, Ron, ed. *The Teachers and Writers Handbook of Poetic Forms*. New York: Teachers and Writers Collaborative, 1987. Print.

Pink, Daniel H. *A Whole New Mind: Moving from the Information Age to the Conceptual Age*. New York: Riverhead, 2005. Print.

Ritter, Kelly, and Stephanie Vanderslice, eds. *Can It Really Be Taught? Resisting Lore in Creative Writing Pedagogy*. Portsmouth, NH: Boynton/Cook Heinemann, 2007. Print.

Robinson, Ken. *Out of Our Minds: Learning to Be Creative*. West Sussex, UK: Capstone, 2011. Print.

The Pedagogy of Creative Writing across the Curriculum

Alexandria Peary

Physicians who lack a passion for language or who fail to see beauty will be at a loss to translate these wonders in the most meaningful terms for their lay patients and into the larger society around us. We need now more than ever to be able to conduct ourselves in the realm of the imagination because what is science if not the dream of something new?
> —Rafael Campo, physician and assistant professor
> at Harvard Medical School, on the relevancy
> of a poetry contest held for medical students

WRITE A TEXT in the voice of an anatomy cadaver, a poem that uses π as an organizational device, a short story that depicts you on the job ten years in the future in a sociology of work course, a one-act play or an advice column that explores a psychological concept, a business memo from the perspective of an adopted persona, an ode that imitates Pablo Neruda in an intermediate Spanish-language class, a burlesque of a play studied in a Modern European literature course. These assignments for creative pieces were generated in introductory courses in majors from all across campus, in general education courses, and in graduate training as part of writing across the curriculum. Many more are detailed in *The WAC Journal* but also in scholarly journals focused on teaching in a range of disciplines, from the *Journal of Medical Humanities, Teaching Sociology, Journal of Chemical Education,* to the *Journal of Education for Business.*

Creative writing—in addition to imaginative self-expression—can provide significant benefits to learning by fostering critical thinking in both low- and high-stakes writing tasks. Through creative writing, students from any major can master course content as well as critically consider information in the disciplines. As a pedagogy established in the United States in the 1970s, writing across the curriculum (WAC), essentially takes the best practices gained from over a century of writing instruction and relays them to academic disciplines that are primarily focused on bodies of knowledge rather than composition. As I have discussed elsewhere, creative writing–based writing across the curriculum (CWAC) helps individual faculty from different disciplines increase and improve the writing assigned in their courses specifically through the genres associated with creative writing—not expository or persuasive (Peary).

It's no secret that the majority of postsecondary educators cite students' writing and communication skills as both top priority and as areas needing development. Most recently, Richard Arum and Josipa Roska in their 2011 *Academically Adrift: Limited Learning on College Campuses* point to the statistic that 50 percent of U.S. undergraduates are not enrolled in a class expecting more than twenty written pages during the semester as one explanation for why 36 percent of students do not show any improvement in critical and analytical learning over four years of college. According to the 2010 National Survey of Student Engagement, when students were asked how many five- to nineteen-page writing assignments they'd completed during the school year, first-year students reported writing a paltry one or two papers or reports, and seniors only slightly higher, at between two and three such assignments.

Creative writing carries enormous potential as an interdisciplinary pedagogy and can improve the learning environment of the twenty-first-century university. Elizabeth Thomas and Anne Mulvey, who teach creative writing in health psychology courses, maintain that the "[i]magination—the ability to form mental images that are independent of present perceptions and the ability to create new images through reorganization of previous experiences—is *critical to advanced study in any discipline*" (emphasis added 243). The role of creative writing in the university is expanding as faculty seek out the "interdisciplinary productions" and "hybrid learning styles" Chad Davidson and Gregory Fraser mention in a 2009 article in the Association of Writers and Writing Program's trade journal, *The Writer's Chronicle* (77).

As Davidson and Fraser indicate, creative writing courses contribute to undergraduates' whole education by enhancing students' performance in other courses. Creative writing is an invaluable transferable skill: students who have taken a creative writing course see improvement specifically in the arenas of critical thinking, the maintenance of a healthy writing process, and close reading. They note that "[c]reative-writing teachers and students have begun to think increasingly in terms of cross-fertilizations between disciplines. Instead of seeing creative and critical classrooms as polar opposites, practicing writers and teachers of writing have begun to test out hybrid learning styles that draw on the strengths of varying discourses" (77). This type of involvement in other fields of thought has long been known to benefit the individual creators of literature—including polymaths such as Nabokov, William Carlos Williams, and Beatrix Potter (Davidson and Fraser 77). On a programmatic level, recent interdisciplinary partnerships between creative writing and other fields include Hamline University's joint JD/MFA degree, in which law students explore sociopolitical concepts through creative nonfiction, and the Games Design and Creative Writing BA at Brunel University in London.

CWAC extends this role by providing the learning benefits of creative writing to students who have never enrolled in a workshop in the English department. As such, versatile creative learning can occur at the course or individual assignment level. In semester-long courses offered to students typically of a single major, including the fiction-writing courses described by Nancy Welch and Sandra Young for education, criminal justice, and nursing majors, students use material from their disciplines to write short stories. Futuristic fictional scenarios afford learners the ability to personally and critically engage with material to the extent that students are able to predict and attempt to shape their professional lives. More frequently, CWAC is used for single assignments, often developed in collaboration and team-taught by a writing faculty member and someone from across the disciplines. The news is good for creative writing specialists since WAC is a way to differentiate oneself on the academic job market. The ability to build interdisciplinary partnerships and to work toward improved student learning and writing are sought-after attributes in applicants for positions inside English departments as well as in administration or learning support services. On a personal note, my ability to engage in WAC helped me obtain my previous teaching and administrative position as a writing program director when I held MFA degrees. At my job interview, I was able to talk about workshops I could develop for faculty from all across the campus to help them with their own writing process and then with strategies to creatively address their students' writing.

Principles of Writing across the Curriculum

Open up nearly any English department's course catalog and your eyes will pass over columns and columns of sections of first-year composition. With 2.135 million first-time students enrolled in college as of the fall of 2010, a conservative estimate for the number of required first-year composition courses is around 67,932 sections at twenty students per section (Hesse). In a fundamental sense, WAC pedagogy can be understood as an attempt to get away from relying on first-year composition courses as the primary or even sole occasion in which students learn about writing. The ubiquitous first-year composition course—nowadays in its one- or two-semester manifestation—arguably arose at Harvard in the late nineteenth century as a way to address the apparent host of writing deficiencies a new demographic of students brought with them upon entering college. Faculty have wanted first-year composition to perform the Sisyphean job of fixing all student writing problems in part because they labored under the misapprehension that writing is a generalizable skill and thus one requiring little practice. In what Mike Rose has called "the myth of transience," faculty think that generalizable writing skills can be acquired through a single (with unstated proviso of "successfully") taught course and be both maintained in and applicable to all future writing tasks. In fact, a one- or two-semester composition course offering *"general writing skills instruction (GWSI)"* doesn't suffice for the complexities of the contemporary university or workplace (Petraglia xi). A chief contribution of WAC has been to shift this perception of student writing, moving it from a pesky matter of remediation ("Why aren't students getting those basic skills in ENL 101? Must be something wrong with them or their teachers") to a developmental perspective (writing is always evolving, changing with context, needing constant instruction) (Russell 15). These views are not intended to disparage first-year writing programs—which typically offer rich instruction in multiple genres and rhetorical situations—but these offerings need to function as the foundation, not finale, of undergraduate writing education. Through research, curriculum development, and outreach to faculty, WAC specialists have worked hard to address some faculty's misperception that first-year composition courses can serve as a one-time inoculation against writing problems and challenges.

Overall, in WAC pedagogy, attention is paid to both the *amount* of writing done by undergraduates throughout their postsecondary education as well as the *types* of writing—genres—they compose. Although WAC pedagogy takes different forms, an underlying principle is that writing must be taught as a process with drafts, staging, and plenty of opportunities for practice and feedback. These are practices well understood by creative writers to be essential to their own growth as writers—we labor for hours over texts, naturally seek feedback, and constantly hone our craft.

Beyond the bedrock of process, WAC operates on three core principles. First, writing is completely intertwined with learning: that the ability to write about something coincides with and confirms one's learning of new material. Second, students need to be given a range of writing experiences with a variety of types of writing—analytical, informational, exploratory, personal, transactional, creative—as well as a spectrum of formal and informal tasks. A third principle of WAC is that students in different majors need explicit, guided instruction in order to write the various genres of their fields.

Writing's Connection to Learning

> I can't guarantee that students remember all that they were taught in lecture, nor that they remember all that they read about in their regular textbook, but I dare say that they don't soon forget Buffy, Elvis, and the Stanovich text. . . . I believe they leave my class a bit wiser about research methods, which renders them more effective consumers of scientific information that increasingly is finding its way into popular media. (Zehr 18)

David Zehr, a psychology professor, has become pedagogically addicted to the creative writing assignments he uses in his introduction to psychology course. In order to help students better understand a key course text on research methods, Zehr asked his students to create a one-act play featuring two fictional students, Buffy and Elvis, at his college. His flesh-and-blood students demonstrated their understanding of the assigned text through the dialog they created between Buffy and Elvis. Zehr was highly pleased with his students' learning:

> The students had a wonderful time writing their responses, and I had a wonderful time reading them. A formal evaluation of

the assignment corroborated what I believed about the effectiveness of this approach to learning research methodology. The written comments by students suggested that the text and the writing connected with them in ways that up to that point I didn't know were possible. (17)

Zehr, seeing the benefits of creative writing assignments, added more of them, including a science fiction or romance-genre short story and advice column, all centered on Buffy and Elvis.

One branch of WAC, *writing-to-learn*, maintains that writing be defined as intrinsically connected to learning. Writing-to-learn tasks are informal writing activities meant to facilitate exploration of course material rather than result in a polished, finished text. Writing is not an add-on component to academic studies but is instead a powerful method for learning and an indicator that learning has actually happened—as Zehr demonstrates. It's that adage: you know you've understood an idea if you can write about it. This view of writing was solidified by Janet Emig in her seminal 1977 article, "Writing as a Mode of Learning" in which she shows how writing corresponds with powerful learning strategies. According to Emig, the writing process is visible and permanent—it creates feedback and reinforcement because the process is visible along with the product. Thus writing is "self-rhythmed," allowing the rereading and reflection that are key to learning. Writing is also beneficial because it's connective to others: a writer must anticipate the needs of her audience and establish permanent lucid connectors in language. Finally, writing, unlike talking, is independent of an action or an actual situation; a writer can respond in words to a situation that is not immediately before him or her—fostering that spectator stance.

Assignments that ask students to demonstrate course concepts by embedding them in a fictional account or in a poetic form inherently invite students to work on their critical thinking capacities. While utilizing the tools of creative writing, a student's attention is turned toward craft matters such as narration, figurative language, and description; the student is able to become a more critical observer to his or her own experience (Britton, "The Spectator Role"). For Lisa Kerr, her medical students benefit more from creative writing than from traditional reflective writing (essays, journaling, or freewriting) precisely because of the increased number of formal devices involved in creative writing (300). For Art Young, poetry-across-the-curriculum produces the cognitive distance characteristic of "an active but disinterested mind," a stance that allows the exploration of multiple points of view that is crucial, for example, in the composing of medical narratives ("Writing across and against" 161; Kerr 300).

Through creative writing, students engage in the foundational activities of the critical thinking so coveted in higher education. These activities include interaction with a problem, identification and critique of assumptions, and a dialogic interchange with the ideas of others (Bean 2–3). Instructors who have worked with CWAC repeatedly point to its ability to strengthen students' personal understanding of course material as well as to draw students' attention to larger social forces and issues and the perspectives of others. For instance, in the field of health psychology, Elizabeth Thomas and Anne Mulvey argue that creative writing provides their students with complex problems to work through and builds "student understandings of the values, goals, and practices of culturally competent work"—crucial qualities in a profession requiring working in the community (240). In two sociology courses (sociology of work and sociology of gender), Laurie Gordy and I found that teaching students to write first-person fiction facilitates what is called "sociological imagination," or the ability to perceive the social forces behind actions and outcomes (Gordy and Peary; Peary).

Faculty appreciate creative writing for its ability to impact learning by increasing student engagement in discussions and projects. One of the unique properties of writing is how it fuels learning because it is "enactive": we learn by doing—and writing helps us "do" (Emig). The sense among instructors is that simply asking students to write causes an immediate spike in student engagement: that writing activates students more than listening to a PowerPoint presentation or studying a textbook. With WAC in general, students are "engaged at higher levels in their studies" (Kinzie). In his study of 20,000 students at 200 schools, Alexander W. Astin determined that students saw writing occurring throughout their undergraduate education as contributing to their cognitive and interpersonal growth (243). In turn, creative writing is equipped to increase engagement even more so than many expository assignments because its craft tools (especially narration) call for activation of concepts. After all, in order to complete, for example, a futuristic account of the professional day of an air traffic controller, elementary-school teacher, veterinarian, or civil engineer, students need to understand course concepts so thoroughly that they can manifest those concepts in characters, settings, and plots.

With creative writing, a course concept can't just be encapsulated in a topic sentence or propped up with an APA in-text citation: the student needs to show that concept in action and subject to change in a particular context. Consequently, faculty have reported their higher satisfaction with undergraduates' written products after replacing conventional research papers with creative assignments. In an adolescent psychology course, Wendy Palmquist reports her ease with grading along with improved quality in student writing: "I did get more poor papers when I assigned traditional term papers. I think that now the vast majority of the students do get involved in the topics, and it is hard to do a really bad job on something you care about!" (44). Although creative writing hasn't been prominent in foreign language education, Lisa Jennings affirms that incorporation of creative nonfiction in an upper-level literature course in German was a pedagogical success: "I can say that these essays were easily the most intriguing and compelling student papers I have read to date. I was pleased with their spirited engagement with issues and the array of creative experimentation" (64). Others become aware of how conventional expository assignments may actually impede students' critical thinking—such as Horst Freyhofer's realization that traditional "[h]istory papers are little more than exercises showing 'how they [our predecessors] did it then'" (48).

The Importance of a Range of Writing Experiences

WAC advocates that students be given opportunity in a comprehensive range of discourse types. In *Language and Learning* (1970) and again in *The Development of Writing Abilities* (1975), James Britton identified three modes of discourse to be taught in schools—*expressive, poetic,* and *transactional. Expressive discourse* most resembles ordinary talk. In its informality, it presumes that the reader is interested in what the writer is saying without too much expectation (such as Twitter or a holiday greeting card). Children's writing or e-mails are examples of expressive discourse, and the important point of expressive writing is that it also serves often as the foundation for poetic and transactional texts in their early drafts (*The Development* 82–83). The purpose of *transactional writing* is to convey content to meet "the demands of some kind of participation in the world's affairs" (*Language and Learning* 174–75; *The Development* 83). Another way of understanding transactional writing is that it seeks to accomplish a concrete end in the world (get offered a job, get a date, convince someone to change his thinking) rather than having any intrinsic merit as a linguistic or self-expressive artifact. Some WAC theorists view transactional writing less than positively as the exam questions, note-taking, and other rote tasks which generally involve the recall of instructor-provided information rather than students generating new thought (Applebee; Fulwiler). *Poetic writing*, or creative writing, is an aesthetic artifact—it's "MAKING something with language rather than doing something with it," and it hopefully evokes an appreciative spectator stance in its reader (Britton "Spectator Role" 158–59). That is, whereas transactional discourse transforms the reader into a participant, someone who is evaluating the ideas in the text for possible real-world use, poetic discourse affords the reader an aesthetic experience, one in which the reader is able to take pleasure in the formal features of the poem or story and in having an emotional reaction—no action required (*The Development* 81).

Research into school-based writing uncovered an imbalance between the types of discourse that students experience. Britton and his co-researchers in 1975 found that the brunt of secondary school writing in England was transactional (63.4 percent), with writing as creative art or poetic at 17.6 percent, and just 5.5 percent allotted to expressive. The disproportion was higher in college-aged students: 84 percent transactional, 4 percent expressive, and 7 percent poetic (*The Development* 163–65). Matters hadn't improved by 1987 when Toby Fulwiler reported that few faculty in the United States perceived writing as important to learning and cited Arthur Applebee's 1981 study indicating that "only three percent of assigned writing tasks required students to compose anything longer than a sentence" in U.S. high schools. Instead of using writing to accomplish substantive learning, 24 percent of students' writing was spent on "mechanical writing" such as filling in blanks and taking notes (Applebee cited by Fulwiler 6–7). In contrast, the poetic function promotes the generation of new ideas, disciplinary knowledge, critical thinking, and engaged student-centered learning.

A skeptic may question the practicality of creative writing as an academic assignment, but in point of fact the "usual" genres of college are a strange import—like a flora or fauna introduced from another environment—that have thrived and pushed out other native species. Thesis-driven documents and expository writing, for instance, didn't guide the early writing courses begun by A. S. Hill or Barrett Wendell at Harvard—daily writings and personal narratives were the order of the day. As David Russell has shown, the trifecta of the lab report, the research paper, and lecture notes that can constitute the bulk of the twenty-first-century college student's writing experience were all imported into the American educational system from the German university model in the late nineteenth century (*Writing* 70–74). The German university model positioned faculty as researchers and utilized three pedagogical set-ups (the lecture course, seminar, and laboratory) to initiate students as apprentices into that research practice (Russell 70). This focus on research at the undergraduate level "narrowed the possibilities for written discourse in the modern curriculum by casting suspicion on genres that were not 'academic,' which is to say research oriented" (Russell 74). As a result, students are predominantly assigned texts that resemble the research journal article rather than creative writing or the workplace genres that a college graduate might encounter such as a memo or client project proposal. Students have been forced to become "mini-Me's"—to replicate the genres of scholarly value produced by faculty.

Creative writing instructors also provide a matchless function in WAC initiatives because of our heightened awareness of genre and our ability to speak on any subject matter. Unlike other disciplines that must carry around the minutiae of content expertise, creative writing brings craft knowledge—or methods for *generating* further knowledge. In this regard, Creative Writing Studies really occupies the generalist position ascribed to the ancient rhetoricians—those earliest of verbal experts. As specialized fields or "technai" arose in the fifth century B.C.E. in Greece, a tension developed between specialized knowledge and the practice of rhetoric, which was seen as lacking subject matter. Aristotle countered that individuals with rhetorical knowledge did not need to be experts in the topic on which they speak; instead, capable rhetors were able to identify the most persuasive devices for a given topic and audience (Bazerman and Russell). Similarly, the ability of creative writing experts to utilize linguistic devices (figurative language, imagery, description, narration, and other creative writing devices) for any occasion allows CWAC to explore concepts inside diverse fields of expertise. For the purposes of our discussion, I will talk about two creative writing devices—narrative and figurative language.

Narrative

Narrative is one of the most prominent craft devices used in creative writing across the curriculum simply because of the sheer number of other writing devices it employs, and in CWAC narrative assignments take the form of diverse subgenres including screenplays, dramatic monologues, short stories, creative nonfiction, memoir, advice columns, love letters, and science fiction, to name a few. For one, its careful selection of detail triggers learning: "Narrators must sort out from such quantity of detail only those events which seem important or significant to the story at hand. . . . This process of selection is a form of understanding" (Kalmbach and Powers 101). The development of a setting "forces students to take account of their environment and see their relationship to that environment": an important outcome in sociology, among other fields (Gordy and Peary 398). The time component inherent in narrative is a powerful learning device, whether students are working with a basic time line or on a futuristic scale (Peterson-Gonzalez; Welch). In her upper-level fiction course for criminal justice, education, and nursing majors, Nancy Welch engages students in "sideshadowing": using the imagination to question the notion that the future—their own or anyone's—is already fixed. Narrative assignments written in the first person in which the student becomes a character effectively activate course concepts since the student is forced to find and express the relevancy of a concept, to see it as personally affecting the self. When teaching narrative in other courses, faculty stage the assignments and provide guidance on how to develop dialog, characters, and setting. In the appendix to this chapter, I have provided an example of one narrative WAC project I co-developed and team-taught with a colleague.

Figurative Language

Figurative language, the core of poetics, is another craft device that can easily spark learning in diverse disciplines. Metaphors and similes can be both generative and analogical: that is, they can help students reach new material as well as develop powerful cognitive comparisons (Miller; Linda Peterson; Seitz; Tobin). In "Magic on the Mind: Physicists' Use of Metaphor," Alan Lightman emphasizes the importance of metaphor to past and present scientific endeavor: "In doing science, it is almost impossible not to reason by physical analogy, not to form mental pictures, not to imagine balls bouncing and pendulums swinging. Metaphor is part of the process of science" (97). Similarly, Meg Petersen has argued that metaphor is helpful in learning chemistry: "The ability to relate seemingly disparate pieces of information, through observing what can be applied from one process to a seemingly unrelated other, allows us to make leaps of understanding. Poetry builds on these processes, thus encouraging this kind of thinking" (100). Figurative language also can foster meta-cognition: in a first-year composition class, Lad Tobin asked students at different points during the semester to describe their writing process with a metaphor in order to help students develop their own perspective on process independent of the one provided by the teacher.

In a Calculus I course, Patrick Bahls employs metaphor to help students better comprehend the terminology of mathematics as well as to increase students' confidence in computation. Bahls uses poetry specifically in introductory-level courses as a matter of retention—to increase the number of students who continue on to degrees in mathematics—and to anticipate the more complex propositions math majors will be asked to perform (78–79). In his assignment, Bahls asks students to write a poem in which mathematics factored into its theme or structure. He offers students models as well as opportunities to receive peer and instructor feedback. One student explored the concept of π through line lengths; another wrote a haiku to explore the everyday relevance of mathematical principles; others wrote free verse to understand their "math phobias." According to Bahls,

> It should not be surprising that students find poetry a useful tool for accessing these mathematical ideas. . . . Both poetry and mathematics deal in images, ideas, and *aha!*s: metaphor is the currency with which poetic trade takes place, and math's economy has the same basis. Spheres, balls, neighborhoods, lattices, chains, nets, sheaves, bundles, sources, sinks, orbits, itineraries, distances, colorings . . . these math metaphors are alive and well, for the active images they evoke aid in mathematical understanding. (82)

Building on the success of this CWAC unit, Bahls plans on using poetry in Abstract Algebra, an upper-level course in the major, in which students will design poems using homomorphism—with structures based on those of algebraic objects (86).

The Importance of a Range of Formal and Informal Tasks

In addition to providing students with opportunities to try out creative as well as expository or analytical assignments, WAC stresses giving students writing experiences of varying impact on their final grades. Many writing-to-learn tasks emphasize student learning rather than evaluating or assigning a grade to student writing, and as such they incorporate *low-stakes* or *informal writing*. Low-stakes writings are "frequent, informal assignments that make students spend time regularly reflecting in written language on what they are learning from discussions, readings, lectures, and their own thinking" (Elbow "High Stakes" 7). Low-stakes tasks are usually loosely graded—for instance, through a check system—or not graded at all. In contrast, *high-stakes* tasks result in a significant portion of a student's final grade and are typically genre specific and in the disciplines, such as a capstone project or one requiring sustained research or drafts. As Art Young describes the difference between low- and high-stakes tasks,

> In most school-based writing, we ask students to write for us in order to improve their writing or to have their knowledge of certain material assessed, and we judge that writing and make suggestions for improvement based on these goals. But writing-to-learn changes this setting by changing the purpose of the writing, the audience for it, the context in which it occurs, and the appropriate response from readers. ("Mentoring" 36)

Low-stakes writings carry several benefits: they reduce student anxiety, allow management of disciplinary jargon, and provide instructors with a window onto student learning. Students have been trained throughout their education to conceive of all writing as automatically high-stakes and risky; writing always feels high stakes because people have mostly written for teachers and for the purpose of evaluation (Elbow 6). Regularly assigning low-stakes writing helps students to be less apprehensive about high-stakes writing assignments. As Peter Elbow praises the effect of low-stakes writing: "we get to throw away the low stakes writing itself but keep the neural changes it produced in students' heads" (5). Low-stakes tasks also resemble Richard Hugo's "triggering devices" in that they can act heuristically and spark the invention of a text.

Another advantage of low-stakes tasks is that they let the student fumble around and experiment, temporarily free of the specialized jargon of a scholarly community. Exploring difficult concepts in one's own natural language (expressive discourse) often fosters and demonstrates real learning of difficult concepts. Poetic discourse serves a similar function in that it provides a strikingly different lens (the approach of creative texts) to discipline-specific content. As a result, students who wrestle with standard academic discourse can gain confidence from creative writing, and at the same time highly proficient students will be thrown the challenge of an additional way of looking at their field. For those students, who "know the 'formula' when they are required to write a lab report or book review, composing a poem occasions disequilibrium because they have learned to mimic the prose of familiar 'school' discourse, and now to write poetry they must rethink form and content" (Welch; Young "Writing across and against the Curriculum" 160). Finally, all low-stakes assignments help faculty gauge student learning in a way not possible with traditional assessments like multiple-choice tests or research papers. Instructors can determine early in the semester where students are floundering with course material and adjust their teaching accordingly (Elbow "High Stakes").

Common examples of low-stakes tasks include freewrites (a composition technique generating private or disposable writing not judged for grammar or cohesion); Muddy Points (in which students tell their instructor which ideas, methods, or terminologies are unclear to them); discussion starters; annotated bibliographies; and process notes. Here are a few others:

> *Class Response Logs* Once or twice a week, I assign questions about course routines, students' sense of their own performance, or how they believe the course is functioning for them. I request that they answer in a class response log (CRL), which I collect four times a semester. . . . I often use CRLs to learn students' reactions to exam grades, whether or not they were satisfied, and how they might alter their exam preparation to improve. (Fishman 62)

> *Five-Minute Essays* At the end of a class period, whether it be a lecture, lab, or discussion, the teacher asks students to write for five minutes about two things: (*1*) what they have learned in class that day and (2) what questions and concerns they still have. (Young, "Mentoring" 28)

> *Letters* Each term, I write weekly letters with one of my classes, composing my syllabus as a letter, requesting letters back. . . . Letters work in all subjects where instructors and students care about each other's thoughts, see the curriculum as exploration, and are willing, at times, to negotiate who is the learner, who is the teacher. . . . After a few weeks of finding *their* ideas featured in *my* letters, nearly all the students enjoy the larger intellectual community that shared ideas create. (Fulwiler "Writing Back" 16)

No matter the genre, low-stakes creative writing carries the same benefits as low-stakes expository tasks: students get to think on the page or screen without the daunting production of polished text. Here are a few examples of informal creative writing tasks, all of which could be implemented to generate class discussion or develop connections to previous course material:

- If *x course concept* were an insect or animal, how would it behave? What would its environment look like?

- Zoom in on the most important moments of *x event*. Recast one minute of that crucial moment in slow motion, describing key actors, setting, and decisions.
- Think of an article or chapter you feel needs to be written on *x topic* from today's assigned reading. Come up with a title for this imaginary article or chapter. Write a two-sentence abstract summarizing its content.
- *X and y course concepts or positions* fall inexplicably in love and enter into a romance. What happens? Write a paragraph in which you describe their love.
- If *x logarithm* were a piece of visual art (painting, photograph, or sculpture), what would it look like?
- Personify two contending positions or innovations, transforming them into children, and put them into conversation at the playground. Write 5–10 lines of that dialog.
- Select an important concept from the last class lecture. Rather than defining that concept, tell a tiny fairy tale about it, giving it characters, a setting, and at least one event or plot turn.

It's important to note that creative low-stakes tasks must remain *informal*: students should be given opportunity to test-drive various craft devices without having their productions be overly critiqued for their artistic quality.

High-stakes creative writing carries the same benefits as expository or transactional high-stakes assignments: it allows students to sustain a project, often through multiple drafts and revisions, and deepen critical thinking and reflection. The main difference again between a low- and high-stakes creative assignment in the disciplines is that the high-stakes or formal project entails effort beyond a single draft, a staging of the work, and graded evaluation. As Peter Elbow has affirmed, high-stakes tasks are important to learning: "It's obvious why we need high stakes assignments in our courses. We can't give trustworthy final grades that reflect whether students actually understand what we want them to understand unless we get them to articulate in writing what they have learned" (*Writing to Learn* 5). In scholarly discussions of CWAC, such as in Art Young's research, creative writing has been generally associated with informal writing-to-learn strategies. However, creative writing actually enjoys unusual flexibility in that it can be used for both low- and high-stakes tasks. While it is possible to encounter a task calling for transactional writing in a low-stakes mode (completing a case study but not as part of a final grade) or to use an expressivist task in a high-stakes mode (a freewrite that receives a numeric grade), these scenarios are difficult to conceive of as classroom practical. In fact, in teaching journals in other disciplines, creative writing is most frequently used as a high-stakes task, typically as a replacement for the traditional term or research paper. For instance, Sandra Young has her nursing students "remember one detail of a patient's case history that did not seem to further the medical history or an aside a patient might have slipped into conversation and then write a poem, short story, or drama from this detail" (81). In another task, Young assigns a "slice-of-life fiction exercise . . . because it calls for close observation, critical analysis, and specific recollections" in which she "asks students to observe and record an episode in the emergency room" in a poem (85). High-stakes projects require students to engage in more complex poetic and narrative strategies—which in turn yield more complex understandings of course content. Here are a few other examples of sustained creative writing–based projects in the disciplines:

- Develop a new trade journal in your field, coming up with a table of contents, article titles, features, and information on fictional contributors to be published ten years into the future.
- Write a script for a pilot of a new reality TV show that explores an issue currently under discussion in your field.
- In a history course, select an actual person and write a series of letters as that person in which you both relay and reflect on an important historical event.
- Develop an imaginary interview between two prominent scholars in your field on *x issue.*
- Describe a day in your life ten years into the future in which you manifest sociological concepts of gender/family/race through the plot, characters, and setting.

Problems have been identified when too much transactional or conventional high-stakes writing is assigned to students, usually as part of an assessment campaign or perceived literacy crisis (Thaiss 304). When writing assignments are skewed toward transactional writing, there's the risk that students are merely being indoctrinated into the hierarchies of the professions. Creative writing avoids the whole conundrum of indoctrination simply by teaching alternative genres. Put plainly, when a professor in medical school assigns a poem in the voice of a heart patient, there is far less chance that traditional hierarchies of knowledge and power, ones encapsulated in the genres of medicine, will be enabled.

Importance of Direct Guidance in Genres
Outside of English Courses

At any moment in a semester, a college student may be juggling several writing assignments, each with a unique set of expectations—a lab report, a persuasive essay, a poem, an annotated bibliography, a literature review—let alone the extracurricular genres of a grad school application or workplace writing at an internship site. Therefore, the professor in the biology department should not assume that her students know the conventions of her field. Whereas in the nineteenth century, a college student at Harvard or Yale—white, mostly male, Protestant, upper-class—would be served the same dish of Latin, oral rhetoric, and math as his roommate, no significant variation in the menu, that's not the case today (Russell *Writing*). The twentieth century ushered in a tremendous bifurcation of professions, one especially pronounced in the United States in which the "numbers of disciplinary and professional workers have increased at rates far more rapid than the already rapid general population growth" (Bazerman and Russell xi). A college education became increasingly more specialized with each academic discipline adopting its own genres, practices, and expectations.

One branch of WAC, variously called *Writing in the Disciplines (WID)* or *"writing-to-communicate,"* is concerned with teaching students about the genre expected in their majors and professions. It bears mentioning this wrinkle in writing education despite the fact that creative writing has not as of yet been involved in this arena of WAC work. Students who are doing poorly at writing in their major courses or fields haven't become acculturated yet—it's not that they're bad writers (Berkenkotter and Huckin, Freedman "Show and Tell"; Carolyn Miller; Devitt "Generalizing"; Swales). As creative writers, our professional training has provided us with whole courses and frequently series of linked courses devoted to the crafting of specific genres; students who strive toward professions other than writing likewise need continuous genre training. We bring this perspective to WID initiatives on campus, and in the future we can use our genre savvy to better communicate the nuances of learning and teaching explicit genre to other faculty.

Setting Up CWAC Partnerships

WAC initiatives are characterized by active collaboration between colleagues in writing-related departments and in any number of other departments across campus. WAC is entirely about interdisciplinary partnership: the word "across" in "writing across the curriculum" indicates how WAC initiatives originate in faculty partnerships and not from an external or administrative mandate (Thaiss 312). WAC typically takes one of two forms: workshops/retreats for faculty to discuss and learn about writing; one-on-one collaboration between someone who teaches writing and someone from another discipline. The latter type of partnership can be a highly rewarding experience for faculty and students alike, and in my experience, CWAC partnerships have easily constituted some of the best moments for me on the job. As Pesche C. Kuriloff describes this phenomena, "With a writing instructor asking the right questions and a content instructor proposing answers, both teachers learn more than they possibly discover alone" (95). The faculty pair meets to identify the objectives in the disciplinary instructor's class which could then be fulfilled by particular creative writing assignments. After designing the lesson or writing project, if team-teaching will be involved, the two instructors work out details of the classroom presentation, determining how feedback and grading will be given, as well as any assessment of their project.

Contact the writing program administrator, WAC director, or English department chair on your campus to learn about existent WAC workshops and opportunities as well as to identify potential colleagues outside your department to invite to join you in designing a CWAC assignment or even a brand new CWAC program. Just spending time with faculty from other departments in the cafeteria or at school functions or while serving on campus committees can give you a sense of who is interested in changing how writing functions in their courses. (I've found that as soon as you mention you're in the English department or are a writer—even while queuing up for commencement—faculty from other fields will without much prompting discuss their students' writing and their own wishes to increase students' ability and writing opportunities.) If you're a graduate student, engaging in this sort of work with WAC provides outstanding training: preparing you to articulate and advance writing outcomes and values when you are eventually hired as faculty, not to mention distinguishing you on the job market. For additional insight the establishment of successful WAC initiatives at postsecondary institutions, Mary T. Segall and Robert A. Smart's *Direct from the Disciplines* and Barbara E. Walvoord et al.'s *In the Long Run* are useful resources. The chapters on setting up faculty workshops and interdisciplinary teams in Susan H. McLeod and Margot Soven's *Writing across the Curriculum: A Guide to Developing Programs*, a free text available at the WAC Clearinghouse website, are also highly useful. Other recommended resources include academic journals like the *WAC Journal*, *Across the Disciplines*, and *Language and Learning across the Disciplines*, the NCTE Series of WAC books (http://wac.colostate.edu/books/ncte.cfm), and the WAC community to be found at the WAC Clearinghouse (http://wac.colostate.edu) and the listserv for the International WAC Network.

Creative writing is a way to enhance a strong WAC tradition by bringing into play the third and occasionally overlooked branch of discourse, the poetic, into writing education. More than simply a series of introductory, intermediate, and advanced workshop courses, creative writing can significantly affect student learning across *all* disciplines. In essence, creative writing sets the stage for the imagination to join critical thinking, self-expression, and disciplinary knowledge in the pantheon that comprises an excellent education and a strong college graduate. What comes to mind is *Clairvoyance (Self-Portrait)*, a 1936 painting by the Belgian surrealist René Magritte in which the painter sits before his easel, staring fixedly at an egg on a table, and yet visible on his canvas is a bird in flight. In a similar way, creative writing across the curriculum is a fundamental act of speculative and critical thinking that can make such leaps of thought possible.

Appendix: Example of Team-Designed/Taught WID High-Stakes Assignment

This high-stakes creative assignment was designed for a first-year seminar course with a sociological focus on identity. Laurie Gordy (sociology professor) and I (writing program director/poet) designed the following prompts for a memoir assignment. Students wrote a 5–7 page memoir that addressed the following question: *What are the factors that have influenced your identity?* The following prompts were spoken to students during a class meeting in which students generated prethinking and prewriting.

1. Gordy/Peary: Instructors explain genre of memoir and assignment expectations: Students' memoirs will use creative devices and scenes from their actual lives to critically evaluate their own identity development and explain how social, historical, and cultural factors affect their own coming-of-age experience. Their pieces will center on one identity factory, though strong memoirs will also mention other social factors as supporting detail. This assignment will undergo a process including revision.

2. Ask students to look at their "résumé" worksheet. (Students were given a handout resembling a résumé to fill out the previous day; instead of the typical information on a résumé, this one had blanks for entries on life experiences, family, gender, race, religion, physical well-being, and so forth.) Gordy asks: Which cultural/social/historical factors received the most writing on your form? In other words, where did you find the most material in your prewriting? Pick the one for which you had the most material.

3. Peary: Brainstorm for five scenes—or particular moments in time— that come to mind pertaining to the cultural/social/historical factors you identified as receiving the most writing on your form. Start each note with the phrase, "The time when. . . ." Just take notes for yourself (no one else needs to understand)—mention people/places/ times for those scenes. For example, "The time when Jim . . ."; "The time when I. . . ." These moments could have lasted for a fairly long time (i.e., several days) or even be as brief as a few seconds. Number the scenes.

4. Alternate between Peary and Gordy: Now pick the most interesting of those moments. "Interesting" means that the moment has some emotional resonance for you—perhaps a negative emotion, even confusion. Pick this moment and brainstorm.

    a. Brainstorm for any objects that come to mind from that moment.
    b. Brainstorm for any gestures or actions made by people from that moment.
    c. Brainstorm for any details about space from that moment.
    d. Brainstorm for details about seasons, weather, date from that moment.
    e. Brainstorm for sensory details—try to remember smell, sight, taste, touch, sound.
    f. What did you look like in that moment? What would you have looked like to others sharing that moment?
    g. What were your thoughts in that moment? Your feelings?

We'll only compose one of these moments in class, but you'll want to do this series of questions once more on your own. Then try to incorporate the material from that other moment into the memoir as further support of the identity point you're illustrating. Right now, circle another moment on your list that seems to have promise for that work to be done later.

5. Have students share one of their brainstorms with the whole class.

6. Instructors differentiate generalized versus specific passages in memoir writing. Generalized parts talk about something that happened more than once—something that is routine or habitual. For instance, generalized writing would happen when a student describes what his or her roommate does every morning. Specific passages refer to moments that never occurred twice. They are specific to a particular time and place. For instance, specific passages would happen when a student describes the moment he or she learned a grandparent had died. Regardless, it's important that students remember that generalizations need to be fresh through two means: the precision of thought and analysis of an idea; and the use of vivid detail.

   Mention key structural point: Memoirs should be organized such that they alternate between generalized and specific passages. Explain that students will create a series of linked moments in time (specific passages) to illustrate the identity factor. Basically, those specific moments will serve as *examples* to support their main point.

7. Peary and Gordy: Let's talk about how to now develop specific passages.

   a. Peary: Using the material generated in prompt 4, write a mini-scene between yourself and at least one other person as though it is happening *now*. Write in the present verb tense. Use dialog. Describe the person's appearance. Describe a bit of the place.

   b. Gordy: Zoom paragraph: Pick an object from the material generated in prompt 4. Using all of your senses, write 5–7 sentences describing that object.

   c. Peary: Panoramic paragraph: Pick a space from the material generated in prompt 4. As though you are a camera moving extremely slowly, panning an entire landscape or room, describe what you would see if you were back in that space. Provide details about the year, season, and hour from that moment and place without explicitly supplying the year, season, or hour.

   d. Ask students to share the details of a specific passage with the class.

8. Developing generalized passages.

   a. Peary: Pick an individual (perhaps yourself) mentioned in prompt 4. Write 4–5 sentences describing something that person *habitually* or *repeatedly* did during the time in which you describe.

   b. Gordy: Start talking about the identity factor. Explain it using the concepts and terms you have been learning in this class. As you're writing, support the sentences with particular people and images from your life generated in the prompts. Incorporate a list sentence. In the next sentence, include two colors. Spend two sentences describing a particular moment in time or object. In the next sentence, provide two sensory details related to this idea.

   c. Explain that this generalized paragraph from prompt 8B could serve as *the first paragraph or start* to your memoir. It could also appear in the middle or at the end of your memoir. You may want to write several such generalized passages. The point is to *interpret your experience through the lens of identity factors.*

9. Gordy: Developing second identity factors: Think of the other identity factors discussed in this course. Of the writing you've done today, think of at least one other identity factor that could be used as a label to describe some detail or event you've written down today. Identify at least one way to slip in discussion of that other identity detail—through implicit concrete, contemporary, and sensory detail.

10. End with discussion on how to organize the piece. Answer any questions. Give deadline for first draft and tell students they have the opportunity to receive feedback with the expectation that they rewrite the piece.

Works Cited

Andrews, Roy. "Writing to Learn in the Music and Theater Department." *WAC Journal* 9 (1998): 89–94. Print.

Applebee, Arthur. *Writing in the Secondary School: English and the Content Areas.* Urbana, IL: NCTE, 1981. Print.

Astin, Alexander W. *What Matters in College? Four Critical Years Revisited.* San Francisco: Jossey-Bass, 1997. Print.

Bahls, Patrick. "Math and Metaphor: Using Poetry to Teach College Mathematics." *WAC Journal* 20 (2009): 75–90. Print.

Bazerman, Charles, and David R. Russell. "The Rhetorical Tradition and Specialized Discourses." *Landmark Essays on Writing across the Curriculum.* Ed. Charles Bazerman and David R. Russell. Davis, CA: Hermagoras Press, 1994. xii–xxxviii. Print.

———. "Writing across the Curriculum as a Challenge to Rhetoric and Composition." *Landmark Essays on Writing across the Curriculum.* Ed. Charles Bazerman and David R. Russell. Davis, CA: Hermagoras Press, 1994. xi–xvi. Print.

Bean, John C. *Engaging Ideas: The Professor's Guide to Integrating Writing, Critical Thinking, and Active Learning in the Classroom.* San Francisco: Jossey-Bass. 2001. Print.

Berkenkotter, Carol, and Thomas N. Huckin. *Genre Knowledge in Disciplinary Communication: Cognition/Culture/Power.* Hillsdale, NJ: Lawrence Erlbaum Associates, 1995. Print.

Blakeslee, Ann M. "Bridging the Workplace and the Academy: Teaching Professional Genres through Classroom-Workplace Collaborations." *Technical Communications Quarterly* 10.2 (2001): 169–92. Print.

Britton, James. *Language and Learning.* Coral Gables, FL: U of Miami P, 1970. Print.

———. "Spectator Role and the Beginnings of Writing." *What Writers Know: The Language, Process, and Structure of Written Discourse.* Ed. Marty Nystrand. New York: Academic, 1982. 149–69. Print.

Britton, James, et al. *The Development of Writing Abilities (11–18).* London: MacMillan, 1975. Print.

Campo, Rafael. *The Journal of Medical Humanities* 27 (2006): 253–54. Print.

Davidson, Chad, and Gregory Fraser. "Out of the Margins: The Expanding Role of Creative Writing in Today's College Curriculum." *The Writer's Chronicle* 42.3 (December 2009): 76–81. Print.

Devitt, Amy J. "Generalizing about Genre: New Conceptions of an Old Concept." *College Composition and Communication* 44 (1993): 573–86. Print.

Elbow, Peter. "High Stakes and Low Stakes in Assigning and Responding to Writing." *Writing to Learn: Strategies for Assigning and Responding to Writing across the Disciplines.* Ed. Mary Dean Sorcinelli and Peter Elbow. San Francisco: Jossey-Bass, 5–14. Print.

———. *Writing with Power: Techniques for Mastering the Writing Process.* 2nd ed. Oxford, UK: Oxford UP, 1998. Print.

Emig, Janet. "Writing as a Mode of Learning." *College Composition and Communication* 28.2 (May 1977): 122–28. Print.

Fishman, Stephen. "Student Writing in Philosophy: A Sketch of Five Techniques." *Writing to Learn: Strategies for Assigning and Responding to Writing across the Disciplines.* Ed. Mary Dean Sorcinelli and Peter Elbow. San Francisco: Jossey-Bass, 53–66. Print.

Freedman, A. "Show and Tell: The Role of Explicit Teaching in the Learning of New Genres." *Research in the Teaching of English* 27.3 (Oct. 1993): 222–51. Print.

Freyhofer, Horst. "I Hate History Papers." *WAC Journal* 11 (April 2000): 47–52. Print.

Fulwiler, Toby. *Teaching with Writing*. Portsmouth, NH: Boynton/Cook Heinemann, 1987. Print.

——. "Writing Back and Forth: Class Letters." *Writing to Learn: Strategies for Assigning and Responding to Writing across the Disciplines*. Eds. Mary Deane Sorcinelli and Peter Elbow. San Francisco: Jossey-Bass, 1997. 15–26. Print.

Fulwiler, Toby, and Art Young, eds. *Language Connections: Writing and Reading across the Curriculum*. Urbana, IL: NCTE, 1982. Print.

Gordy, Laurie, and Alexandria Peary. "Bringing Creativity into the Classroom: Using Sociology to Writer First-Person Fiction." *Teaching Sociology* 33.4 (Oct. 2005): 396–402. Print.

Hesse, Doug. "Number of FYC courses taught each year?" *WPA list-serv*. WPA-L@asu.edu. Web. 23 Jan. 2012.

Hugo, Richard. *Triggering Town: Lectures and Essays on Poetry and Writing*. New York: W. W. Norton, 1982. Print.

Jennings, Lisa. "Making the Connection: A 'Lived History' Assignment in an Upper-Division German Course." *WAC Journal* 16 (Sept. 2005): 61–69. Print.

Kalmbach, James, and William Powers. "Shaping Experience: Narration and Understanding." *Language Connections: Writing and Reading across the Curriculum*. Ed. Toby Fulwiler and Art Young. Urbana, IL: NCTE, 1982. 99–106. Print.

Kerr, Lisa. "More than Words: Applying the Discipline of Literary Creative Writing to the Practice of Reflective Writing in Health Care Education." *Journal of Medical Humanities* 31 (2010): 295–301. Print.

Kinzie, J. *Promoting Student Success: What Faculty Members Can Do*. (Occasional Paper No. 6). Bloomington: Indiana University Center for Postsecondary Research, 2005. Print.

Kuriloff, Peshe C. "The Writing Consultant: Collaboration and Team Teaching." In *Writing across the Curriculum: A Guide to Developing Programs*. Ed. Susan H. McLeod and Margot Soven. Newberry Park, CA: Sage, 1992. 94–108. Print.

Laufer, Doug, and Rick Crosser. "The 'Writing-across-the-Curriculum' Concept in Accounting and Tax Courses." *Journal of Education for Business* 66.2 (Nov.-Dec. 1990): 83–88. Print.

Lightman, Alan. "Magic on the Mind: Physicists' Use of Metaphor." *American Scholar* 58.1 (Winter 1989): 97–102. Print.

Lopez-Mayhew, Barbara. "Writing in the Foreign Languages Department." *WAC Journal* 9 (Aug. 1998): 68–81. Print.

Magnotto Joyce Neff, and Barbara R. Stout. "Faculty Workshops." *Writing across the Curriculum: A Guide to Developing Programs*. Ed. Susan H. McLeod and Margot Soven. Newberry Park, CA: Sage, 1992. 32–45. Print.

McLeod, Susan H. "The Pedagogy of Writing across the Curriculum." *A Guide to Composition Pedagogies*. Ed. Gary Tate, Amy Rupiper, and Kurt Schick. New York: Oxford UP, 2001. 149–64. Print.

———. *Strengthening Programs for Writing across the Curriculum*. San Francisco: Jossey-Bass, 1988. Print.

McLeod, Susan H., and Elaine Maimon. "Clearing the Air: WAC Myths and Realities." *College English* 62 (2000): 573–83. Print.

McLeod, Susan H., and Margot Soven, eds. *A History of Writing across the Curriculum: Composing a Community*. West Lafayette, IN: Parlor Press, 2006. Print.

———. *Writing across the Curriculum: A Guide to Developing Programs*. Newberry Park, CA: Sage, 1992. Print.

McLeod, Susan H., and Eric Miraglia. "Writing across the Curriculum in a Time of Change." *WAC for the New Millennium: Strategies for Continuing Writing-across-the-Curriculum Programs*. Ed. Susan H. McLeod, et al. Urbana, IL: NCTE, 2001. 1–27. Print.

Miller, Carolyn. "Genre as Social Action." *Quarterly Journal of Speech* 70 (1984): 151–67. Print.

Miller, Hildy. "Metaphoric Components of Composing Processes." *Metaphor and Symbolic Activity* 8.2 (1993): 79–95. Print.

Palmquist, Wendy J. "Using Writing in the Adolescent Psychology Course." *Writing across the Curriculum* 7. (Aug. 1996): 33–48. Print.

Peary, Alexandria. "Spectators at Their Own Future: Creative Writing Assignments in the Disciplines and the Fostering of Critical Thinking." *The WAC Journal* 23 (2012): 65–81. Print.

Petersen, Meg. "The Atomic Weight of Metaphor: Writing Poetry across the Curriculum." *Writing across the Curriculum* 12 (May 2001): 97–100. Print.

Peterson-Gonzalez, Meg. "In Defense of Storytelling." *WAC Journal* 6 (Aug. 1995): 63–70. Print.

Peterson, Linda. "Repetition and Metaphor in the Early Stages of Composing." *College Composition and Communication* 36.4 (Dec. 1985): 429–43. Print.

Petraglia, Joseph, ed. *Reconceiving Writing, Rethinking Writing Instruction*. Mahwah, NJ: Lawrence Erlbaum Associates, 1995. Print.

Rose, Mike. "The Language of Exclusion: Writing Instruction at the University." *College English* 47 (1985): 341–59. Print.

Russell, David R. "American Origins of the Writing-across-the-Curriculum Movement." *Landmark Essays on Writing across the Curriculum*. Ed. Charles Bazerman and David R. Russell. Davis, CA: Hermagoras Press. 1994. 3–22. Print.

——. "Where Do Naturalistic Studies of WAC/WID Point? A Research Review." *WAC for the New Millennium: Strategies for Continuing Writing-across-the-Curriculum Programs*. Ed. Susan H. McLeod, Eric Miraglia, Margot Soven, and Christopher Thaiss. Urbana, IL: NCTE, 2001.

——. *Writing in the Academic Disciplines: A Curricular History*. 2nd ed. Carbondale: Southern Illinois UP, 2002. Print.

Russell, David R., and Charles Bazerman, eds. *Landmark Essays on Writing across the Curriculum*. Davis, CA: Hermagoras Press, 1994. Print.

Segal, Marty T., and Robert A. Smart, eds. *Direct from the Disciplines: Writing across the Curriculum*. Portsmouth, NH: Boynton/Cook Heinemann, 2005. Print.

Seitz, James. "Composition's Misunderstanding of Metaphor." *College Composition and Communication* 42.3 (Oct. 1991): 288–98.

Sorcinelli, Mary Deane, and Peter Elbow, eds. *Writing to Learn: Strategies for Assigning and Responding to Writing across the Disciplines*. San Francisco: Jossey-Bass, 1997.

Swales, John M. *Genre Analysis: English in Academic and Research Settings*. Cambridge, UK: Cambridge UP, 1990.

Thaiss, Christopher. "Theory in WAC: Where Have We Been, Where Are We Going?" *WAC for the New Millennium: Strategies for Continuing Writing-across-the-Curriculum Programs*. Ed. Susan H. McLeod, Eric Miraglia, Margot Soven, and Christopher Thaiss. Urbana, IL: NCTE, 2001. 299–323. Print.

Thomas, Elizabeth, and Anne Mulvey. "Using the Arts in Teaching and Learning: Building Student Capacity for Community-Based Work in Health Psychology." *Journal of Health Psychology* 13.2 (2008): 239–50. Print.

Tobin, Lad. "Bridging Gaps: Analyzing Our Students' Metaphors for Composing." *College Composition and Communication* 40.4 (Dec. 1989): 444–58. Print.

WAC Clearinghouse. Ed. Mike Palmquist. 1997. Colorado State University. 15 July 2011. Web. <http://wac.colostate.edu/theses/index.cfm?category=20>.

Walvoord, Barbara E., et al. *In the Long Run: A Study of Faculty in Three Writing-across-the-Curriculum Programs*. Urbana, IL: NCTE, 1997. Print.

Welch, Nancy. "No Apology: Challenging the 'Uselessness' of Creative Writing." *JAC: A Journal of Composition Theory* 19 (1999): 117–34. Print.

Young, Art. "Considering Values: The Poetic Function of Language." *Language Connections: Writing and Reading across the Curriculum*. Ed. Toby Fulwiler and Art Young. Urbana, IL: NCTE, 1982. 77–97. Print.

———. "Mentoring, Modeling, Monitoring, Motivating: Response to Students' Ungraded Writing as Academic Conversation." *Writing to Learn: Strategies for Assigning and Responding to Writing across the Disciplines*. Ed. Mary Deane Sorcinelli and Peter Elbow. San Francisco: Jossey-Bass, 1997. 27–40. Print.

———. "Writing across and against the Curriculum." *Writing across the Curriculum: A Critical Sourcebook*. Ed. Terry Myers Zawacki and Paul M. Rogers. Boston: Bedford/St. Martin's. 2012. 158–67. Print.

Young, Sandra. "Beyond 'Hot Lips' and 'Big Nurse': Creative Writing and Nursing." *Composition Studies* 33.1 (Spring 2005): 75–91. Print.

Zehr, David. "Buffy and Elvis: The Sequel." *WAC Journal* 6 (Aug. 1995): 15–22.

A Basic Writing Teacher Teaches Creative Writing

Clyde Moneyhun

BASIC WRITING—SOMETIMES called *developmental writing* or (less often these days) *remedial writing*—has in my experience been a fountain of pedagogical ideas for the teaching of all writing. In my particular case, teaching basic writing has definitely given me ideas about how to teach my creative writing classes with fresh methods that respond to the needs of writing students better than the usual workshop method. In this essay, I'll explore the ways in which pedagogy used in basic writing courses can inform the teaching of creative writing, drawing on literature in the field of basic writing pedagogy and also my own classroom experiences in both kinds of courses. Before I talk about basic writing and what it might have to offer creative writing, however, I should note that *basic writing* is a controversial, contested, and much-debated term. What is basic writing, or rather, in how many ways can it be defined? Discussions of basic writing may focus on the writing itself, or on the writers who produce such writing, or on the pedagogy employed to teach such writers.

What Is Basic Writing?

Basic writing defined by text features. Some scholars try to define basic writing by what we find on a page, and also by what we do not find, by what is lacking. An early effort to characterize the texts we called basic writing is from Mina Shaughnessy, whose book *Errors and Expectations*

(1977) is foundational to the field. According to Shaughnessy, basic writing tends to be represented by "small numbers of words with large numbers of errors," including "errors with the so-called regular features of English" such as problems with number agreement in verbs, capricious spelling and punctuation, and "sentence boundary" issues that lead to fragments and run-ons. Basic writers also seem to be "restricted as writers . . . to a very narrow range of syntactic, semantic, and rhetorical options, which forces them into either a rudimentary style of discourse that belies their real maturity or a dense and tangled prose with which neither they nor their readers can cope" (139).

Many problems arise from trying to define basic writing in these ways. The first one is simple: how many errors are too many errors, and what kinds of errors will we say are serious enough? Every piece of writing contains errors by someone's definition of error. Where's the threshold that would label a piece of writing as "basic"? More important, defining basic writing by the countable, measurable errors it contains or by the rhetorical qualities it seems to lack can lead us to characterize such writing as simple in its ideas, its reasoning, its maturity. In many essays (for example, "The Study of Error" and "Inventing the University"), another basic writing pioneer, David Bartholomae, analyzes his basic writing students' texts and finds sophisticated thinking patterns and mature reasoning. Basic writing, in other words, may fool us by its errors and linguistic awkwardness into thinking that there's nothing worth reading in it.

Basic writing defined by who writes it. If it's hard to define what text features characterize basic writing, can we at least say something about the people who write it? Are there common traits, attitudes, backgrounds, or experiences that can help us define them? Shaughnessy says that we can "infer that they have never written much," that "they come from families and neighborhoods where people speak other languages or variant, non-prestigious forms of English," and that "while they have doubtless been sensitive to the differences between their ways of speaking and their teachers'," they have not had the opportunity or inclination to learn "standard English," especially in its academic form (139). This definition clearly delineates certain populations: minority students, working-class students, immigrant students, and, increasingly in American education, nontraditional students.

Here too, however, the definition gets slippery when we examine it. For starters, if we define basic writers by what they lack—basically, a white, middle-class upbringing—we fail to account for white middle-class students who somehow end up in basic writing classes anyway, and there are many of them. At the same time, we discount the experiences and insights of people raised in "different" ways because they may express their wisdom in "different" ways, which is the thesis of Shirley Brice Heath's *Ways with Words*, an ethnography of three small rural communities in the Piedmont area of the Carolinas, and a book that has become central to discussions of multiple literacies and alternative knowledges. Either way, whether we define basic writers in ways that exclude who many of them actually are (i.e., white and middle class) or in ways that devalue who they are (i.e., minorities from the wrong side of the tracks), we stigmatize and traumatize students by locating the problem not in their writing but in them; they don't just write the wrong way, they're the wrong kind of people. Rather than lacking in literacy, basic writing scholar Mike Rose reminds us in his influential *Lives on the Boundary*, the majority of people in basic writing courses are for the most part "completely literate" people in nonacademic ways, "literate people straining at the boundaries of their ability, trying to move into the unfamiliar, to approximate a kind of writing they can't yet command" (188). And this could be any of us.

Basic writing defined by its pedagogy. Since basic writing is most often characterized as writing that is riddled with errors, and basic writers as people who habitually make errors, basic writing pedagogy can be focused on the identification and remediation of errors. Basic writing textbooks are often heavy on sentence-level work, and basic writing classes may focus heavily, if not primarily, on grammar. As documented by basic writing scholars from Robert Connors to Andrea Lunsford, basic writers are often restricted to reading and writing short texts, producing free-standing sentences (most often as examples of "correctness" rather than communicativeness), or short paragraphs, or at most short essays (Connors; Lunsford). Worse, since basic writing courses are considered remedial and below the level of college work, they are often required but carry no course credit, and so are "clearly punitive in nature" (Lunsford 249).

Fortunately, there is a vigorous critique of this view of basic writing pedagogy. Resource books such as *A Sourcebook for Basic Writing Teachers* (edited by Theresa Enos) and *Landmark Essays on Basic Writing* (edited by Kay Halasek and Nels P. Highberg) offer many alternatives to a grammar-based, minimalist teaching plan, as does the back catalog of the *Journal of Basic Writing*. The ineffectiveness of a grammar-based curriculum has been thoroughly documented, and teachers have learned to challenge basic writers with more rigorous reading and writing assignments, to have higher expectations for their writing, and generally to recognize and utilize the life experiences and mature insights they bring with them into the classroom. Sadly, though, such pedagogies have been slow to catch on.

Basic writing as a social construct. Finally, in addition to discussions of the nature of basic writing, basic writers, and basic writing pedagogy, it has been suggested that all of it—the entire world of basic writing—is not simply discovered, but created. As Bartholomae famously put it, "I think basic writing programs have become expressions of our desire to produce basic writers, to maintain the course, the argument, the slot in the university community" (315). In other words, the definitions above are variable, adaptable, fungible, according to our purposes. Shaughnessy notes that "one school's remedial students may be another's regular or even advanced freshman" (137). This point of view questions everything about our definitions, since, as Kelly Ritter asks, if we imagine we can somehow define basic writing and basic writers accurately, if there is "an agreed-upon societal and institutional demarcation for 'basic' writers that diagnoses a lack of something specific," then "why does the course vary so dramatically from institution to institution?" (7). Why? Because each institution has its own way of defining basic writing and basic writers, and so its own way of "labeling them 'not ready' for what first-year writing entails at that location" (9). If you look for basic writers, in other words, you will find them.

No matter how basic writing and its writers are defined, and no matter how they are chosen for a specially designated basic writing class, they come to us in such great numbers that an entire subfield of composition studies has grown up around us. The discussions that have raged (and still rage) in basic writing take us down to the root assumptions of our teaching, no matter what kind of writing we teach, cause us to question our methods, and give us new ways of doing things.

Basic Writing Pedagogy in the Creative Writing Classroom

Two events happened to me—at the same time—that shaped my writing pedagogy more than anything else. When I was an MFA student at the University of Arizona in the 1980s, I was also a TA, and though I was dedicated to writing and teaching fiction, as soon as I taught my first basic writing class, I was hooked. I spent half my life in fiction workshops, giving revision feedback to my fellow MFA candidates, and teaching the occasional introductory course in short story writing. But I spent the other half teaching English 100, the basic writing course taken by about a third of all UA students, eventually participating as a graduate student member of the *ad hoc* committee that completely overhauled the course curriculum across all sections.

I continue to walk on both paths, sometimes alternating, but more often straddling. On the one hand, I've researched and written about basic writing pedagogy and, as a director of composition, have shaped basic writing curricula and trained instructors to teach basic writing courses. On the other hand, I've led conference workshops on creative writing pedagogy and coauthored a text for use in fiction writing classes. And while I still teach creative writing (these days, usually creative nonfiction), I also still teach basic writing whenever I get the chance. The pedagogies of creative writing (with their emphasis on peer sharing) continue to inform my teaching of basic writing, but I'm realizing that my teaching of basic writing (with its emerging emphasis on deep revision) has an even greater impact on my teaching of fiction and creative nonfiction in very specific ways.

Assignments

Good student writing begins with good assignments. In the teaching of composition, I find that too many assignments are far too long and exhaustive, as they attempt to spell out in long detail everything a paper needs to be. There's much description of the final product, its length and format, its necessary parts, the shape and purpose of its content. Particularly with basic writers, the well-intentioned teacher, imagining that such students need everything explained down to the tiniest detail, more often in fact stifle their students' ability to produce good writing. Mike Rose notes that "rigid rules" for writing "impeded rather than enhanced the composing process" of basic writing students he observed (Rose, "Rigid Rules" 390). This should come as no surprise, since basic writers are more likely to be slavish in their devotion to what they imagine are the rules, terrified of error, and tied in knots of self-doubt when they try to write.

Therefore, rather than providing my basic writers with exhaustively complete assignments, I present them with short prompts that help them generate exploratory first drafts. Since basic writers are more likely to get stuck, to experience what they call "writer's block," I like assignments that use what composition teachers call *heuristic devices*, questions and challenges that get the juices flowing, or that get the flow unstuck, or that carry us to places we didn't know we were going.

I find that in too many creative writing classes, the problem is the opposite of the maniacally detailed assignment: no assignment at all, other than "story due on Wednesday." I think students, even graduate students, deserve to be set on a path, as we set ourselves on a path when we sit down to write our own stories. In creative nonfiction classes, I usually lay out a series of subgenres for students to explore: travel writing, nature writing, sports writing, food writing, profiles, reviews. Sometimes we stick to one genre for a whole class, such as memoir, but try out different approaches to it, from a fast-paced, present-tense, you-are-there method to a leisurely, after-the-fact, reflective approach. In a beginning fiction class, I sometimes set out a series of story types or techniques to try, from point-of-view exercises to style exercises to genre exercises. In a more advanced class, I often encourage students to explore a set of story possibilities (a 300-word story, a story in dialogue, a story set in history), but don't specify the order in which they should share them with the class.

While some of my creative writing colleagues may think that assignments stifle creativity, I would argue that they encourage it. Because my creative writing students often complain of the same problems as my basic writing students ("I don't have any ideas" and "I don't know what happens next"), I think my assignments are heuristic in the same ways that basic writing assignments can be. Rather than close doors, they can open them; they can tamp down anxiety, get students unstuck, and help them imagine new possibilities for their pieces.

Research

My composition classes usually require students to do at least some research, and sometimes a lot, in order to write their papers. My basic writing students tend to have as much anxiety about research as they have about writing in general, and as little interest. I've learned to help basic writing students be more enthusiastic about the usual stultifying library search for sources by helping them locate topics that mean something to them, and also by expanding the meaning of research.

Many basic writing teachers are fond of starting with personal narrative, and some of them end there as well. I sometimes use a four-essay sequence that begins with a personal essay, but then moves to an essay based on interviews, followed by an essay informed by library research, and ending with a paper that synthesizes all the previous essays—since they're all on the same topic. One student once wrote a comic piece about being a single mother of two small children; then became more serious while interviewing her single mother friends; then wrote about a "deadbeat dad" bill pending in Congress that would free up court-ordered child support to improve all their lives; and then put it all together in a piece that made you laugh, made you cry, and made you angry all at the same time.

The idea of doing research for a creative writing class, including a fiction class, is rare, though fiction writers and especially nonfiction writers know that we do it all the time. Some of my creative students have resisted doing research for their pieces, even in nonfiction classes. I generally ask them to proceed through the same three-part process from the "I experience" to the "we experience" to the "all-of-us-experience." Are you writing about the desert? I ask. Go to the desert. Hike there, picnic there, spend the night there. Then talk to people who live there, work there, do research there. Then read Edward Abbey's *Desert Solitaire*, or anything by John Muir, or even Annie Dillard's *Pilgrim at Tinker Creek*, to see how it's done. Is your fictional character a soldier like you were? Draw on your experiences, but also talk to a range of other people who have served in other times and places, and try reading Tim O'Brien's stories, or Anthony Swofford's *Jarhead*, or Michael Herr's *Dispatches*.

Peer Response

We all know that the foundation of many (if not most) creative writing classes is the workshop. In my early teaching of fiction workshops, I did with my students what my teachers had done with me. The students read each other's stories out of class and came in ready for a discussion. The writer remained silent from beginning to end. I sometimes asked them to focus their comments on certain elements of fiction (scene-setting, characterizing details, dialogue), but there were no real guidelines for the discussion. We've all seen workshop discussions that wander aimlessly, sometimes misinterpret the writer's intentions, occasionally offer tactless assessments of a story's (or a writer's) worth.

Teaching basic writing has shown me how to vary the routine of the usual workshop method to help students provide more focused, more helpful, and more diplomatic feedback to student writers.

A lot of peer work in basic writing classes involves not whole-class discussions, but instead small-group peer response sessions. However, I quickly learned that peer response sessions among basic writers would crash and burn if I didn't teach them how to do it. In their experiences as basic writing students, they had seldom been asked to turn a teacher's eye on a classmate's piece of writing, to look for ways in which it might be improved, so some of them tended to be completely uncritical ("I loved it and wouldn't change a thing"). Others mimicked the harsh comments they'd received from teachers and were thoughtlessly critical ("I think your main idea is just stupid"). The largest group, after years of teachers marking their errors with red pens, attempted haphazardly to correct minor and mostly nonexistent problems.

Along the way, I developed a peer response routine for basic writing classes that worked well, and I've starting using its details when I teach creative writing, whether we use small-group or whole-class workshop sessions. From basic writing scholars including Nancy Sommers (especially her "Responding to Student Writing"), Elaine O. Lees (especially "Evaluating Student Writing" and "Proofreading as Reading, Errors as Embarrassments"), and Lil Brannon and Cy Knoblauch (especially "On Students' Rights to Their Own Texts: A Model of Teacher Response"), I gleaned a number of attitudes that I could ask my students to use with each other's work: (*1*) respect the writer's intentions for a piece, and avoid imposing your own; (*2*) honor what is working well in a piece; (*3*) base your suggestions for change on what the writer is already trying to do.

I enact these principles in both my basic writing classes and creative writing classes by asking students to do the following:

1. Try to figure out the writer's intentions and repeat them back to the writer. This is harder than it may sound, since a writer's intentions may be obscure or scattered. We also have to fight our tendency to impose our own intentions on a piece, rewriting it in our heads to the piece we would have written.
2. Tell the writer what's working well toward realizing the intentions, as well as they can be guessed. In our usual comments on what we don't like or isn't working, we can neglect to let writers know what we do appreciate.
3. Help the writer find ways to sharpen the focus on the intentions. Which passages or elements seem superfluous? What information is still needed? This helps divert attention away from a post mortem of an as-yet unfinished story and direct it toward what the story can become.

I find that these guidelines help students walk a line between being too soft and too edgy in their comments, expressing what they have to say in the context of the writer's goals, framing it as constructive ideas for revision.

In a break with most workshop teachers, while I ask the writer to remain silent during the discussion as in the usual workshop, I also carve out time at the end for the writer to respond to what's been said. I let them know that defending a piece (and accusing us of simply being poor readers) is bad form, but that they are free to comment on our understanding of intentions, to ask for clarification, to ask follow-up questions. I find that this step is crucial in fulfilling our promise to respect what writers are trying to do and offer constructive criticism toward helping them fulfill their own intentions.

Teacher Feedback

It may be clear by now what principles guide my own teacher response to student writing. Teaching basic writing has taught me to give the right response at the right time. In early drafts, a basic writing student in particular needs someone to ignore language errors and pay attention to the broad "global" issues. Is the topic appropriate to the assignment, is it promising, is it narrow enough? Is there a main idea either stated or lurking, and if so is it more than superficial, is it mature, is it important? And so on. Later, after large issues have been addressed, we can turn our attention to narrower "local" issues of language. I translate this into the teaching of creative writing, for example, by taking a student fiction down to the most basic choices that have been made. Might a different point of view work better? Has the most promising character been chosen as the main character? Does the story start at the right moment? Until the big questions have been answered, it makes no sense to me to talk about how to punctuate dialogue.

I've also learned from teaching basic writing, and learned it the hard way, that it is both unethical and ineffective to damage a writer's confidence. Basic writing scholars including Patricia McCarthy, Scott Meier, and Regina Rinderer have drawn on the theories of psychologist Albert Bandura about self-efficacy to show how success at a given task is related to how capable we feel about doing well at it (466). Basic writers are famously sensitive writers with low self-esteem and poor confidence in their abilities as writers; if we expect them to write well, therefore, we need attend to the affective realm and help them see themselves as successful. As Ed Jones puts it: "Teachers need to be cognizant that, according to social cognitive theory, students' self-confidence depends in no small measure upon the feedback that teachers can provide" (234).

I find that since creative writing can be so personal for students, and so much of their personal lives is exposed in what they write for a workshop, they can experience similar feelings of anxiety about their writing abilities, feelings that can be exacerbated with harsh critical comments. Some creative writing classes amount to a school of hard knocks where one of the goals is helping students develop a tough skin. I don't want my students to be wary, tough, and competitive. I want them to be open, sensitive, and trusting. They need to be confident enough to take risks and not get slammed for it. They need to experience the success of approval and admiration, even as they learn to work harder to improve their writing through revision. Therefore, as I ask them to do when they criticize each other's work, I start with what's good, what's working, what delighted me, and I key all other comments to that. I hope, in short, that my students know what John Butler says his students know about him: that "I am in their corner instead of at the opposite side of the ring" (564).

Revision

Most teachers of writing require revisions, usually one or two. In my basic writing courses, I often require six or seven revisions. My assignments are keyed to what students should focus on for each version of the essay, and my feedback on each version focuses on that goal. I once collected the umpteenth draft of a set of papers in a basic writing class, and remarked (as I often do) that I was looking forward to reading them, as they were really getting good after all the revision. A student raised his hand. "Why did we have to write all these drafts to get to this point? Why didn't you just tell us how to fix everything on the first draft?"

The answer is, of course, that I couldn't have, even if I'd wanted to. Ann Berthoff feels that basic writers are particularly susceptible to the belief, instilled by teachers who build in only one chance to revise, that revision is merely "a chance to get 'it' right the second time around" (545). If, on the other hand (as most professional writers believe and experience), writing is a process of discovery, then important discoveries can happen only across the work of revising, reworking, cutting some things and adding others, finding our way. I give comments aimed not at "fixing" texts but at helping writers explore the possibilities of their ideas. Basic writers in particular need time to attend to a few ideas at a time across many drafts, bracketing the language issues that can inhibit their writing and prevent them from exploring ideas.

Creative writing students need a similar process if we expect them to develop as writers. While some teachers require (or at least allow) some revision, in my most recent creative writing classes, I work in four versions of every piece. The first one is brainstorming, exploring every direction that a piece might go—for fiction, making lists of settings, events, characters, combinations of characters; for creative nonfiction, making lists of possible topics, possible ways to narrow a topic, possible research to do. The students share these with each other, then come back with a rough draft. This draft we workshop in the usual way, helping the writer discover his or her intentions, pointing to unexplored but possibly fruitful paths, encouraging revision. The third version finally comes to me, and I do my best to make the same kind of supportive, respectful comments. The final version is a revision for the end-of-class portfolio of all a student's work.

Sharing

My basic writers tend to divide the world into two groups: people who can write and people who can't. They, of course, belong to the second group. People who can write just do it: write with ease and joy, never have to revise, and get good grades or publication. People who can't write actually have to work at it, often in frustration and sometimes in agony, have to revise again and again, and never quite get it right no matter what.

For a number of reasons (including testing my assignments), I nearly always write along with my students, and I share my process and my drafts with them as I bounce along. I tell them how I reject topic after topic until I find the right one; how I wander around looking for a main idea; how I get frustrated, run out of ideas, hit dead ends, find solutions, forge ahead. One semester while I was teaching a basic writing course, I had to write an entry to an encyclopedia of rhetoric and composition. There was a severe word limit and many other specific requirements. I labored. I printed out what I had, took scissors to it, scribbled all over it, typed in the corrections, printed again, and repeated the process—many times. I saved all the drafts and thumbtacked them to the wall of my office for students to see when they came in for appointments. It made an effect.

I write along with my creative writing students too, sharing my drafts and revision process. Only once in my extended time (undergraduate and graduate) as a creative writing student did a teacher do this; it was Tobias Wolff sharing with us a draft that would become "Hunters in the Snow." It was astonishing to hear him talk about what he was trying to do, what he still considered the story's weaknesses, what he thought he might try next. I share that anecdote with my students, along with the testimony of other writers who struggle, suffer, and persevere, from Virginia Woolf in her letters and diaries to Anne Lamott in *Bird by Bird*.

Reading

The first basic writing course I taught as a TA many years ago was a product of the bad old days of basic writing pedagogy. We had a grammar book and accompanying workbook, and we were expected to "teach" grammar with lectures, assign the workbook exercises as homework, and test the students' progress with preprinted exams. We were also to teach the students to build paragraphs out of individual (and grammatically sound) sentences, and then to teach them how to build a five-paragraph essay out of perfectly rounded paragraphs. (There was no reader, but if there had been, it would have been one of the several readers marketed for basic writing courses, with either very short pieces or even short excerpts.)

The committee charged with changing this paleolithic curriculum didn't so much revise it as replace it. I don't remember the discussions that led us to decide that students in the university's basic writing course would now read three nonfiction books. Many composition theorists have explored "the reading-writing connection" (notably Nancy Nelson, Robert Calfee, Mariolina Salvatori, Sandra Stotsky, David Bartholomae, and Anthony Petrosky). Basic writing scholars Sugie Goen and Helen Gillotte-Tropp assert that reading is even more important for basic writers, citing dramatic improvement in the progress of basic writers they studied whose classes incorporated substantial reading. As I taught basic writing over the next several years after our curriculum revision, we developed a growing list of books to choose from: Maya Angelou's *I Know Why the Caged Bird Sings*, Luis Rodriguez's *Always Running*, Ernesto Galarza's *Barrio Boy*, Richard Rodriguez's *Hunger of Memory*, Lorene Cary's *Black Ice*. Adding serious, substantial readings was part of our approach to not treating basic writers as if they were children who couldn't handle grown-up books.

I've learned from teaching basic writing in this way that all writers, including and maybe especially student writers, need to be readers. We tend to remember and mention writers in our creative workshops, to recommend writers, but we rarely make reading and analysis of texts a formal part of the class. For entry-level fiction writing classes, I'm partial to collections like James Moffett and Kenneth R. McElheny's *Points of View*, while for more advanced students I like choosing three or four collections by writers both classic and contemporary, from Hawthorne and Melville to Flannery O'Connor, Raymond Carver, and Anthony Doerr. It gives us a chance to see how other writers have addressed the same problems that we struggle with ourselves as writers, and it encourages students to place their writing on a continuum with published professional work.

Publishing

I was teaching at a working-class urban university, and one semester was handed a sophomore-level basic writing course for education majors who had not done well in first-year writing. Many had taken not just one but two first-year basic writing classes, then two mainstream composition classes, so this was their fifth required writing course, one into which they were placed as a result of poor grades so far. Morale was not good.

Syllabi from previous teachers of the course showed that it was developed as a grammar brush-up. I couldn't imagine a greater exercise in masochism than leading a soulless, stultifying semester of grammar drills with this group of people. I decided that we would at least read something good, and for these future teachers I chose Jonathan Kozol's *Savage Inequalities*, an exposé of the injustices of school funding in America. We also visited several well-funded suburban high schools and several underfunded urban high schools to observe for ourselves the results of unfair funding patterns. Reading the local newspaper one day, I ran across a particularly lame-brained op-ed column claiming that inequities in school funding were irrelevant. It all came down to the quality of the teachers, the columnist claimed, and the work ethic of the students. The implication was that minority and working-class schools were bad because of teacher ineptitude and student laziness, not because they were funded at half the levels of their whiter, middle-class neighbors.

When I brought the column to class, my students were livid. I ditched the lesson plan I had made and invited each of them to write a letter to the editor replying to the column. They started, individually or in small groups. Soon, though, they ended up crowded around one computer, with three or four of them taking turns at the keyboard while others shouted suggestions. When the letter was done, they demanded that I sit down and "fix" it. I worked at the sentence level, changing what they told me to change, correcting only a few small errors that they didn't catch themselves.

We mailed the letter and it was published in the newspaper.

I'm not alone in finding ways for my students to publish their writing. There's a journal devoted to undergraduate research, *Young Scholars in Writing*; recent anthologies of examples of excellent student writing are available for use in writing classrooms; and in general, there's strong interest in what Margaret Mansfield calls "real world writing" and the opportunity for student writers to reach audiences beyond the classroom. Such writing, Mansfield says, enables students "to grapple with notions of audience, authority, and 'real' (i.e., serious) writing; to reflect upon their roles as writers; and to discover much about themselves, their topics, and the writing process" (70). Rosemary Arca observes that these effects are even stronger for basic writers, who can, though real-world writing and publication, pass from "a diminished view of themselves" as writers to writers who "compose for real audiences," producing "public texts" for a wide readership (133).

I've carried this belief in the power of publishing student writing into the teaching of creative writing. I want my creative writers to experience the same sense of writing for a real audience that I try to give to my basic writers. At the low end, in this age of electronic texts, we always put together at least a virtual class anthology, with each student contributing his or her best piece to a collection that I compile and distribute over e-mail. In the past, and again recently with the ease of self-publishing a great little perfect-bound volume, we sometimes do the thing in print, a sort of special issue devoted to their work, with an introduction by me. And of course, since I'm constantly feeding them opportunities small and large to submit their work for publication at small journals and national magazines, to enter their work into contests, and to apply for student writing fellowships, students do end up publishing, winning prizes, and getting recognition for their work.

Teaching Specific Students

Basic writing students are famously diverse—and not just in the sense of being members of minority groups or speakers of minority languages. Any given basic writing class is liable to have a much greater variety of students than a standard composition class: white middle-class kids who managed to have checkered experiences with writing, sons and daughters of migrant workers, gifted students from underfunded schools that failed to serve them, children of refugee families, working parents, veterans. Each one of them has a particular and sometimes idiosyncratic background, very specific talents and challenges, and individual needs for instruction and guidance.

My basic writing students have taught me to see all my classes this way. Sometimes homogeneity disguises difference: a room full of artsy, ambitious creative writing majors that includes a laid-off software engineer coming back to school, a twenty-year-old who wants to be a sports writer, an empty-nester working on her novel, a goth girl recovering from child abuse, a small-town boy adrift in what he sees as the big city of the campus, an impossibly young-looking GI just home from war. What stories will seem urgent to tell for each of them? What approach will help them tell the most of what they have to say? What support—critical and moral—will they need along the way? The answers will be different for every student.

High Expectations

Sean had failed to do the assignment that was due on the second day of class. The students were surprised that I'd made an assignment on the very first day, but the rest of them turned up with it. After I'd collected them, and while they did a small group activity, I counted them, found one missing, and determined whose piece it was. I quietly slipped into a desk next to Sean, who was sitting by himself rather than joining a group. He was a tough guy, with a crude tattoo showing through the V-neck collar of his T-shirt. I asked, "Sean, did you forget to turn in your writing?" He looked at me with a blank expression. "Or did you not get a chance to do it yet?" "Yeah, I didn't do it yet," he said. "That's cool this time," I said, "but you'll need to bring it next time, along with the other thing I'll assign today." The next class, he showed up with both pieces—poor efforts at best, but a small victory for both of us. In my office a few weeks later, he told me that no teacher had ever called him on missing work or absences. "They just left me alone," he said.

Some years back, I started telling my basic writing students: "In this class, you're going to do the best writing you've ever done in your life." By the end of every semester, at least some of them tell me that this prophecy turns out to be true. I support them in all the ways I've described, with guidance as they brainstorm, research, draft, and revise their work, but most of all I set the bar high. They often tell me that teachers don't expect them to do well, have lower expectations for them, dumb down assignments for them, let them get away with a C or a D for a course grade. In the tasks I set for my students, in my comments on their writing, in our class discussions of their writing, I let them know that we will have high standards and expect grown-up writing from grown-ups.

I say the same thing to my creative writing students. "We're writing literature here," I tell them. Like many fiction writing teachers, I discourage them from writing genre fiction like fantasy or romance, because too much of it is written for children or adults who aren't very bright. The characters in it tend not to have adult problems to solve, adult lives to live. If they insist on doing it, I ask that they set their sights high and measure themselves against the best genre writers, to compete with Tolkien and C. S. Lewis. I steer them away from cheap plot devices, most of them involving the horrible and ironic death of a character. A student once wrote a draft about a sad loner who falls in love for the first time with a wonderful woman, only to see her stabbed to death before his eyes. The End. I asked him to revise by (*a*) letting the poor woman live and (*b*) beginning the story with her wounding. How will our hero handle it? The resulting second draft still needed a lot of work, but at least it was a story about real life, not just a joke with a groaner of a punch line.

Most of all, I think that teaching basic writing has forced me to step up my game, to have higher expectations not just for my students but for myself. If you're doing it right, there's no coasting in teaching basic writers. They demand your attention and your creativity and your very best work. While it's much easier to coast in a creative writing workshop—just setting due dates, presiding over a student-led workshop, and pontificating off the cuff from time to time—those students too deserve the planning, thought, and attention that I try to give my basic writing classes.

Creative Writing Gets Creative

I can sum up what I've said here by saying that we should bring to the creative writing classroom the same level of engagement, experiment, and—yes—creativity that we bring to the challenging task of teaching basic writing. The creative writing community is oddly conservative in its pedagogy, set in its workshop ways, reluctant to try teaching methods that might emerge from the composition world or, heaven forbid, the basic writing world. I'm heartened by attention to pedagogy among creative writers, though limited, that goes beyond the workshop, from Joseph Moxley's 1989 collection *Creative Writing in America* to Wendy Bishop's more recent work. The online *Director's Handbook* from the Association of Writers and Writing Programs (AWP) calls for some of the methods I've outlined here, including the requirement of "extensive and diverse reading," "peer review" that includes patterns other than workshop, instructor comments that "convey respect for the intentions of the writer" and offer suggestions for revision, and the requirement that students revise (AWP). I hope that creative writing teachers will remain open to pedagogical ideas from their colleagues in composition and especially to those of us teaching basic writing, which has been the mother of invention for so many innovations in the teaching of writing.

Appendix

Assignments

1. Ask students to imagine an assignment that could have prompted a writer to produce any classic piece of fiction, from Hemingway's "Hills Like White Elephants" to O'Connor's "A Good Man Is Hard to Find," or any classic piece of creative nonfiction, from White's "Once More to the Lake" to Orwell's "Shooting an Elephant." What tasks might an imaginary writing teacher have set in order to elicit the piece of writing? They can have fun writing the assignment sheet in a teacher voice.

2. Ask students to investigate (in the authors' essays, interviews, and diaries) assignments that writers claimed they had given themselves. For example, Hemingway famously described making himself write in a way that showed only "the tip of the iceberg"; Woolf said she tried to write as her character Lily Briscoe (in *To the Lighthouse*) painted, like "the colour burning on a framework of steel; the light of a butterfly's wing lying upon the arches of a cathedral"; Faulkner said (in his *Paris Review* interview) that he wrote *The Sound and the Fury* to explain to himself why a little girl was up a tree at night, looking through a window at her grandmother's wake.

Research

3. As either homework or an in-class activity, as individuals or in groups, ask students to use the Internet to investigate details they can use to describe a journey taken by the real (creative nonfiction) or imaginary (fiction) people they're writing about. I once asked a class to come up with everything I'd need to describe a drive from downtown Boise, Idaho, to Ketchum in Sun Valley. One group found the roads; another found the geography along the way, complete with names of mountains and valleys; another found names of flowers and animals I might see during the season they chose; another came up with some history of the region, including a nineteenth-century all-woman surveying crew. Then each group wrote a one-paragraph version of the drive.

4. In creative nonfiction classes, I sometimes assign the genre of "profile." Since most profiles are based on interviews, we practice performing interviews as research. (The Internet is full of advice for performing interviews, especially for journalists.) We go through the steps of brainstorming questions, finding ways to set a subject at ease, transcribing a recorded interview, editing the transcription, and turning a raw interview into a profile.

Peer Response

5. The intention of the writer is the foundation of the responses I ask students to give each other, but a writer's intention can be hard to guess. To drive the point home, I often give students both a published story by a friend and one of mine. The friend comes to class and leads the discussion on my piece, while I lead the discussion on his. The discussion is focused on what each writer intended with the story—with style, with emotion, with meaning. Then each of us has a chance to say what we tried to do, measuring our intentions against what the class was able to guess about our intentions.

Teacher Feedback

6. So much of my feedback on student writing is an effort to counteract the feedback they've gotten from teachers in the past—feedback focused on error and on "fixing" a problem rather than on finding creative paths to follow. I've asked both my basic writers and my creative writers to share bad teacher feedback—either really received in the past or imagined—to get a sense of what they don't find helpful. One class spontaneously compiled their details into a "What Not to Do" list for me as I read their work.

Revision

I adapt many revision exercises from my textbook with Marvin Diogenes (*Crafting Fiction*, Mayfield, 2001):

7. Choose a character you want to understand more fully. In the first person or close third person point of view, complete at least three of the following prompts, writing up to a paragraph for each one.

- "I still don't understand why I . . ." (He still didn't understand why . . .)
- "The best birthday I ever had was . . ." (The best birthday she ever had was . . .)

- "I'd like to look good in . . ." (He'd like to look good in . . .)
- "In elevators I always stand . . ." (In elevators he always stood . . .)
- "I'll never get caught . . ." (She'd never get caught . . .)
- "I used to be sure that . . . (He used to be sure that . . .)
- "By this time next year . . ."
- "A little thing I couldn't do without . . ." (A little thing he couldn't do without . . .)
- "I'm afraid of getting what I want because . . ." (He was afraid of getting what he wanted because . . .)
- "One thing I remember from school is . . ." (One thing she remembered from school was . . .)

8. Imagine two of your characters in a domestic setting; the setting can be one that they share or one that belongs mostly to one of the characters. For each of the activities listed below, describe one character doing the activity from the perspective of the other character. What does the observing character notice? How does the observing character interpret or judge the actions of the other?

   A. First, describe character B doing the following things from character A's point of view:

   - Watering a plant
   - Watching the news on television
   - Putting away groceries
   - Getting dressed on a Sunday morning
   - Sweeping the porch or patio or driveway
   - Talking on the telephone
   - Washing dishes
   - Drying hair after a bath or shower

   B. Second, describe character A doing the following things from character B's point of view:

   - Putting on shoes
   - Vacuuming
   - Reading the newspaper
   - Chopping vegetables to make a salad
   - Making the bed
   - Looking in a mirror before going to work
   - Folding laundry
   - Playing with the family pet

239

9. Make a list of all the characters who appear in your story; this list should include characters who are thought about by other characters, even if they haven't been shown yet. Then make another list for each scene in your story, listing the characters who interact in each scene. This exercise can show you groupings that you haven't explored yet; you might find that you have been avoiding certain groupings, keeping characters apart because you're not sure how they will behave with each other. These avoided interactions are often the key to moving the story forward into the next draft.

Reading

10. I'm always asking students what they're reading, or what they've read in the past that was memorable or influential. Sometimes I institutionalize this into a "What Are You Reading?" discussion during the last fifteen minutes of the last class of the week. Each student comes prepared to talk about one item (story, novel, nonfiction piece) that they've just read that week or that they read in the past, explaining what is impressive about it, what they learned about writing from it, and what they might in fact borrow in the future.

Publishing

11. One thing published writers do is give public readings. A culminating event in all my creative writing classes is a reading. We practice for it by watching readings on YouTube (from Anne Lamott to Tobias Wolff to Toni Morrison); by attending readings on campus or in the area; and by having formal weekly readings in class (brief—just a page or so—but with a podium). The final reading is usually at a local coffee shop, and friends and loved ones are invited.

Works Cited

Arca, Rosemary L. "Systems Thinking, Symbiosis, and Serve: The Road to Authority for Basic Writers." *Writing the Community: Concepts and Models for Service Learning in Composition.* Ed. Linda Adler-Kassner, Robert Crooks, and Ann Watters. Urbana, IL: NCTE, 2006. 133–42. Print.

Association of Writers and Writing Programs (AWP). "Recommendations on the Teaching of Creative Writing to Undergraduates." Program Director's Handbook. 2012. 20 June 2013. Web. <https://www.awpwriter.org/library/directors_handbook_recommendations_on_the_teaching_of_creative_writing_to_undergraduates>.

Bartholomae, David. "The Tidy House: Basic Writing in the American Curriculum." *Writing on the Margins: Essays on Composition and Teaching.* Boston: Bedford/St. Martin's, 2005. 312–26. Print.

Berthoff, Ann E. "Recognition, Representation, and Revision." Enos 545–56. Print.

Brannon, Lil, and C. H. Knoblauch. "On Students' Rights to Their Own Texts: A Model of Teacher Response." *College Composition and Communication* 33.2 (May 1982): 157–66. Print.

Butler, John. "Remedial Writers: The Teacher's Job as Corrector of Papers." Enos 557–64. Print.

Connors, Robert J. "Basic Writing Textbooks." Enos 259–74. Print.

Enos, Theresa, ed. *A Sourcebook for Basic Writing Teachers.* New York: Random House, 1987. Print.

Goen, Sugie, and Helen Gillotte-Tropp. "Integrating Reading and Writing: A Response to the Basic Writing 'Crisis.'" *Journal of Basic Writing* 22.2 (2003): 90–113. Print.

Halasek, Kay, and Nels P. Highberg. *Landmark Essays on Basic Writing.* Mahwah, NJ: Erlbaum, 2001. Print.

Heath, Shirley Brice. *Ways with Words: Life and Work in Communities and Classrooms.* Cambridge, UK: Cambridge UP, 1983. Print.

Jones, Ed. "Predicting performance in first-semester college basic writers: Revisiting the role of self-beliefs." *Contemporary Educational Psychology* 33.2 (2008): 209–38. Print.

Lees, Elaine O. "Evaluating Student Writing." *College Communication and Communication* 30.4 (1979): 370–74. Print.

Lees, Elaine O. "Proofreading as Reading, Errors as Embarrassments." Enos 216–30. Print.

Lunsford, Andrea. "Politics and Practices in Basic Writing." Enos 246–58. Print.

Mansfield, Margaret A. "Real World Writing and the English Curriculum." *College Composition and Communication* 44.1 (1993): 69–83. Print.

McCarthy, Patricia, Scott Meier, Regina Rinderer. "Self-Efficacy and Writing: A Different View of Self-Evaluation." *College Composition and Communication* 36.4 (1985): 465–71. Print.

Ritter, Kelly. *Before Shaughnessy: Basic Writing and Yale and Harvard, 1920–1960.* Carbondale: Southern Illinois UP, 2009. Print.

Rose, Mike. *Lives on the Boundary.* New York: Penguin, 1989. Print.

Rose, Mike. "Rigid Rules, Inflexible Plans, and the Stifling of Language: A Cognitivist Analysis of Writer's Block." *College Composition and Communication* 31.4 (1980): 389–401. Print.

Shaughnessy, Mina. "Basic Writing." *Teaching Composition: Ten Bibliographical Essays*. Ed. Gary Tate. Fort Worth: Texas Christian UP, 1976. 137–68. Print.

Sommers, Nancy. "Responding to Student Writing," *College Communication and Communication* 33.2 (May 1982): 148–56. Print.

11
Digital Technologies and Creative Writing Pedagogy

Bronwyn T. Williams

VISIT THE WEBPAGES of most university creative writing programs and you'll find similar images. Time and again you'll see pictures of print books and journals, of students in a classroom talking about the printed manuscripts in front of them, of writers giving readings from their books, even of students sitting in scenic campus settings, writing with pens on the paper of their journals. But you'll rarely see any images that include digital technology. There are no pictures of students at computers—even simply word processing—or of wikis or blogs or digital compositions. Even low-residency creative writing programs that depend on digital technology rely primarily on images of print on paper. What these images remind us is that, in the conception of creative writing faculty within the academy as well as in the public imagination, few academic endeavors may be more closely connected to the technology of print on paper than the creative writing classroom. The image of the creative writing class, a circle of desks where students and teacher discuss words on printed pages, is both grounded in traditional literacy technologies of the academy, but also reinforces a traditional conception of pedagogy where communication is controlled by the teacher. The creative writing teacher is not only the person with the experience and wisdom of writing, but also the gatekeeper and conduit to connections about publishing. Certainly a great many creative writing classes continue to run the way they have for decades, except that the works have been produced on word processors (and maybe now read by some students on smartphones).

Creative writing teachers have had the reputation—sometimes warranted, sometimes not—of resisting the integration of digital technologies into their pedagogies. The reductive depiction is of the creative writing classroom clinging desperately to ink, paper, and the face-to-face workshop as digital technologies transform the world around them. The perception is often that many creative writing faculty are, if not curmudgeonly Luddites, certainly dragging their feet in terms of engaging with digital technologies in their teaching. Of course, no discipline in the academy has been untouched by the ways in which digital technologies are changing everything from genre to composition to response to the relationship to audience and more. Some creative writing teachers have embraced these developments, while other developments have entered the classrooms unbidden and changed the way the teaching happens anyway.

The contrast between the traditional print-and-paper pedagogies of the creative writing classroom and what has happened with creative writing and digital media could not be more dramatic. With the advent of the Internet and the World Wide Web, there has been an explosion of creative writing activity and innovation. On fan fiction sites, writers build their stories while receiving crowd-sourced feedback from their audiences. Projects such as National Novel Writing Month (NaNoWriMo) engage thousands of writers in writing and responding to each other's work. Online journals break down the material constraints to publication and offer new models of distribution, while writers, whether on blogs or through e-books, increasingly choose to publish themselves. Meanwhile, digital storytelling, podcasts, and other multimodal approaches to texts change conceptions of genre and what should be defined as a creative writing text. What's more, students engage with digital media outside the classroom and such activities shape their writing and reading habits. It is imperative, then, to explore in both innovative and critical ways how best to connect digital technologies with creative writing pedagogy.

In this chapter I quickly chart the intersections of digital technologies and teaching. Then, rather than focusing on a few specific technologies or practices—which may quickly become outdated—I examine how concepts that digital media allow intersect with concepts particularly relevant to creative writing pedagogy. I focus on four central concepts: collaboration, multimodality, publishing, and sampling and remixing. These concepts will remain important elements of digital media even as specific technologies evolve. I will discuss digital media in terms of the affordances (Selfe and Hawisher 2004) they offer to teachers and writers. In other words, how are different media and technologies best suited to particular ends for writers and teachers? Considering these affordances raises important questions of how to approach digital media in terms of our goals for the creative writing classroom. Where do such affordances allow us to do things we do now more effectively? Where do they offer us new ways to think about writing and teaching? I illustrate how digital media concepts can connect with existing approaches to creative writing pedagogy and discuss how digital technologies also challenge those practices and provide new opportunities for how creative writing courses work.

Word Processing and Hypertext

As soon as computers began to be used for writing, there were attempts to address their use in teaching creative writing. As early as 1985, Mike Sharples, in *Cognition, Computers, and Creative Writing,* began to explore the effects of new technologies on student writing and to imagine how such changes could be used in teaching. Sharples, as is typical of early research in this area (Casella 1989), focused most of his work on the uses of word processing software for teaching of creating writing. During this same period there was a growth in computer software such as Storytree or Survive, developed as tools to help creative writers with composing and organization.

The first significant change in creative writing pedagogy came with the development of hypertext. Michael Joyce's "Afternoon, A Story" (1990) is marked as one of the first significant achievements in experimenting with what digital media could enable that would be different in terms of creative writing by creating a linked, nonlinear text. The story is a series of fragments of writing, connected with hyperlinks. The reader moves through the text by choosing links that move in multiple directions among the fragments, rather than in a more traditional linear narrative. The development of hypertext, at first created on disks for individual computers, generated a great deal of discussion about how narrative, authorship, and reading might evolve in a digital world (Douglass 1989; Henney 1988). If print-on-paper narrative conventionally "moves toward providing its readers with greater autonomy in deciding which developments and conclusions are more preferable or probable than others . . . hypertext presents its audience with discrete pieces of information and ellipses, requiring a participatory act by the reader nearly tantamount to the creative effort expended by the author" (Douglass 1989, 97). As is often the case in innovations of any kind, much of the most vocal discussion about hypertext was dominated by voices that viewed the new communication technologies in particularly hyperbolic utopian or dystopian terms. Over the years, however, more thoughtful discussions of how hypertext might fit into writing classrooms began to take place (Fischer 1996; Russell 1998; Monroe 1999; Howard 1999), although more of this scholarship focused on writing classes in general, rather than creative writing in particular. The software Storyspace, designed for the creation of hypertext, found use in some K–12 and university writing classrooms as a new way of approaching writing.

The discussion of associative structures of writing that made use of the capacity of computers to layer and link information led to discussions of how the experience of reading and writing on the screen was different from the technologies of print and paper. Proponents of hypertext (Russell 1998; Howard 1999; Stephenson 2011) argued that the associative connections that could be made by linking pieces of text disrupted the traditional linearity and narrative logic of print on the page. As Gunther Kress (2003) writes, "The ease with which texts can be brought into conjunction, and elements of texts reconstituted as new texts, changes the notion of authorship. If it was a myth to see the author as originator, it is now a myth that cannot any longer be sustained in this new environment" (6). The reader of a hypertext story could now easily make active choices that would disrupt the structures and hierarchies of meaning designed by the author.

Hypertext narratives, in their early forms of linked segments of words, did not gain much long-term traction in creative writing pedagogy as they were overtaken by new technological possibilities. Even as the possibilities created by links became an integral part of webpage design, the capacity of the Web to incorporate multiple media took the creation of online texts quickly beyond the print hypertext model. As online technologies were established that also allowed individuals to respond to each other, the development of what is often called Web 2.0 or New Media, the balance of agency between the author and reader became all the more fluid. Rather than be limited to choosing links in a hypertext, a reader could now be an active respondent or even collaborator with an author. The real emergence of hypertext came not in the composing of linked narratives by individual writers, but in the collaborative spaces of forums, wikis, and blogs. At the same time, interactive games and virtual communities further complicated the nature of narrative online. Now a person sitting at a computer could inhabit a character within a text and make decisions about the actions of those characters. Janet Murray (1997) argued that this capacity for shifting perspectives might lead to forms of literature that would combine the interactive capacities of games with the depth of character and style of traditional novels, plays, and poems. Although Murray's vision of the fusion of game and literature may not yet have taken place, the experimentation of digital creative writing has led to a wide and varied range of texts and genres, some of which I will address in the discussion of multimodality later in the chapter. In fact, Petrelli and Wright (2008) note the futility of trying to find a workable definition of "digital fiction" for their study of authors and editors. They note that some people or organizations point to any text composed on a computer, while others find multimodality to be a defining concept, and still others point to the interactive nature of texts to be essential.

Gaps in the Digital Conversations

It is possible, given the discussion above, to think that digital media have been an active, ongoing part of the discussions of creative writing pedagogy. Unfortunately, the scholarship in creative writing pedagogy remains remarkably unengaged with digital technologies. A search through the most recent AWP conference program reveals sessions on electronic publishing, but rare discussions of digital media in pedagogy sessions. In the journals such as *The Writer's Chronicle, New Writing: The International Journal for the Practice and Theory of Creative Writing,* or even the short-lived *Creative Writing: Teaching Theory and Practice,* there are only occasional articles here and there about digital media and writing (Gilligan and Street 2011; Harper 2011; McLoughlin 2009) but even fewer about digital media and creative writing pedagogy. Articles about creative writing and pedagogy continue to focus on questions such as how to compose print texts more effectively, with the only difference being that the focus has moved from basic word processing to discussing the use of organizational software such as Scrivener. Some articles discuss the new media writing of published authors as models for students (Koehler 2013; Smith 2012) and pieces addressing online publishing are not uncommon. In textbooks about teaching creative writing, digital technologies, when they are mentioned at all, tend to be covered in a single chapter (Nieves and Moxley 2012; Smith 2012). There have also been occasional articles that address some of the institutional issues in terms of digital media facing creative writing studies. Koehler (2013), for example, argues that digital creative writing studies can potentially integrate the work of literary criticism and writing studies in work of "digital craft criticism" that pays attention not only to the rhetorical affordances of digital media, but to the aesthetic implications as well. Harper (2012), meanwhile, notes the ways in which digital media can allow for collaboration over distance, both as teaching and as a creative endeavor for creative writers. Still, articles such as these remain fairly uncommon.

What is important to understand is much of the conversation about creative writing pedagogy continues to be conducted as if the technologies of writing and reading had not changed since 1985. In the recent collection *Does the Writing Workshop Still Work?* (Donnelly 2010), for example, the only time digital media are addressed at any length in the sixteen chapters on creative writing pedagogy is a brief discussion in Donnelly's introduction about whether digital media has had a deleterious effect on students' attention spans. It is entirely possible that there is a much broader range of practices involving digital media taking place in creative writing courses that is not reflected in publications about pedagogy. The fact that courses such as "Experimental Writing Workshop" are offered at the University of Massachusetts–Amherst and "Digital Storytelling" at George Mason University, to name just two examples (Koehler 2013), would seem to be an indication that more is happening than is being written about. Still, the lack of a scholarly conversation about digital media and creative writing is disappointing and means that all teachers would benefit from a wider circulation of these practices and ideas.

By contrast to the limited impact new technologies seem to have made on creative writing pedagogy, outside of the university, digital media have had a profound and transformative impact on creative writing. Online technologies have changed every aspect of creative writing, from invention to publication. While self-publishing has been one important part of the digital revolution, it is also important to understand how online technologies have facilitated and encouraged the writing of countless people. It isn't difficult to find websites offering writing advice, communities of writers trading feedback and response, and social media networks for writers in every genre on sites such as Facebook and Twitter. As one example, fan fiction sites offer a form of writing workshop for the thousands of people involved, where work is read, responded to, and revised. Other sites, in other genres, take similar approaches. The innovation and energy taking place in creative writing online is breathtaking and global. Of course, writing and discussions of writing on such a vast scale mean that the quality and utility of what is written and responded to varies widely. Simply put, it can be as easy to find bad writing online as good. Still, many writers produce compelling work online and use digital media in productive and innovative ways that largely remain outside of the conversation about how writing is taught in universities. Kathleen Yancey notes that students writing with digital media outside the classroom "have learned—in this case, to write, to think together, to organize and to act within these forums—largely without instruction, and more to the point here, largely without *our* instruction" (2004, 301). While there is scholarly attention being paid to online creative writing practices (Black 2008; Gee 2004; Williams 2009), it tends to be more ethnographic-style studies of literacy practices rather than explorations of how connections can be made between out-of-school writing and teaching and what is happening in the classroom or workshop.

The literacy-focused studies of online creative writing illustrate that the rarity with which the scholarship in creative writing pedagogy addresses the uses of digital media stands in contrast to the complex and varied conversation that has been taking place in rhetoric and composition and literacy studies over the past quarter century. Journals such as *Computers and Composition, Kairos,* and *E-Learning* have focused on how digital technologies can be used in teaching writing. In addition there have been numerous books written on the issues of digital media and writing, as well as articles in the central journals in the field, such as *College English* and *College Composition and Communication.* This rich, ongoing conversation began with questions of how computers might influence the act of writing— hence the names such as *Computers and Composition*—and soon expanded to incorporate examinations of how computers and, eventually, online digital media could be used as pedagogical tools in writing classrooms.

Today many first-year and professional writing courses include the use of some kind of digital technology, and it is not unusual to see such courses taught in computer classrooms (or to see images on first-year writing websites of students and teachers using computers). In general, the fields of rhetoric and composition and literacy studies have heeded the call Cynthia Selfe made in the 1990s: "Composition studies faculty have a much larger and more complicated obligation to fulfill—that of trying to understand and make sense of, to pay attention to, how technology is now inextricably linked to literacy and literacy education in this country" (1999, 414). As a consequence, many scholars have explored how technology shapes composing practices from invention to revision, both in and out of school, as well as conducting scholarship on hypertext, webpage writing, and multimodal writing. At the same time, other scholars have focused on how digital technologies can be used for teaching through peer-editing software, distance learning, collaborative writing, and online publication such as blogs and additional social media. It's not possible to review here the broad range of literature on digital technology and writing pedagogy, but some of the ideas and research from rhetoric and composition can be productive in the creative writing classroom, and I will discuss them in more detail below.

Yet just as the scholarship about creative writing pedagogy rarely includes digital technology, the robust conversation about computers and writing pedagogy has rarely addressed the creative writing classroom. There have been some notable exceptions. Adam Koehler's (2013) essay in *College English*, "Digitizing Craft: Creative Writing Studies and New Media," offers a thoughtful exploration of how digital media can figure in the institutional identity of creative writing studies. The online journal *Kairos* devoted a 1999 special issue to hypertext fiction and poetry, and journals such as *Computers and Composition* have published the occasional article connected to creative writing issues (Brown 2012; Jones 2002; Stephenson 2011). It's also important to note that some articles in K–12 writing pedagogy have addressed digital creative writing pedagogy and offer some useful ideas (Callahan and King 2011; Dymoke and Hughes 2009; Gerber and Hughes 2011), though do not usually make the connection to university-level approaches or issues.

The focus of this chapter is not to make anecdotal and possibly reductive guesses as to why there has been such a difference between the way creative writing and rhetoric and composition have incorporated digital media into writing pedagogy. I would rather make a call, as others have done before me, for more conversation and integration among the various writing-related fields in the academy. As I've argued before (Williams 2010), we would all benefit from a more capacious and inclusive conception of writing and literacy studies that includes a variety of fields. Such large-scale arguments about the field are not the focus of this chapter, however. Instead I want to turn to exploring where digital media offer opportunities for the kinds of writing and teaching valued in creative writing.

Approaches to Digital Media and Pedagogy

As far back as 1985, Sharples recognized that computers might offer possibilities for teaching creative writing beyond word processing. In talking about Writer's Aid, a software package for word processing and organization, he imagined other uses for computers: "The Writer's Aid could be one of a set of 'Tools for Learning,' a package of software to help a child to acquire, store and manipulate knowledge, to investigate language, sound and pictures, and to communicate at a distance with other children" (109). Sharples recognizes, at this early stage, what Lev Manovich (2000) points out fifteen years later, that as soon as information is encoded in digital ones and zeroes, it has the potential to be changed into a variety of representations and transported more easily. In thinking about digital technologies and writing pedagogy, then, it is important that we not focus too narrowly on the popular technologies of the moment. Such technologies are changing so rapidly that what seems to be the "hot" technology or website of a moment can very quickly disappear (MySpace, for example). Or, new technologies such as mobile devices can change the nature of how and when and why we use digital media. The important question to consider is, what do digital technologies allow us to do more effectively?

Four ways in which we can think about the affordances offered by digital media are in terms of Response and Collaboration, Publication and Distribution, Multimodality, and Sampling and Remixing. The first two categories mark ways in which digital media offer changes to activities, such as collaboration and response or publishing and distribution, that have always been central to creative writing pedagogy. The second two areas of Multimodality and Sampling and Remixing are substantially different from the traditional focus of the creative writing classroom, but worth exploring in terms of contemporary creative writing courses.

Response and Collaboration

Response is at the core of teaching writing. In the creative writing classroom the typical workshop setting elicits response from both peers and instructors. Traditionally, and as is often still the case, this response involved face-to-face conversations and annotations on paper drafts. Along with the importance of response in offering a sense of what works, or doesn't, with a particular audience, it is almost of equal value to a writer to learn through responding thoughtfully to other writers' work. Digital technologies both enable the kinds of response that have been part of writing workshops, and they offer enhanced opportunities for other kinds of response in other settings.

Perhaps the most significant changes digital media bring to response involve distance, time, and modes of responding. In the print-on-paper writing course of the past, most response was limited to the confines of the classroom. Outside of a workshop it was almost impossible to get response except when an editor replied to a submission or a review was published about a book. Today, however, response has become a central element of life online, including creative writing. The audience online is, more often than not, no longer a group of silent readers. Instead, words and other content posted online often are created with response as an integral function of the text. Whether on a blog or wiki or social media, the relationship between creator and audience is now often dialogic. In some areas, such as some online forums or wikis, "within the communities that engage in the collaborative creation and extension of information and knowledge . . . the role of the 'consumer' and even that of the 'end user' have long disappeared and the distinctions between producers and users of content have faded into comparative insignificance" (Bruns 2008, 2). Indeed, among many younger people, there is an expectation that response will be possible, whether they decide to engage in it or not (Williams 2009). The result of this dialogic capacity of text is that the writer not only can imagine an audience, but also hear from it at different points along the writing process in ways not possible before, while the reader knows that, at any time, talking back to the writer—or talking to other writers—is possible. Within a given writing situation, the reader and writer often shift roles back and forth as a text is read, responded to, and revised.

I believe in the value of face-to-face response in a classroom and would not argue for eliminating it. Digital technologies, however, allow for different forms and spaces for response. For example, digital technologies allow response to expand beyond the classroom in productive ways. In its most straightforward form, circulating drafts by e-mail before a class session, on which students can comment in tracked changes, gives individuals more time to read and respond to drafts, though it essentially is just an electronic reconstruction of the traditional workshop. What is potentially more exciting is that other forms of response outside the classroom can productively disrupt the traditional timelines of the workshop. For example, a class Twitter account (or blog or wiki) can create a space for ongoing, informal response to take place before and after a piece is talked about in class. Online responses before a class session can offer the class, and the instructor, a set of ideas from which to begin the in-class discussion— whether continuing the conversation that began online, or pushing off in a new direction if the online conversation seems to have covered one concern thoroughly. Once the in-class session is over, the opportunity to continue the conversation can also be productive. We've all experienced having an insight about a work after a workshop, and wanting to communicate it to the author before the next class session, and digital communications create a space for that. In the traditional workshop, conversations about a particular draft often ended with the end of the class session. Digital media allow for conversations to continue as works, and responses to those works and responses to the responses, evolve during the semester. Different technologies privilege different kinds of response. A Twitter exchange will be less formal and enforce brevity and immediacy. A wiki site allows for response through which it is easy for the author and others to keep track of who made the responses and when. Individual blog sites allow for more length as well as response more focused on an individual writer.

Although many in creative writing may scoff at the material posted on fan fiction sites, the model of online reading and response presented on these sites offers approaches of ongoing response and revision that could be adopted in writing courses. Most fan fiction writers have "beta readers," experienced writers who read and respond to work before it is published. Writers often search around before finding a beta reader—or readers—with whom they can establish a working relationship. Writers gaining in experience, in turn, often become beta readers themselves and the community of response grows. Once work is published, active response does not end as readers often post reviews of published pieces. Writers talk about how reviews can lead them to revise work further, or shape their future writing (Black 2008; Williams 2009). Clearly the model of response used on fan fiction sites drew from the creative writing workshop, but it also allows a way to see how this model of response to writing can work in digital environments.

Digital technologies also offer the possibility of using different modes of communication to alter and enhance how readers respond to writing. For example, it is now possible to create digital audio responses to work and circulate comments to writers or entire classes. Talking through responses as one reads through a text offers a writer a different way of experiencing the immediate impact of the work on a reader. Audio responses also allow for a difference in tone and formality. Digital technologies permit the embedding of links or even images in written responses so that writers can easily access resources or models of writing. Most important, using different modes for response allows individuals to employ other ways of creating knowledge and communication. Images, sound, and multimodal writing can engage a wider range of metaphor and representation in order to challenge students in their writing.

The same technologies that have facilitated a fluid and dialogic approach to response online create opportunities for collaboration among student writers. Collaborative writing has not necessarily been the focus of creative writing classrooms, which have more typically focused on the model of the individual writer creating autonomous texts. At the same time, however, other fields have focused on the academic and social benefits of having students work cooperatively on projects. Collaboration in creative writing can certainly help students learn how to work together, shaping ideas through negotiation and dialogue. The more exciting possibilities of collaborative work in creative writing, however, may exist in the way collaboration shakes up the traditional conceptions of single authorship and challenges students to rethink ideas of voice and point of view. Whether on blogs, wikis, social media, or other digital media, students writing together must explicitly confront questions of vision and voice. Like other collaborative art forms such as theater or film, writing becomes a process where writers must consider other potential positions or points of view, as well as articulate clearly their own. They learn from others' strengths, as well as come to more clearly recognize some of their own. Collaborative writing might only be used at the brainstorming stage, or could be used to create larger pieces, whether in fragments or more coherent narratives. Different media create different possibilities. The speed of Twitter might be better suited for invention work, while a wiki allows for the creation of texts with a more integrated collaboration.

Collaboration through digital media also allows for a form of problem solving. As Henry Jenkins (2006) has pointed out, online technologies have created spaces for "collective intelligence." The point of collective intelligence is not that everyone online knows everything, but that people all can contribute some knowledge and help solve mutual problems. Online forums, whether on medical issues or popular culture or home repair, for example, bring people together who can offer responses to questions and ideas and collaborate on finding possible answers. Using digital media as a way of employing the collective intelligence of students in a class is a way of working through writing or other course-related problems as a course is proceeding. Resources and links can be shared, such as connections to other forums, or simply brief and more timely responses to a writer trying to work through a particularly knotty place in a story or poem. Again, different technologies, whether forums on course-management systems or social media, offer differences in speed and depth in terms of these conversations. It is also true that online conversations can turn negative and harmful very quickly. As Jenkins points out, the often unorganized, even unruly, nature of collective intelligence is both a strength and a weakness. In the classroom, then, it is useful to establish models and ground rules for the kinds of interactions that are expected in this kind of collaboration in a class (Sidler, Overman, and Morris 2007; Takayoshi and Huot 2003). That said, conversation and response are crucial in a good writing classroom, and digital media allow for sharing and reworking texts and response in ways that are more flexible and egalitarian.

Publication and Distribution

If there is any area where digital media have been discussed at length in creative writing, it is in terms of publication and distribution. A robust discussion has occurred about how platforms such as e-books will affect the profession of writing (Goldfarb 2012; Lacey 2010; Smith 2012). Less discussion has ensued about how to think about digital publication in terms of pedagogy. One of the obvious benefits for students of online technologies is the ability for students to post work for an audience outside the classroom. Posting by itself is not enough, however, and there are more productive ways to think about how publishing and distribution can be used in teaching.

One aspect of publishing online can be connected to the previous discussion of response. In the traditional print-on-paper paradigm, publishing was something that happened as an end process, after response, revision, and editing happened backstage. Now, however, with the capacity for digital response that I previously discussed, it is possible to think of publishing as a process. In other words, as with the example of fan fiction sites, a work can be published in stages and receive response as those pieces are published. For example, students posting their drafts of stories or poems on a blog can use that space simultaneously for publication and for response and revision. Such a model requires a different conception of what is meant by "publication" where it is regarded as a process that includes revision, as well as a willingness to live with the idea of the "published" work as more impermanent and malleable and potentially under continuing development and revision. In some ways this is not as radical an idea as it may initially seem, as many writers have revised and republished works in the past. As a pedagogical tool, the idea of publishing as a process emphasizes the importance of response and revision. In addition, student writers become more explicitly conscious of audience and how audiences may vary in different contexts. Finally, publishing as a process may help students regard publishing as a less-harrowing, high-stakes endeavor.

A different aspect of digital media and publishing that can be useful in a creative writing course is the idea of *transmedia*. Transmedia texts are works about the same content that are produced in different media and modes. In popular culture, transmedia storytelling has come to mean a world in which a film is just one narrative in a fictional world, and it is complemented by additional narratives in games or online spaces (Jenkins 2006). In terms of creative writing, an example might be a person who would write a poem and also create a video on the same themes or metaphors. The two works could be encountered and interpreted independently, yet when both were read would mutually complement and extend the meaning of each text. Another example might be of a writer who creates a short story on one site and a linked, complementary graphic narrative on another. While I will discuss the value of multimodal work below, it is important to see how different digital publishing platforms, such as blogs and You-Tube, can allow for transmedia approaches to creative writing. A writing portfolio for a course does not have to be restricted to print on paper now, but can use multiple media to explore different aspects of the same ideas, emotions, or narratives.

Another aspect of digital publishing that should be part of creative writing pedagogy is teaching students how to think strategically and rhetorically about where to publish, and how to be read. The egalitarian promise of online technologies is that many of the walls to distributing work to a reading audience have come down. It is true that, sitting at a laptop, anyone can put out writing to be read by others. It is also true that, with so much writing and other content being posted every minute of every day, it is very easy for the work that is posted to vanish unnoticed in the vast ocean of online content. Or, to put it another way, a popular T-shirt says, "More people have read my T-shirt than your blog." As a number of scholars have pointed out, it is a misunderstanding to think we are in an "information economy." Information is plentiful and easy to access. Instead, with so much information flooding the digital world, it is more accurate to think of the vital factor as being "attention" (Knobel and Lankshear 2007; Lanham 2007). In other words, publishing your work is not enough; you have to find a way to get people to read it. (Although the anxiety that occasionally surfaces among creative writers that online technologies are producing "too many" writers strikes me as bizarre. People who write are people who read and we should be celebrating, not worrying about, an increase in their numbers. I can't imagine people in other creative endeavors ever worry about there being "too many" musicians, or dancers, or cooks.)

Part of our work in the creative writing classroom has always been helping students understand how to reach an audience for their writing, by teaching them about how to identify and submit work to journals or agents or publishers. Such discussions of publishing now should include ideas about how to reach an audience online. It is useful to talk about how to identify a good online journal, or site, on which to publish, or to explain how social media sites can be used to connect people to published writing, or how to connect to groups online that can draw readers to published work. Ridolfo and DeVoss (2009) talk about the necessity of considering "rhetorical velocity," when publishing online, in which the composer writes with a strategic awareness of how the work may circulate or be reused online. Making these kinds of connections, and using sites such as social media effectively, is part of the world of being a writer today and part of the education we should be providing students.

Multimodality

If response and publishing are familiar ground for creative writing pedagogy, multimodality is largely new territory. Since the advent of the printing press, writers have generally had one option for creating work, and that has been print on paper, which remains an important medium that offers distinctive opportunities for a creative artist. The explosion of digital media, however, offers choices in how to communicate ideas to an audience. Video, sound, and images, which were once limited to the capital-intensive companies that could produce and distribute them, are now available to anyone with a computer. As Kathleen Welch (1999) has pointed out, digital media has highlighted again the importance of the delivery of ideas. We have choices to make now, when it comes to communicating ideas, with different modes offering different affordances in terms of communicating our ideas. For example, while print on paper may excel at portraying the internal emotions or consciousness of a character, video allows for the layers of information to be apprehended quickly and simultaneously. In other areas of teaching writing, courses are helping students understand how to think critically and creatively about the affordances of different modes and media, and then to produce work in more than just one mode (Selfe 2007; Wysocki 2004).

In creative writing, one individual can now produce creative work in more than one mode. Jane Nelson in *Wide and Widely Branded*, for example, combines animations, music, video, and words to create an interactive, multimodal piece in which the elements work together to explore issues of space, history, and identity in Australia (Smith 2012). Other writers produce print texts but also embark on digital storytelling projects. Some writers produce their own video book trailers to promote their work, while others create and post podcasts of their work. Some online videos are combinations of poetry, music, and image, while others are more in the tradition of the literary essay of exploring an idea through a combination of memoir and reflection. Digital media allow for an exploration of multimodal composing that is challenging all of us to keep up with it. As Petrelli and Wright (2008) note in their study on digital fiction, trying to define what multimodal works are in a time when the possibilities are evolving so quickly is a challenge in itself. New genres and new ways of creating and portraying imaginative work are emerging online virtually every day. The definition of what it means to "write" is changing. Increasingly we will come to regard "writing" to include both print, but other forms of composing as well.

Engaging with multimodality in the classroom makes some creative writing instructors anxious or resistant. They may feel they lack the expertise to teach or evaluate modes other than print. They may feel that the creative writing classroom is an important place to focus on print and the affordances it provides and that other modes of communication are only a distraction. They may feel that print remains superior to other modes, or that modes such as sound and video are too closely connected to popular culture. For those, and other, reasons, I often hear from writing teachers about a reluctance or resistance to multimodal writing. I am not unsympathetic to these concerns and have shared parts of all of them at different times. When new technologies of literacy and technology emerge, they are disruptive because they do alter cultural practices and values (Cope and Kalantzis 2000; Kittler 1999; Stephens 1998). Something is always lost, even as other things are gained. Ever since Socrates argued against print literacy, there have always been individuals who do not trust the innovations and lament at what will fade away because of new technologies (Stephens 1998). The concerns about change are often valid—print literacy led to less memorization and, in turn, the decline of the epic poem; the telephone and e-mail meant the end of the telegraph—but other times only reflect an anxiety about change and nostalgia for the imagined past. At the same time, there are always those who embrace the new technologies with fervent predictions of the great, and relentlessly positive, changes they will bring to our lives. The truth, as always, lies somewhere in between dystopia and utopia. It takes time and exploration for new genres to emerge and great work to emerge in those genres, and creative writing should be part of that process. Rather than giving in to the anxieties about change, or accepting at face value the grandest claims for the future, we should be working with our students to figure out how other modes of communication fit within our work as creative writers.

Making multimodal work part of a creative writing course may mean having to think about some other ways of communicating ideas and emotions. For example, Gunther Kress points out that new multimodal literacies mean considering visual arrangement as well as the arrangement of words in a sentence. Where we place things in space has meaning: "Placing something centrally means that other things will be marginal, at least relatively speaking" (2). We will have to consider how visual rhetoric and poetics work as well as those we have learned through words (Handa 2004; Hill and Helmers 2004). Other writers have focused on how writing can engage with sound and podcasts (Keller 2007; Selfe 2009). Effective and helpful scholarship on the grading and assessment of multimodal work is available to help those of us initially intimidated at evaluating work outside of our backgrounds (Borton and Huot 2007; Yancey 2004). In addition there are books that contain straightforward, nuts-and-bolts advice and support for creating multimodal compositions (Burn 2009; Lankshear and Knobel 2010). These citations only scratch the surface of the work available on teaching multimodal texts. Increasingly, resources are available online, such as the Center for Digital Storytelling, that offer valuable resources for both instructors and students.

Even if the production of multimodal texts does not become a central part of a creative writing course, it can still contribute to the pedagogy. For example, if students are asked to take a print text and "remediate" it—translate it in to another medium—it can offer them insights and metaphors they can bring back to the revisions of their print text (Williams 2014). Something as simple as finding images online to remediate a work as a collage on a Tumblr site can help students re-see and reimagine what they are writing about in print, engaging with new images, new metaphors, and new structures.

Sampling and Remix

A final way to consider the use of digital media in teaching creative writing comes through practices of sampling and remixing. Most people in creative writing now work from the understanding that no work is completely original. We all work from the influences, references, and intertextual connections of the work we have encountered before. We may write our own story of love or death or alienation or farce, but we draw on conventions, images, ideas, and other elements of writing we have read in the past. As writers, we take from that past and weave it together with our ideas into something new. Of course, some writers borrow more explicitly from the characters or themes of stories and poems that have come before them, and, going back to Shakespeare, we understand that is part of the nature of creative writing. In recent years, however, the question of sampling and remixing to create new work has become more explicit and more contentious. In some artistic fields, such as music (especially hip-hop), sampling has become a central part of the artistic ethos: "Hip hop producers don't try to pretend that they wrote or performed all the sounds on their records, but instead pride themselves on their unique recombination of sources within a new composition" (Hess 2004). And some writers have worked with more explicit sampling and remixing. One recent example from creative writing is David Shields's *Reality Hunger: A Manifesto* (2010) in which he used unattributed quotations to create a new text through a form of collage. Shields's work resulted in significant argument and debate about the "creative" nature of the work.

Digital media have made copying, sampling, and remixing commonplace. The same qualities of digital technologies that allow for copying and distributing work also make it easy to copy and rework into something new. Sampled and remixed videos on YouTube such as "40 Inspirational Speeches in Two Minutes," which mixes together bits from such speeches in film to create a new text, have become a genre of their own. Social media pages, such as Facebook, are often collages of sampled and reused images, words, and music that individuals use to create collages of identity (Williams 2009). And memes have become brief compositions of images and words, whose popularity stem at least in part from the participatory nature of the phenomenon—everyone gets to take part (Knobel and Lankshear 2007). Whether we choose to acknowledge it or not, it is clear that we all now live in a culture of sampling and remix. What's more, for our students—who may be actively engaged in these activities, at least on social media pages if nowhere else—the aesthetics and ethics of sampling and remixing may be very different than they are for some instructors. I want to stress that I am not making a moral judgment but simply pointing out the results of new and emerging practices of reading and writing. In fact, the ability to copy and paste digital material has blurred the lines between reading and writing (Williams 2009) in ways that have significant implications for how we talk about those practices with students. If a student sitting at a computer can switch from reading material on a website, to copying it, to pasting it on another site or document, all within a few quick clicks, then we are facing new ways of thinking about interpreting and creating.

We have to be aware, as instructors, of how perceptions of writing and ownership may have changed. What's more, part of this change may involve thinking in different ways about the impermanence of texts in a world of sampling and remix. And the culture of remix that is most prevalent around us is deeply embedded in popular culture. So it may also be useful not only to think about the ways in which the content of popular culture has become a resource many draw on to create new texts, but also to consider how the experiences with the rhetorical conventions of popular remix are shaping how students approach their own creative work (Burn 2009; Knobel and Lankshear 2007; Williams 2014).

Using sampling and remix explicitly in a creative writing class, whether as things to read or as assignments to create, can engage students in thinking about how they read and draw on work, and how they use what they have encountered to make something new. Digital media, with the capacity for creating links and associative structures, also allow for explorations of collage and mosaic-like structures that can be exciting and challenging in the classroom. Taking apart and reworking an existing genre, like a movie trailer (Burn 2009), to tell a new story, create new images, teaches about narrative structure and genre conventions in innovative ways.

The growth of sampling and remixing has led to many debates covering everything from intellectual property to the nature of creativity. One of the simplest, yet perhaps most important, acts we can do in our classrooms is to engage students in conversations about these ideas over the course of a semester. If sampling has made us ask questions about creativity and ownership of ideas, where does a new story or poem or play come from? If digital media allow us to sample and remix some other person's work, what does that mean about the stability of a text? Is the work never really finished? Never fully whole? And, if any work can be sampled and remixed and re-re-re-remixed, what is the "work" in the end anyway? Not all the work involving digital media and the creative writing classroom necessarily has to happen on computers.

It is a mistake to think that we have a choice about "bringing" digital media into a creative writing course. In a world where most students walk about with powerful hand-held computers, and all of us encounter, time and again during a day, digital technologies that mediate our lives, the digital world enters our classes whether we want it to or not. Instead, what we have are choices we must make. It is a defensible position to say that, in a world where digital media is pervasive, the creative writing classroom should be a space for exploring the distinctive affordances of print on paper. In the digital world of speed and rapid juxtaposition, having a space for slowing down in writing and reading is a justifiable argument. If an instructor chooses to have a print-on-paper classroom, I think it would be helpful to the students for the instructor to explain why this is the choice she or he is making for the course, so that students can understand that there is a rationale behind the decision, and not just a reflexive resistance.

I am persuaded, however, that addressing the advances and affordances of digital media needs to be part of our job as writing teachers. The world of writing—the world of *creative* writing—is changing all around us, because of digital media. Ways of producing and distributing texts are changing. Habits of reading are changing, and possibly habits of mind as well. If we think we can draw stable lines between different modes of expression, leaving print narrative and poetry over here and multimodal digital work over there, we are engaged in a futile effort. Instead we should recognize that creative work is becoming ever more fluid and multimodal and that, in the near future, artists will routinely move from one medium or mode to another, depending on what they want to express. This is an evolution from the way that so many writers have for centuries moved between genres such as poetry, fiction, drama, and the essay. I would argue that our job is not to try to maintain boundaries, but to be central figures in the educational journeys of our students as we help them explore the creative—and digital—world around them in inspired and imaginative ways.

Appendix: Ways to Engage Digital Media in the Creative Writing Classroom

In addition to the ideas presented below, many good resources address the practical, nuts-and-bolts details of using digital media in teaching writing (Burn 2009; Lankshear and Knobel 2010; Nieves and Moxley 2012).

Response and Collaboration

Student Response. Multiple technologies now offer ways for students to respond to writing out of class. Three popular technologies offer different opportunities for student response. All of these sites offer the possibility of linking among posts and to outside resources. All of these technologies also allow for the insertion of links and images that may provide useful additional resources or other modes of response for students. A note: While course management systems, such as Blackboard, may offer these functions, online spaces that are easier to navigate—and free—such as Twitter, Wikispaces, or Wordpress, will create a much more productive and engaged classroom.

- Microblogs, such as Twitter, offer spaces for quick and fluid discussions. The strength of such sites is speed and the ability to build conversations about linked ideas. Microblogs can be particularly effective for brainstorming and invention activities and mini workshops. The 140-character limit of a site such as Twitter also encourages concise and focused comments.
- Blogs, such as Wordpress, have the space for longer posts, as well as the functionality to include comments at the end. Such sites can be better at creating opportunities for lengthier posts and responses. Blogs may be particularly well suited for building a portfolio of work over the course of a semester. They can also be used for informal writing, journaling, and reading responses.
- Wikis are particularly well suited for collaborative writing. A wiki will track the changes made by participants, but also allow for individuals to revise and edit others' words. This kind of site is effective for editing work, invention exercises, or collaborative writing. Collaborative writing projects on wikis help students work on negotiating voice and point of view. Editing exercises allow students to help each other with the polishing of writing projects.

Collective Intelligence. The key to using crowd-sourcing in a classroom is to establish a sense of community—and sometimes some ground rules—and to help students understand when they can use the space to solve problems. Online forums offer spaces where students can post questions about, and get answers to, everything from course logistics, to how to solve a particular writing issue that comes up outside of class. Wikis offer spaces where students can combine information. For example, a wiki page of good introductions to short stories or effective metaphors would allow students to compile such resources, including links to other pages, if they like.

Publication and Distribution

Transmedia Writing. Ask students to create different materials that are part of the same project: for example, a poem, a video, and a creative wiki that are all part of the same set of ideas or themes, but can all stand on their own as individual works of art. The pieces are linked and can be read either together or separately. Have students reflect on the experience of exploring the themes in different media.

Gaining Attention. Ask students to commit to either posting a finished work online, or creating a class publication. As part of the project, have the students create a plan for drawing people to the site. For example, posts on Twitter accounts could be linked to the publication, or a Facebook page could be created about the publication. Links to the site can be circulated online, or QR codes could be created and posted on campus. Have students track the "rhetorical velocity" of how the social media efforts bring people to the site. Most social media pages, including blogs and Facebook, can track the number of visits to a page.

Online Writing Conventions and Genres. Ask students to explore online writing sites and forums and see what the conventions and rules are for responding and taking part. Have students visit different online writing sites—from literary to fan fiction—and to see how those sites create and reproduce their genres and communities.

Multimodality

Remediation. Ask students to reproduce a poem or narrative in a different medium—turning the poem into a video, or the story into a webpage, etc. Have them use the experience to think about ways of revising the original print work, and then reflect on the differences in working in various media. Which medium seemed most effective for communicating particular ideas or emotions?

Podcasts. Students can create podcasts of their work. The easiest thing to do is to simply create readings of the work and post them online for others to hear. But podcasts can also include other sound or music, and students can be encouraged to see how the affordances of sound, voice, and music can alter and enhance the work they have written.

Graphic Works. Students can create their own graphic works easily. Images can be embedded in text on everything from word-processing software to PowerPoint to online blogs such as Tumblr. Have students make the words and images work in a complementary, integrated way, and not as a set of unrelated elements.

Story Trailers or Book Posters. Ask students to create video "trailers"—like movie trailers—or posters using software available online, for their stories or poems. Examples can be found online.

Digital Storytelling. There is no end to the kinds of digital texts students can create in the classroom. But the digital storytelling sites that are widely available online allow for one way of approaching working with narratives and poetry online.

Sampling and Remix

Sampled Narrative or Poem. Ask students to create a sampled work by drawing from images, music, and video online. This can allow them to think about the nature of creativity and how their work builds on the work of others. Then have the students create new work that builds from the ideas or themes of the sampled work, but uses their own words and images and sound and have them reflect on the experiences.

Works Cited

Black, Rebecca W. *Adolescents and Online Fan Fiction.* London: Peter Lang, 2008. Print.

Borton, Sonya C., and Brian Huot. "Responding and Assessing." Selfe 99–112. Print.

Brown, James J. "Composition in the Dromosphere." *Computers and Composition* 29 (2012): 79–91. Print.

Bruns, Axel. *Blogs, Wikipedia, Second Life, and Beyond.* London: Peter Lang, 2008. Print.

Burn, Andrew. *Making New Media: Creative Production and Digital Literacies.* London: Peter Lang, 2009. Print.

Callahan, Meg, and Jennifer M. King. "Classroom Remix: Patterns of Pedagogy in a Techno-Literacies Poetry Unit." *Journal of Adolescent and Adult Literacy* 55.2 (2011): 134–44. Print.

Casella, Vicki. "Poetry and Word Processing Inspire Good Writing." *Instructor* 98.9 (1989): 28. Print.

Cope, Bill, and Mary Kalantzis, eds. *Multiliteracies: Literacy, Learning, and the Design of Social Futures.* London: Routledge, 2000. Print.

Donnelly, Dianne. *Does the Writing Workshop Still Work?* Bristol, UK: Multilingual Matters, 2010. Print.

Donnelly, Dianne, and Graeme Harper. *Key Issues in Creative Writing.* Bristol, UK: Multilingual Matters, 2012. Print.

Douglass, Jane Yellowlees. "Wandering through the Labyrinth: Encountering Interactive Fiction." *Computers and Composition* 6.3 (1989): 93–101. Print.

Dymoke, Sue, and Janette Hughes. "Using a poetry wiki: How can the medium support pre-service teachers of English in their professional learning about writing poetry and teaching poetry writing in a digital age?" *English Teaching: Practice and Critique* 8.3 (2009): 91–106. Print.

Fischer, Katherine M. "Down the Yellow Chip Road: Hypertext Portfolios in Oz." *Computers and Composition* 13.2 (1996): 169–83. Print.

Gee, James Paul. *Situated Language and Learning: A Critique of Traditional Schooling*. London: Routledge, 2004. Print.

Gerber, Hannah R, and Debra P Price. "Twenty-First-Century Adolescents, Writing, and New Media: Meeting the Challenge with Game Controllers and Laptops." *English Journal* 101.2 (2011): 68–73. Print.

Gilligan, Shauna Busto, and Karen Lee Street. "Critical Reflection on Creative Collaborations: Imagining the Image and Wording the Work." *New Writing: The International Journal for the Practice and Theory of Creative Writing* 8.1 (2011): 43–58. Print.

Goldfarb, Ronald. "What Writers Need to Know about Electronic Publishing." *The Writer's Chronicle* (Summer 2012). Print.

Handa, Carolyn. *Visual Rhetoric in a Digital World*. Boston: Bedford/St. Martin's, 2004. Print.

Harper, Graeme. "'Unmade' Virtual Collaboration Creation Report on an International Experiment." *New Writing: The International Journal for the Practice and Theory of Creative Writing* 8.3 (2011): 321–31. Print.

Hess, Mickey. *Is Hip Hop Dead? The Past, Present, and Future of America's Most Wanted Music*. Westport, CT: Greenwood Press, 2007. Print.

Hill, Charles A., and Marguerite Helmers. *Defining Visual Rhetorics*. Mahwah, NJ: Lawrence Erlbaum, 2004. Print.

Howard, Diane. "The Dynamics of Constructing and Reconstructing On-line Identities." *Kairos* 4.1 (1999). Print.

Jenkins, Henry. *Convergence Culture: Where Old and New Media Collide*. New York: New York UP, 2006. Print.

Jones, Gwyneth. "Secret Characters: The Interaction of Narrative and Technology." *Computers and Composition* 19 (2002): 7–17. Print.

Joyce, Michael. *Afternoon—A Story*. Watertown, MA: Eastgate Systems, 1990.

Keller, Daniel. "Thinking Rhetorically." *Selfe* 49–63. Print.

Kittler, Friedrich. *Gramophone, Film, Typewriter*. Trans. Geoffrey Winthrop Young and Michael Wutz. Palo Alto, CA: Stanford UP, 1999. Print.

Knobel, Michele, and Colin Lankshear. "Online Memes, Affinities, and Cultural Production." *A New Literacies Sampler*. Ed. Michele Knobel and Colin Lankshear. London: Peter Lang, 2007. 199–228. Print.

Koehler, Adam. "Digitizing Craft: Creative Writing Studies and New Media: A Proposal." *College English* 75.4 (2013). 379–97. Print.

Kress, Gunther. *Literacy in the New Media Age*. London: Routledge, 2003. Print.

Lacey, Christopher. "The Rise of Digital Thinking." *New Writing: The International Journal for the Practice and Theory of Creative Writing* 6.3 (2009): 290–99. Print.

Lanham, Richard A. *The Economics of Attention: Style and Substance in the Age of Information*. Chicago: U of Chicago P, 2007. Print.

Lankshear, Colin, and Michele Knobel. *DIY Media: Creating, Sharing, and Learning with New Technologies*. London: Peter Lang, 2010. Print.

Manovich, Lev. *The Language of New Media*. Cambridge, MA: MIT Press, 2001. Print.

McLoughlin, Nigel. "Cellular Teaching: The Creation of a Flexible Curriculum Design and Mode of Delivery in Response to the Effects of Higher Education Policy on the Way We Teach Creative Writing." *New Writing: The International Journal for the Practice and Theory of Creative Writing* 6.2 (2009): 124–32. Print.

Monroe, Barbara. "Compromising on the Web: Evolving Standards and Pedagogy for an Evolving Rhetoric." *Kairos* 4.1 (1999).

Murray, Janet. *Hamlet on the Holodeck: The Future of Narrative in Cyberspace*. New York: Free Press. 1998. Print.

Nieves, J. A., and J. Moxley. "New Tools for Timeless Work: Technological Advances in Creative Writing Pedagogy." *Teaching Creative Writing*. Ed. Heather Beck. New York: Palgrave Macmillan, 2012. 169–73. Print.

Petrelli, Daniela, and Hazel Wright. "On the Writing, Reading, and Publishing of Digital Stories." *Library Review* 58.7 (2008): 509–26. Print.

Ridolfo, Jim, and Dànielle Nicole DeVoss. "Composing for Recomposition: Rhetorical Velocity and Delivery." *Kairos* 13.2 (2009).

Russell, G. "Elements and Implications of a Hypertext Pedagogy." *Computers and Education* 31.2 (1998): 185–93. Print.

Selfe, Cynthia L. "Technology and Literacy: A Story about the Perils of Not Paying Attention." *College Composition and Communication* 50.3 (1999): 411–36. Print.

———. *Multimodal Composition: Resources for Teachers*. New York: Hampton Press, 2007. Print.

———. "The Movement of Air, the Breath of Meaning: Aurality and Multimodal Composing." *College Composition and Communication* 60.4 (2009): 616–63. Print.

Selfe, Cynthia L, and Gail E. Hawisher. *Literate Lives in the Information Age: Narratives of Literacy from the United States*. Mahwah, NJ: Lawrence Erlbaum, 2004. Print.

Sharples, Mike. *Cognition, Computers, and Creative Writing*. Chichester, UK: Ellis Horwood, 1985. Print.

Shields, David. *Reality Hunger: A Manifesto*. London: Hamish Hamilton, 2010.

Sidler, Michelle, Elizabeth Overman, Richard Morris. *Computers in the Composition Classroom*. Boston: Bedford/St. Martin's, 2007. Print.

Smith, Hazel. "Creative Writing and New Media." *The Cambridge Companion to Creative Writing*. Ed. David Morley and Philip Neilsen. Cambridge, UK: Cambridge UP, 2012. 102–17. Print.

Stephens, Mitchell. *The Rise of the Image, the Fall of the Word*. Oxford, UK: Oxford UP, 1998. Print.

Stephenson, Lynda R. "Road Trip: A Writer's Exploration of Cyberspace as Literary Space." *Kairos* 15.2 (2011).

Takayoshi, Pamela, and Brian Huot. *Teaching Writing with Computers*. Boston: Houghton Mifflin, 2003. Print.

Welch, Kathleen. *Electric Rhetoric: Classical Rhetoric, Oralism, and a New Literacy*. Cambridge, MA: The MIT Press, 1999. Print.

Williams, Bronwyn T. *Shimmering Literacies: Popular Culture and Reading and Writing Online*. London: Peter Lang, 2009. Print.

———. "Seeking New Worlds: The Study of Writing beyond Our Classrooms." *College Composition and Communication* 62.1 (2010): 127–46. Print.

———. "From Screen to Screen: Students' Use of Popular Culture Genres in Multimodal Writing Assignments." *Computers and Composition*. 34. 2014. 110-121.

Wysocki, Anne. *Writing New Media: Theory and Applications for Expanding the Teaching of Composition*. Logan: Utah State UP, 2004. Print.

Yancey, Kathleen Blake. "Made Not Only in Words: Composition in a New Key" *College Composition and Communication* 56.2 (2004): 297–328. Print.

Yancey, Kathleen Blake. "Looking for Sources of Coherence in a Fragmented World: Notes toward a New Assessment Design." *Computers and Composition* 21 (2004): 89–102. Print.

12

Ecological Creative Writing

James Engelhardt and Jeremy Schraffenberger

> One can graduate from our best universities without knowing
> why the ozone layer matters, without understanding the
> greenhouse effect or the extinction crisis, without recognizing
> the impact of human population growth. . . . Such learning
> can occur in any course, in any discipline, if the teacher is
> committed to helping students recognize that we all belong to
> this greater community, that we humans are merely one tribe
> among the host of living tribes.
> —Scott Russell Sanders, essayist and fiction writer,
> "Stories for the Earth"

ON EARLY SUMMER weekends, very few people in the park are thinking
about locally sourced food, water crises, or an increase in extreme weather
events. Why should they? They're gathered with friends and family enjoying
the long, warm days. Summer romances and family vacations will follow,
all to evaporate by the time the school year comes around.

Most writers are taught to focus on what we might call the "summertime
issues." Family and friends fall in and out of love; they clash over choices of
destination and goals. Summer becomes autumn, and regrets, anger, and
disappointment drive the Christmas vacation narrative.

These issues are central to writing about people just as they are central
to the creative writing classroom. But in this era, our human stories are

caught up in a much larger story, and human concerns feel a bit smaller and less significant. We're living in a world in which the degradation of the environment leaves us with fewer, and more dire, choices. New research in the sciences underscores our interconnections locally and globally. Faced with this new reality, how should we respond? And more importantly for this essay, how should we respond as writers and teachers of writing? These are important questions, and the answers lead to creative and compelling practices that will result in both better teaching and better writing—for ourselves and our students.

Ecological Creative Writing and Place

We look to ecology for answers to these pressing questions because when creative writing is transformed by ecological principles, students begin to understand that they are indeed a part of—and not apart from—the world around them. These principles might transform an entire creative writing class, a specific unit, or even just an individual assignment, but in the end it's crucial that we teach and write in ways that acknowledge our ecological interconnectedness. There are simple and pedagogically beneficial ways to incorporate this central insight of ecology into creative writing classes. As Scott Russell Sanders reminds us in the epigraph above, doing so in any discipline, creative writing included, is not an unreasonable goal, so long as we as teachers remain committed.

It should be noted here that we're not proposing we all teach "nature writing" classes; in fact, it's important to challenge the very concept of "nature." We agree with our ecocompositionist brethren Sidney I. Dobrin and Christian R. Weisser when they describe their field as "not a study of nature writing but a study of writing and ecology and the ecology of writing" (62). Conventionally, the word ecology is used to refer to the nonhuman world, the plants, insects, and animals that interact "out there" in the environment, but the practice of ecology helps us and our students understand the ways our lives and writing practices are interconnected with other lives and other writers, with books and culture, with the many (obvious and not so obvious) ways the world and history inform our existence. We all bring our intellectual histories as well as our bodies into the classroom, and the texts we create arise in an environment, that is, within a particular time and place, influenced by what we are reading and the status of our various relationships.

We should be clear about what the word "environment" is supposed to mean. Is it the place where we live? The state or national park a short drive from campus that has some "wilderness"? That trash vortex in the Pacific Ocean? Weather? "Environment" stretches and shrinks to cover many ideas, but we'll try to pin it down. To "environ" literally means to surround or encircle, and so for us "environment" refers to whatever is around you. You may be reading this essay from a glowing tablet screen after a catalog search in your local library. Or you may be holding a paperback copy as you swing on your front porch. Or perhaps you're up late at night in a tiny cinder-block dorm room trying to read a blurry photocopy. Environment is always about where you happen to be. Ecological creative writing, therefore, focuses attention on the environments that surround and influence us as writers.

This focus on environment establishes place as a central and ongoing concern, not only as a subject of writing, but also as a way of reconsidering and recontextualizing creative writing as a discipline within the academic community. Beneath and behind the familiar concerns of craft and technique, considering place can help us think ecologically in creative writing. Cheryll Glotfelty offers a useful definition of place as "a relationship of land and stories about land. A place is a dynamic concept. Places are always being made" (269). Students write in place, their writing is placed, and we teach in particular places. But place is cultural as well as literal, changing as we change, shaped by our behavior and by the stories we tell each other and ourselves.

Focusing on the dynamics of place changes much of what we might do in the classroom. For instance, the familiar advice creative writing students often hear to "write what you know" can be quite helpful to new writers who may be daunted by the prospect of having to write creatively; however, this advice not only might limit what a student is allowed to imagine, but it also usually means that they're asked to render images, ideas, characters, and narratives from a decidedly anthropocentric, or human-centered, perspective. Focusing on place and thinking ecologically asks creative writers to consider the possibilities of an ecocentric perspective, one that decenters human concerns and interests and recognizes the self as only part of a larger interconnected ecosystem. Such a shift in thinking inevitably transforms "what you know," challenging what it means to "know" at all, even at the level of identity; instead of thinking of oneself as a separate, stable individual (or character), we begin to understand ourselves as a complex set of interdependent relationships, acknowledging our embeddedness and interconnectedness *in a place*.

Place can also inform other familiar pieces of creative writing advice. The mantra "show, don't tell" now urges students to avoid too much abstraction or exposition not just because those practices can deflate the writing, but also (and perhaps primarily) because concrete language reminds us that we're in a place, that whatever is being written about on the page has an antecedent in some place or other. There are other problems, of course, with the unthinking repetition of "write what you know" or "show, don't tell"; no piece of advice is valid all the time. In this context, however, we only want to demonstrate how paying attention to our relationship to place can alter what we say to our students and why we say it. Considering this often-overlooked category of place leads inevitably to the insight that writing is deeply part of the world and cannot be severed from it.

Perhaps most obviously, focusing on place requires a reconsideration of setting in stories, essays, and poems. In his essay "Speaking a Word for Nature," Sanders complains that much contemporary fiction is "barren" because it "pretends that nothing lies beyond its timid boundaries. . . . What is missing in much recent fiction . . . is a sense of nature, any acknowledgement of a nonhuman context" (649). Our goal as teachers and writers, then, should be to move beyond "timid boundaries," to find "what is missing" in the setting, and to put it on the page. Lawrence Buell describes a similar situation, claiming that a text's environment should be presented "not merely as a framing device but as a presence that begins to suggest that human history is implicated in natural history" (7). The challenge in the classroom is to render setting not as a discrete, easily ignored element within a piece of creative writing but as an interactive participant or guiding force in the narrative. We might start by asking the following questions of a text: Is there an explicit setting at all? Is the setting merely an inert backdrop or stage for the more important human concerns in the foreground? How might the setting be used "not merely as a framing device"? How could the setting offer a sense of the nonhuman natural world? How does the setting suggest what is and isn't possible within the world of the text? Coming to definite answers to these kinds of questions may not be possible, but reflecting on them might suffice.

Ecological Creative Writing as Ecotone

As a result of thinking ecologically and focusing on place, the creative writing class becomes an *ecotone*, the region where two distinct ecosystems meet. The easiest example of this region is a beach, where the watery environment encounters land. Because they are transitional areas or "between" places, ecotones are in a state of dynamic tension. In the classroom, ecotones might be a model for the students themselves encountering new aesthetics and interests among each other. And other cultural ecotones are at play as students and instructor continue to interact with each other, with new writing, and with the assigned texts. Because ecotones are places of natural tension, the classroom can also become a site of great creative foment as ideas and practices are explored and executed.

As a way to emphasize and take advantage of this ecotone between our language and the world, students can be asked to visit some natural or built environment near campus (waterway, coffee shop, parking lot, cornfield) noting all the words they have for the things and phenomena they observe (cutbank, alcove, asphalt, tassel) as well as those things they don't have words for. Not only might this exercise be a valuable stylistic lesson in rendering precise concrete images, but ideally it will also lead to a discussion of the relationship between the intellectual and linguistic world on the one hand and the environmental and physical world on the other. In this way, the ecotone of ecological creative writing expands out into the campus and the community as students leave the classroom charged with engaging the world off the page. When students bring their writing back to share with the class, we might look for how their words intersect with the world, how they serve or influence each other. It's a refiguring of Coleridge's adage that poetry is the "best words in their best order" to encompass the nonhuman world. That is, the best words are no longer relegated solely to the page but exist now in those many places: campus, classroom, community. Writing born of this ecotone compels students to weigh words against world.

Another important implication of the ecotone is that the dynamism of the contact zone extends back into the ecosystems involved. Of course, as with any complex system, repercussions will be difficult to predict, and so it is with our students. We cannot be sure that any of our students will ever do another piece of creative writing or that they will ever think much about the world around them once they leave our classes, but as teachers we are ourselves in the ecotone as well, with similar open-ended questions. What can we do but keep going into the uncertain future? But this uncertainty can be exciting, too, because the ecotone presents a useful metaphor for the discipline of creative writing itself as it relates to the rest of the work we do as writers and teachers inside and outside university communities.

James Englehardt and Jeremy Schraffenberger

Ecological Creative Writing and Interdisciplinarity

When embraced as an ecotone, creative writing allows students to have a more vital, holistic educational experience because it's already a site conducive to interdisciplinary exploration. Creative writing as a discipline is in a unique, somewhat marginal, but, to our minds, particularly advantageous position in the university. Like a trickster, it can easily traverse seemingly rigid disciplinary boundaries, revealing the inherent connections between and among different academic pursuits, connections we sometimes, to our detriment, ignore. It's quite easy to imagine a poem, for instance, about quantum physics, a short story informed by Darwinian evolution, a lyrical essay meditating on some mathematical principle or other. Creative writing has this tricksterish ability because it can't be said to have a proper "subject" at all; writers plumb whatever depths they desire. While we certainly look to exemplary poems, stories, and essays for the sake of modeling this or that technique, these assigned texts don't constitute a "subject." Each semester students will write about a wide (and unpredictable) range of things: stocking shelves in a grocery store, becoming a zombie, crashing a car, climbing a mountain, trimming one's toenails, eating a peach. The true "subject" of creative writing is always brought to the classroom by students themselves, carried in their memories, their experiences, and their imaginations. We can, therefore, take advantage of this inherently interdisciplinary position by asking students to think ecologically, directing their attention to the memories, experiences, and images they carry of the place(s) around them.

As we incorporate ecological principles into creative writing, we should ask if the inverse is also true, that ecology needs creative writers. Peter Hay points out a troubling contradiction in contemporary ecological scholarship that "denies the subjectivity and relationality that an ecological perspective enjoins" (194). Rather than completely dismissing the "rigour, rationality, [and] linear case-making" of academic scholarship, however, Hay argues for a pluralistic ecological discourse, one that would not only include various forms of analytical writing, but also modes (lyrical, dramatic, narrative) and genres (poetry, fiction, creative nonfiction) of creative writing (202).

It's clear that ecology can benefit from what creative writers have to offer, and as a discipline, creative writing seems particularly well suited to become a negotiated space for both scientific and artistic endeavor, hosting the cooperative, interdisciplinary work Hay is calling for. Gary Snyder describes much the same kind of work when suggesting that writers should "fear not science," urging them to "[g]o *beyond* nature literacy into the emergent new territories in science" (262, italics in the original). And in his essay "The Language Habitat," James points out other benefits to creative writers embracing science: "Science . . . allows the poet to name things carefully. And it looks into the mind that makes and reads poems and points the poet toward compositional, structural, and aesthetic strategies" (par. 2). In other words, science has much to offer our writing, not only the development of a more precise vocabulary but also the development of different ways of knowing the world we write about in the first place.

While their respective methods and discourses might sometimes differ, science and creative writing should never be considered mutually exclusive because each relies on the human capacity to imagine. As Edward O. Wilson puts it, "The two vocations draw from the same subconscious wellsprings and depend upon similar primal stories and images" (62). By entering these "new territories in science" and tapping into these "same subconscious wellsprings," creative writing teachers and students will deepen their own engagement with the world around them while also cultivating creative writing itself as a site where meaningful interdisciplinary work can be done.

The Critical Work of Ecological Creative Writing

It's important to note that we want to *broaden* the focus of creative writing, not *shift* it completely from matters of craft and technique. This broadening entails asking deeper questions of our texts than we otherwise might: What are the ecological implications of our human-centered metaphors? How does point of view overlook or incorporate environment? Does the plot ignore, glorify, or otherwise approve of ecological destruction? Are the characters or narrator oblivious to the physical world around them? Are ecological interconnections written into the text? Asking such questions signals to students that the creative writing class is a place where they can expect to do the hard work of critical thinking.

An easy (and we would add lazy) critique of ecological creative writing might be that its teachers are simply looking to wander out into a copse of trees, probably hug them, and demand that their students write uselessly soulful pagan odes celebrating nature. Such an attitude, though, comes from unexamined dismissals of the pastoral or, more recently, the non-fiction nature ramble. While we admire these modes, the classroom we're describing interrogates them more carefully than outsiders might expect and asks for meaningful critical work to be done; ecological thinking resists eco-nostalgia, the all-too-familiar pining for a past when life was simpler and easier, a past, we might add, that has never really existed. A focus on the here and now pushes students to think more clearly and critically about what the past might have actually looked like.

Of even greater importance is a critical consideration of what any of us might mean by "nature." "Nature" is not a stable thing that exists "out there" in the world; "nature" is how humans talk about the thing that exists out there. Attention to nature, then, is attention to how we *think* about nature. We use the term *nonhuman nature* to refer to that part of the world that exists no matter how much or little we think about it. Stepping out of your house at forty below zero in flip-flops, shorts, and a t-shirt will be a bad choice—whether you're using Celsius or Fahrenheit to construct your understanding of temperature. By asking students to separate and differentiate between these concepts, we're giving them the tools to compose and think critically.

When students engage with nature as they find it, they must reconsider their own unexamined claims, filters, models, myths, and preconceptions, especially when it comes to nostalgic idealization and celebration of nature. The ecological creative writing classroom encourages this kind of deep critical thinking as students work through their own ideas about "nature" set against nonhuman nature. By complicating and interrogating their expanding world through classroom discussion and their own writing, students gain insight and perhaps a new attitude about how they should act and engage that world.

Ecological Consciousness and Ethics

Even though ecological creative writing transforms the classroom into a place where critical, interdisciplinary work can be done, students are also allowed to explore nonrational, one might say "wild," approaches to the world, to language itself, and to their own writing in particular. The creative writing class is a particularly fitting place for an ecological consciousness and ethics not just to emerge, but to also be properly appreciated and integrated into a student's understanding of the world.

Regrettably, the phrase "expand consciousness" rings vaguely of New Age spirituality or psychedelic drugs, but we simply mean that students will develop a deeper understanding of their minds in their environment, enriching their understanding of the relationship between self and ecosystem. Hay argues that an ecological consciousness and ethical commitment to an environment "are not, in the first instance, theoretical; nor even intellectual.

They are, rather, pre-rational" (*Main Currents* 2); this "pre-rational impulse" is responsible for "an instinctual and deep-felt horror" at environmental destruction (2, 3). Likewise, Wilson coins the term *biophilia* to describe "the innate tendency to focus on life and lifelike processes"; he goes on to make the case that "to explore and affiliate with life is a deep and complicated process in mental development" and that "our existence depends on this propensity, our spirit is woven from it, hope rises on its current" (1). Wilson claims that ecology "has produced a genuinely new way of looking at the world that is incidentally congenial to the inner direction of biophilia" (2). The ecological creative writing class is by no means anti-intellectual, nor is it an aimless and pedagogically wild free-for-all, but it is a particularly suitable, nurturing place to heed Hay's "pre-rational impulse," to follow Wilson's "inner direction of biophilia," and to expand consciousness.

Tapping into one's creativity naturally feeds the development of consciousness, and ecological creative writing guides this work because thinking about larger and more complicated contexts pushes students to see that, to pull an aphorism from the larger culture, it isn't about them. And the "it" in this case refers to pretty much everything: class, the university, food, water, birds, beer, and on and on. This deliberate move opens the discussion, and their writing, to the idea that maybe "it" can reach deeper, that the nonhuman natural world doesn't care about people—doesn't *care* at all. This insight can be folded back into student writing: If the rising river doesn't care about the protagonist, how would it act? Why should it rain when a character is sad? How might we better describe that ferocious, man-eating tiger?

If the foundation of teaching is, as Derrick Jensen suggests, "to respect and love [our] students into becoming who they are," then we should be working to help them develop a new understanding of the self as contingent (33). In this way, "who they are" might lead to a new understanding of humanity's place within the ecosystem, not apart from it, and certainly not controlling or ruling it. We are nature within culture; the most compelling story might be filtered through our minds, but it remains the story of the world around us. We act within ecosystems, not as solitary geniuses exhibiting our creative gifts but as equal members within a community.

An ecological consciousness in which humans are seen as equal members within the community of an ecosystem inevitably leads to the development of a new ethics. Ethics is generally only invoked in creative writing classrooms when we start to write family and friends into our work, but an ecological exploration of humanity's place in the world requires a greater awareness of our responsibilities to the nonhuman natural world. We understand that students may not follow us into more involved, activist roles, but ecological creative writing makes a critical move when it asks students to consider how their words interact with their world, and that abstract-to-concrete jump is important for education generally. That is, while the larger philosophical issues may or may not fire up a student's imagination, we can nevertheless help students to situate themselves in their local place(s), urging them to become involved with the local community and nonhuman nature. The ethical shift may not be inevitable, but it follows that when we know and experience a place intimately—even when we think about it more deeply— we are more likely to think twice about the consequences of our actions.

Another ethical question emerges from the very local ecology of the classroom and what we all bring there with us. As instructors, we have a strangely public role within the seemingly private class space. Students are always aware of our bodies, and we must, in turn, be aware of what that means to them. As it happens, both of us are white men, and we recognize that students bring different ethnicities, races, genders, abilities, and life histories to our classes—and to our discussion of the environment. While all people have a complicated relationship to place, the histories of some places carry additional weight and challenges depending on a person's race, ethnicity, and/or gender, not to mention issues of safety and accessibility that must be negotiated. In the introduction to their important collection of essays, Alison Deming and Lauret Savoy put the question succinctly, "[w]hat is the American Earth to people of color?" (9). Thus, we are reminded that ecological creative writing must always be aware of its own cultural niche.

While creative writers might sometimes be dismissed as ethereal dreamers or the quintessential expressivists devoted to their own emotional morass, ecological creative writing sets us in direct opposition to these accusations. By developing an ecological consciousness and ethics, we confront and struggle with our place and our responsibilities to that place and its inhabitants. Further, we confront ourselves and our own histories, as well as the history of our place. It is a rich and difficult engagement.

Ecological Creative Writing and Time

Another crucial but perhaps unexpected consequence of creative writing becoming an interdisciplinary ecotone where we might do critical work is a transformation of our experience and understanding of time, namely in slowing things down. Just as the slow-food movement challenges the fast-food industry, ecological creative writing responds to "the fast take-away, virtual, globalized, download/uptake versions of electronic peda-gogy," which can lead to "disembodiment, displacement, disembedding, and decontextualizing" in the classroom (Payne and Wattchow 17, 18). All of us experience and are subject to the rhythms of natural biological time in our everyday lives—walking, sleeping, eating, speaking—but we're also increasingly (and unavoidably) pressed into the digital immediacy of tech-nological time. Ecological creative writing isn't about stubbornly resisting change—on the whole, when implemented ethically and strategically, digital technologies are a boon to higher education—but nor does it unthinkingly endorse more and more (and ever more) technological mediation in our and our students' experiences of the world.

The inevitable conflict that emerges between biological and technological orientations to time leads to an unhealthy experience of what sociologist Alberto Melucci calls "time dissonance" (qtd. in Payne and Wattchow 29). Wendell Berry describes his own stark experience of "time dissonance" while on a solo camping trip to the Daniel Boone National Forest in his essay "An Entrance to the Woods":

> Once off the freeway, my pace gradually slowed, as the roads became progressively more primitive, from seventy miles an hour to a walk. And now, here at my camping place, I have stopped altogether. But my mind is still keyed to seventy miles an hour. And having come here so fast, it is still busy with the work I am usually doing. (721)

This passage echoes Henry David Thoreau's frustration in his famous essay "Walking" of being "not where my body is" and feeling "out of my senses," eventually asking, "What business have I in the woods, if I am thinking of something out of the woods?" (78–79). Both Thoreau and Berry want to be "in the woods," to experience the "deep pleasure in being here" (Berry 722). Eventually, Berry's mind slows down to his body's natural rhythms, such that he is able to experience the place around him more immediately through his senses. The "entrance to the woods" suggests a parallel entrance to his own living skin. When we urge our creative writing students to render vivid, sensory images, we are implicitly asking them to slow themselves down enough to pay attention to such details, to be mindful and observant. In other words, a lesson in concrete vs. abstract language can transcend mere stylistic preference, containing within it a lesson in paying attention to our bodies as they experience the material world around us.

But slowing down doesn't stop at the body. Ecological thinking invites us to consider the entire range of temporal orientations, from historical time (tens, hundreds, thousands of years), to geological time (tens of thousands, hundreds of thousands of years), to cosmological time (millions, billions of years). Once Berry's mind slows down to his body's natural rhythms, he reflects on time in just this way: "And because the natural processes are here so little qualified by anything human, this fragment of the wilderness is also joined to other times; there flows over it a nonhuman time to be told by the growth and death of the forest and the wearing of the stream" (723). A reflection on humanity's *place* in the world leads to a reflection of humanity's *time* in the world, such that "men's history in the world, their brief clearing of the ground, will seem no more than the opening and shutting of an eye" (723). When we realize that human existence (much less human civilization) has been around for a relatively short period of time, we bring ourselves, humbled, back down to earth.

By thinking about time in this way, ecological creative writing can also explore how we might move sustainably into the future. *Sustainability* is a popular buzzword that captures a lot of anxiety about our interdependent path forward. We see this word applied to energy, to institutions, to our food, but for our purposes sustainability is simply a way of thinking about the present in terms of the future. We agree with compositionist Derek Owens, who predicts that "sustainability—as a metaphor, a design problem, a cultural imperative, and a social and ecological necessity—will become one of the new paradigms shaping much of our work as teachers and scholars" (1). Creative writing teachers need to begin considering how the long-term, intergenerational thinking of sustainability will change our practices.

For our students, sustainability means that they develop certain habits of thinking and leave our classrooms with some strategies for exploring their cultural, textual, social, and physical ecosystems with the future in mind. These habits might have a number of implications in creative writing. For instance, when writing a narrative, can a student project into the future to imagine how the actions currently taking place will eventually affect the characters? And can that future be integrated into the narrative, or can it at least help in the revision process? Students can be asked to think of how their own creative writing and language use participates in the evolution of English. They might also consider how the very act of writing and thinking about poetry, for example, helps to sustain it as a vital genre. Similarly, writing in and about local environments, because of the intimate attachments writers and readers develop, can lead to a more passionate desire to sustain them for the future. These are all ways sustainability can inform what we do in creative writing classes.

Applications

The Vignette as Ecological Genre

The literary vignette is a short piece of writing that focuses on describing a single subject. Some might call it a snapshot or a sketch because it doesn't develop a conventional plot. A vignette could be classified as a short-short story, a brief lyrical essay, a prose poem, or even a monologue. Because the vignette defies easy definition and stymies our attempts to place it neatly in one category or another, it is an inherently blurred genre.

The word *vignette* literally means "little vine" in French. In the late eighteenth century, it was used as a term for the decorative vines that would wind and twist around the borders of pages in a picture book, creating a decorative frame for the picture, as though the viewer is peeking through some ornamental shrubbery to catch a glimpse of the image that lay at the center of the page. In the latter half of the nineteenth century, with the invention of the camera, some of the decorative vines began to disappear in favor of an image that faded out around the edges so that there was no longer a definite border. Instead, the image emerged from the page as though from mist. Most of us have seen small photographic portraits from the nineteenth century with those hazy edges; these pictures themselves came to be called vignettes. Eventually, from this photographic sense, *vignette* was used as a term for a short literary sketch.

In "The Ecology of Genre" Anis Bawarshi argues that when writers

> use genres, they are interpreting and enacting the social motives (embedded rhetorically within it) that sustain an environment and make it meaningful, and so are becoming socialized into producing not only certain kinds of texts, but also certain kinds of contexts, practices, and identities—ways of being and acting in the world, socially and rhetorically. (78)

The inherent blurriness of the vignette, then, suggests that we can call it an ecological genre because its "contexts, practices, and identities" are ecological, asking that we dwell on (and perhaps in) margins, edges, borders, limits. As editor and ecocritic Jonathan Skinner argues, "Ecopoetics is border living, an irrepressible border practice" (111). The vignette as a "border practice" draws our attention to ecotones in ways that other genres don't. It also compels us to reconsider the larger implications of literary representation itself. That is, what do we put inside our various frames, and how do these frames change our relationship to a subject? How does writing about a specific place transform it into a singular object rather than a dynamic process of interconnections? How might rendering a place into language change or distort its actuality?

Students in an ecological creative writing class engage these concepts when they write vignettes even if they're not consciously aware of doing so, but they can be given more specific guidance to emphasize the ecology of the genre. For instance, students might be asked to consult a map of their school's campus and then to divide it into roughly equal sections, following particular natural (or human-made) borders and boundaries rather than slicing it up neatly into a grid. Each student would then choose a section to visit, spending enough time there over the course of days or weeks to become familiar with it. When writing their vignettes, students should note specific landscape features, plants and animals present, weather conditions, human and nonhuman structures and accommodations, people who frequent the place, what these people do there, and how all of these observed elements are related. Each student's vignette can then be collected with the others in one document, creating a new, more intimately drawn campus map.

There are, of course, any number of other ways to use vignettes in the creative writing classroom, whether consciously ecological or not. Reading a collection of vignettes that focuses on a specific place—like Mary Austin's *The Land of Little Rain* (1903), which describes a region in southeastern California, or Sandra Cisneros's *The House on Mango Street* (1984), which describes a neighborhood in Chicago—can give students apt models for their own writing. Vignettes from a nineteenth-century picture book might also be used as points of departure for writing about imagined people and places. Students could also revisit some of their own old writing and attempt to blur its edges, metaphorically or otherwise. Either way, the vignette is a useful and compelling genre in the context of ecological creative writing.

A Storied Relationship to Place

One of the main goals of the ecological creative writing class is to encourage a process of writing derived from close attention to whatever environments students find themselves living and working in. In this way, the local is embraced, not at the expense of being aware of global crises but as a means to develop an ecological consciousness that might then turn to such crises later. An emphasis on the local also prevents writing that tends to idealize the nonhuman natural world. We want our students to write against nostalgia, against the hyperreal, against fetishized pastoral fantasy. The ecological thinking we want to develop in creative writing doesn't require a radical retreat from civilization into nature; rather, we ask students to attend to their real physical environments, their everyday lived experiences, instead of trying to recreate the grand romance of wilderness adventure.

Few students have access to genuine wilderness adventure anyway. For instance, Jeremy lives and teaches in a state (Iowa) that sets aside only 2 percent of its land for outdoor recreation. And of that 2 percent, only 5 percent is native prairie, which represents a tenth of a percent of the total land in the state that remains as it was before the plow that broke the plains initiated the age of modern agriculture. In other words, even if it were for some reason desirable to design a creative writing class around recreating pastoral fantasies or wilderness retreat narratives, it would be nearly (if not completely) impossible in a place like Iowa because today's farms are far from pastoral, and the wild prairie has long since been cultivated and turned into private property.

Barry Lopez defines in his essay "A Literature of Place" the kind of writing that might emerge from an ecological creative writing class, proposing what he calls a *"storied* relationship to place" (25, italics in the original). Such a relationship not only requires intimacy, attentiveness, and vulnerability—such that a writer will develop a sense of belonging and identification with a place—but also a deep familiarity with its history. While it might be difficult in a single semester for students to develop a storied relationship and become what Lopez calls elsewhere "local geniuses of American landscape," they can at least begin the process ("American Geographies" 53). Places, as critic Kent C. Ryden tells us, "are myriad and inexhaustible; each of us carries within our head our own personal geography of countless numbers of significant places, and any one geographical location can be seen and interpreted, can be made significant, by different people in different ways" (103). If places are considered "sets of narratives, or of objects that invoke narratives," then students can contribute their own experiences, their "own personal geography," to the stories we tell about local places (3).

Students should choose a local place that will become the subject of their writing. This place should be as specific as possible, and it will be useful for the purposes of research if it has an identifiable name. At first, when students spend time in their chosen places, they should, as Lopez advises, "[p]ut aside the bird book, the analytic state of mind, any compulsion to identify, and sit still. Concentrate instead on *feeling* a place" ("Literature"

25, italics in the original). Once students have felt and experienced their places over the course of days, weeks, or months, they can begin to research them, trying to learn as much as possible about their histories. How have humans interacted with these places in the past? What historical events might have happened there? Where did they get their names? How have the places changed? How have they stayed the same? Who has owned these places? Students might find answers to these questions at historical societies, in the archives in university and public libraries, or even from longtime residents, "local geniuses" able to tell unrecorded but informative stories.

The poetry, fiction, or creative nonfiction that comes from this assignment will combine a student's intimate experience of the place with historical information about it. The writing will be grounded in the kind of close observation and attention to everyday environments that not only counters conventional nostalgic images and idealized narratives of the nonhuman natural world, but also helps students to develop an ecological consciousness.

Origin Stories

Ecological creative writing focuses a lot of its attention on place and where we find ourselves in the "here and now," but we've also demonstrated how it reconsiders our relationship to time, specifically asking that we try to experience (or imagine) a fuller range of temporal orientations, which mainly demands slowing down from the rapidity of technological time. Often, this attention to time results in contemplating not just the present but also the future and how our decisions, attitudes, and behaviors might affect the well-being of coming generations on the planet. As Skinner claims, "Ecopoetics takes responsibility for the future from now on . . . it is visionary, future-oriented" (112).

While attending closely to the present, creative writing as we've been imagining it is certainly also "visionary" and "future-oriented," but ecological thinking must look back to the distant past as well, back to our human origins and beyond, not for the sake of nostalgia, nor to discover some secret about how our hominid ancestors lived in perfect harmony with nature, but because doing so deepens our understanding of the world we currently inhabit and the world that future generations will inherit. Considering the distant past in this way is beneficial to the ecological creative writing class for a number of reasons. For one, when students are reminded of our origins as a species, they're reminded at the same time of our ultimate interconnectedness; humans are placed alongside other animals in the evolutionary tree of life. From these realizations arise a deep and powerful humility that should inform the way we think (and write) about ourselves—as individuals, as a species, and as members of our human and nonhuman communities. Finally, thinking about the distant, evolutionary past makes us reflect on some of the characteristics that define us as a species, namely language and imagination, without which there would be no writing in the first place, much less creative writing.

Applying such thinking in a creative writing classroom might simply entail reflection or discussion in class about the origins of human creativity. But one might also devise certain assignments that engage these ideas. For instance, students could be asked to freewrite a page or two, trying to render specific, vivid images. Then as a revision exercise they could be asked to investigate (or imagine) the origins of all the concrete things they've included, integrating the information into their writing. If a student writes about dandelions dotting her lawn, she would then research how the plant likely arrived in North America with the English settlers on the *Mayflower*. If a student writes about an apple eaten at lunch, he would then research industrial food chains in the United States, perhaps even moving back through time until he discovered that the apple's original home as a wild species was in the mountains of Kazakhstan. Another version of this exercise focuses not on things but words themselves, as students are asked to research etymologies, noting how words might be related to each other. For instance, if a student writes about an avocado, she will learn that the word is derived from the Nahuatl (Aztec) word *ahuakatl*, meaning "testicle," not only because avocados are shaped like testicles but also because they were believed to be an aphrodisiac; the Spanish colonizers thought the word sounded like *avocado*, which means "advocate." Embedded in the strange history of this word are these other interesting histories we can learn from. Everything we observe and every word we use has some origin story that can enrich our writing while also emphasizing the interconnectedness of ecological thinking.

We want to end by reminding the reader, and ourselves, that creative writing can be about anything, that in addition to craft we can—indeed, we have to—bring other subjects into the classroom. In order to make sense of a changing and degrading planet, we owe our students the opportunity to engage their world. Creative writing offers insights into the world that can be useful for other disciplines, including the natural sciences, and the process of coming to those insights is rigorous. In other words, the creative writing classroom is ecologically linked to the rest of the academy. Ecological thinking helps students understand their place in the world at many levels. They engage their campus, their bioregion, their history, and their culture. We must remind ourselves that students are undergoing complex transformations within their academic ecosystems, and we have responsibilities as instructors that cannot be ignored. In the end, the practices we have suggested are merely sketches, but sketches, we believe, that reinforce an ecological approach to creative writing.

In his essay "Creative Writing in the Academy," David Radavich asserts that creative writing classes should be "brought into deeper and wider relationship with other courses in the curriculum . . . emphasizing reading skills, critical thinking, language awareness, and historical consciousness" so that programs "can be made to foster more understanding of public concerns and social responsibility" (112). As a part of the university ecosystem and the academic world, the discipline of creative writing should demonstrate "a commitment to social betterment of a troubled world" (112). The most appropriate and compelling way to achieve these aims is to broaden our focus as creative writing teachers from familiar questions of craft and technique so that it encompasses ecological principles as well, crossing disciplinary boundaries as we engage the world around us. No longer does it seem sufficient (or even ethical) to teach students simply *how to* write a successful poem, story, or essay; now we must ask what it means if an otherwise "successful" piece of writing blindly perpetuates a conventional model of the nonhuman natural world as mechanistic, atomistic, or merely utilitarian, if it doesn't integrate place as a significant or informing element in its composition, if it doesn't somehow acknowledge or contend with our inevitable interconnectedness.

And so in the face of our current and ongoing global environmental crisis, teachers of creative writing should acknowledge and incorporate ecological principles into the design of their classes, because to do otherwise is to ignore the obvious and in turn be indirectly complicit in environmental degradation. To do otherwise is to assume that creative writing as a discipline can only be concerned with aesthetic questions of craft and technique rather than how our poetics might relate to and affect the world around us. To do otherwise is to forget how the work we do as teachers and writers might address the most pressing (we're tempted to say *de*pressing) issues of the day. To do otherwise, finally, is to retreat and lock ourselves in a disciplinary garret, fiddling away while the world burns. David W. Orr reminds us that "all education is environmental education.

By what is included or excluded, students are taught that they are part of or apart from the natural world" (12). The only ethical pedagogical choice is to teach creative writing, in whole or in part, with an emphasis on our ecological interconnectedness and interdependence.

Works Cited

Bawarshi, Anis. "The Ecology of Genre." *Ecocomposition: Theoretical and Pedagogical Approaches*. Eds. Christian R. Weisser and Sidney I. Dobrin. Albany: SUNY P, 2001. 69–80. Print.

Berry, Wendell. "An Entrance to the Woods." *Nature Writing: The Tradition in English*. Eds. John Elder and Robert Finch. New York: Norton, 2002. 718–28. Print.

Buell, Lawrence. *The Environmental Imagination: Thoreau, Nature Writing, and the Formation of American Culture*. Cambridge, MA: Harvard UP, 1995. Print.

Deming, Alison H., and Lauret E. Savoy, eds. *The Colors of Nature: Culture, Identity, and the Natural World*. Minneapolis, MN: Milkweed, 2002. Print.

Dobrin, Sidney I., and Christopher J. Keller, eds. *Writing Environments*. Albany: SUNY P, 2005. Print.

Dobrin, Sidney I., and Christian R. Weisser. *Natural Discourse: Toward Ecocomposition*. Albany: SUNY P, 2002. Print.

Engelhardt, James. "The Language Habitat: An Ecopoetry Manifesto." *Octopus Magazine* 9. 10 July 2007. Web. 15 May 2013.

Glotfelty, Cheryll. "Ecocriticism, Writing, and Academia: An Interview with Cheryll Glotfelty." Dobrin and Keller 255–72.

Hay, Peter. "Academic Discourse or Personal Essay? Reflecting on Rival (?) Discursive Modes for Place and Nature." *Interdisciplinary Studies in Literature and Environment* 10.2: 193–202. Print.

———. *Main Currents in Western Environmental Thought*. Bloomington: Indiana UP, 2002. Print.

Jensen, Derrick. *Walking on Water: Reading, Writing, and Revolution*. White River Junction, VT: Chelsea Green Publishing Company, 2004. Print.

Lopez, Barry. "The American Geographies." *Orion*, Autumn 1989: 52–61. Print.

———. "A Literature of Place." *Portland: The University of Portland Magazine*, Summer 1997: 22–25. Print.

Orr, David W. *Earth in Mind: On Education, Environment, and the Human Prospect*. 1994. Washington, DC: Island P, 2004. Print.

Owens, Derek. *Composition and Sustainability: Teaching for a Threatened Generation*. Urbana, IL: NCTE, 2001. Print.

Radavich, David. "Creative Writing in the Academy." *Profession 1999.* New York: MLA, 1999. 106–12. Print.

Ryden, Kent C. *Sum of the Parts: The Mathematics and Politics of Region, Place, and Writing.* Iowa City: U of Iowa P. American Land and Life Series. 2011. Print.

Sanders, Scott Russell. "Speaking a Word for Nature." *Michigan Quarterly Review* 26.4 (1987): 648–62. Print.

———. "Stories for the Earth: An Interview with Scott Russell Sanders." Dobrin and Keller 223–36.

Skinner, Jonathan. "Small Fish Big Pond: Lines on Some Ecopoetics." *Angelaki: Journal of the Theoretical Humanities* 14.2: 111–13. Print.

Snyder, Gary. "Unnatural Writing." *The Gary Snyder Reader: Prose, Poetry, and Translations.* New York: Counterpoint, 1999. 257–62. Print.

Thoreau, Henry David. "Walking." *Nature / Walking.* 1862. Boston: Beacon P, 1991. Print.

Wilson, Edward O. *Biophilia: The Human Bond with Other Species.* Cambridge, MA: Harvard UP, 1984. Print.

Afterword

WHAT HAPPENED AS you read this book? We're curious. Were you left with a different image of the creative writing classroom? Did one pedagogy particularly resonate with you, perhaps energizing your approach to an upcoming semester or your lesson plan for next week's class? Did an interesting combination of two or more pedagogies, as suggested in our prologue to this book, cause you to inch your chair closer to your teaching?

We're hoping readers, no matter what stage of their teaching career they're in, will appreciate gaining this window into so many rich pedagogical approaches to creative writing. If you're a veteran instructor, each of these chapters can offer a glimpse at a whole set of other seasoned instructors' practices—a bit like observing a really interesting class or team-teaching. If you're just starting out on a career as a creative writing instructor, your options may have just increased exponentially beyond managing an in-class workshop. What would it be like to tutor poetry in a writing center or partner with a biology professor to teach a science-fiction unit? To ask students to come up with new language to express female or working-class experience? To get your students involved in a community micropress or strengthen their short stories by paying attention to setting as an ecosystem? To help students give better readings of their work through attention to the fifth canon in classical Greco-Roman rhetoric of delivery or *pronuntiatio*? You can see creative writing *and* creative writers differently through the lenses of these pedagogies. Over time, it's also possible that your pedagogical leanings will shift, and you will pick up new interests. What once was perhaps uninteresting to you suddenly becomes relevant with changes in the classroom, in higher education, in the demographics of the discipline of creative writing studies.

Here's what we're also hoping happens after you read this book. The chapter authors have initiated conversations to which many new voices will join. We hope that as each of these pedagogies evolves, it takes on its own conversations, arguments, research questions, terminology, empirical and archival research, praxis, issues, and controversies, to become a fully formed and distinct branch inside creative writing studies. In a few years, we expect to see these pedagogies appear as titles of conference talks and books, as the focus of undergraduate and graduate courses, as discussion topics in professional organizations and listservs, stimulating even whole new journals and eponymous conferences in the way variants of these pedagogies have done in composition studies. Our purpose is to prompt nuanced conversations about praxis which will propel creative writing studies after its own pedagogies. Not every pedagogy is meant to sit well with the next; several of these pedagogies are in opposition in composition studies, and yet all of these pedagogies have been extremely influential inside that field. Several arose in reaction to perceived offenses in other pedagogies, and many a heated discussion has occurred on folding chairs at conferences and in journal issues between proponents of different composition pedagogies. That sort of lively debate, however, is part of the health of composition studies and not a sign of troubles.

Indeed, just as we sent out a call several years ago for chapter proposals for this book, we're sending out a call to readers. Pick the pedagogy (or two) that interests you the most from this collection and begin to investigate, dive deeper, and explore the history and theories beyond the Works Cited provided here. Did you perhaps notice a crack, an omission, a pedagogical strand for creative writing that was not covered in this collection? Go to it. Expand the conversation.

Contributors

Pamela Annas is a professor emerita of English and formerly an associate dean of the College of Liberal Arts at the University of Massachusetts, Boston. She directed the English MA program at the University of Massachusetts Boston and helped develop the school's MFA program. Her books include *A Disturbance in Mirrors: The Poetry of Sylvia Plath*; the anthology *Against the Current*; the textbook/anthology *Literature and Society*; and a poetry chapbook, *Mud Season*.

Patrick Bizzaro has published nine books and chapbooks of poetry (with two more forthcoming), two critical studies of Fred Chappell's poetry and fiction, a book on the pedagogy of academic creative writing, four textbooks, and a couple hundred poems in magazines. He lives quite happily with Resa Crane and their seven-year-old son, Antonio, in Indiana, Pennsylvania, where he is currently a professor of English in Indiana University of Pennsylvania's doctoral program in composition and TESOL. His articles on creative writing studies have appeared regularly in *College English* and *College Composition and Communication*. His coedited book on poet and pedagogue Wendy Bishop, *Composing Ourselves as Writer-Teacher-Writers*, was published in spring 2011 by Hampton Press.

James Engelhardt's poetry has appeared in the *North American Review*, *Natural Bridge*, *Terrain.org*, and many other journals. His critical work has appeared in the *Journal of the Midwest Modern Language Association* and *Mid-American Review*. He is the acquisitions editor at the University of Alaska Press and continues to teach at writers conferences.

Contributors

Sandra Giles is an associate professor of English at Abraham Baldwin Agricultural College (ABAC). She has had work published in such journals and anthologies as *Wilderness House Literary Review, Southeast Review, Writing Spaces, The AWP Pedagogy Papers, On Writing: A Process Reader,* and *Feeling Our Way: a Writing Teacher's Sourcebook.* She has presented at the Association of Writers and Writing Programs Conference (AWP) and the Conference on College Composition and Communication (CCCC), as well as other writing and teaching conferences. She also serves as a teacher-consultant for the Blackwater Writing Project, a unit of the National Writing Project out of Valdosta State University, and is a faculty advisor for ABAC's college literary magazine *Pegasus.*

Steve Healey's poetry collections are *Earthling* and *10 Mississippi*, both from Coffee House Press. His work has appeared in *American Poetry Review, Boston Review, Fence,* and the anthology *Legitimate Dangers: American Poets of the New Century.* Previous essays about creative writing pedagogy have appeared in *Key Issues in Creative Writing* (Multilingual Matters, 2012) and *The Writer's Chronicle.* He teaches at Minneapolis Community and Technical College.

Tom C. Hunley is a professor of English at Western Kentucky University. He is the author of four full-length poetry collections and six chapbooks. His previous books of creative writing pedagogy include *Teaching Poetry Writing: A Five-Canon Approach* (Multilingual Matters, New Writing Viewpoints Series, 2007) and *The Poetry Gymnasium: 94 Proven Exercises to Shape Your Best Verse* (McFarland, 2012). His work has been featured three times on *The Writer's Almanac with Garrison Keillor* as well as in *Poetry Daily, Verse Daily, TriQuarterly, Five Points, Virginia Quarterly Review, New York Quarterly, North American Review,* and *The Writer's Chronicle.*

Kate Kostelnik earned her PhD in English from the University of Nebraska, Lincoln, where she also served as the associate coordinator of the writing center. She currently teaches at the University of Virginia. Her fiction, which earned a 2007 New Jersey State Arts Council Fellowship, has appeared in *Hayden's Ferry* and *Fifth Wednesday*, among others. Her scholarship has been published in *Creative Writing Teaching: Theory and Practice* and in *Pedagogy.* She thanks Dr. Bobbi Olson for invaluable assistance in the development of this chapter, which was discussed and revised in the UNL writing center.

Tim Mayers is an associate professor of English at Millersville University. He is the author of *(Re)Writing Craft: Composition, Creative Writing, and the Future of English Studies,* as well as several scholarly articles and book chapters on creative writing. His novel manuscript, "Intelligence Manifesto," won the 2007 Paradigm Prize.

Andrew Melrose, DPhil, is a professor of children's writing at the University of Winchester, United Kingdom. Andrew has more than 150 film, fiction, nonfiction, research, song, poem, and other writing credits, including the *Story Keepers* film series; a "textual intervention" on the New Testament, broadcast worldwide; and thirty-three scholarly or creative books. He is also the editor of the online journal *Writing4Children* and an inaugural member of the international advisory boards for *TEXT: Journal of Writing and Writing Courses* and *Axon: Creative Explorations*. In addition to his creative writing, Andrew has written a number of books, articles, and book chapters on various aspects of critical and creative writing and on the cult and culture of the child, children, and childhood. *Here Comes the Bogeyman: Exploring Contemporary Issues in Writing for Children* and *Monsters under the Bed: Critically Investigating Early Years Writing* were published by Routledge in 2012.

Clyde Moneyhun's MFA in fiction and PhD in rhetoric and composition are from the University of Arizona. He is an associate professor of English at Boise State University, where he teaches writing and directs the Boise State Writing Center. He is a coauthor of the composition textbook *Living Languages* and the creative writing textbook *Crafting Fiction*; has published scholarly articles in *College Composition and Communication*, *Rhetoric Review*, and the *Journal of Advanced Composition*; and has published fiction, travel writing, and translations in many venues. His current projects include translations of contemporary Catalan poetry, which have appeared in the *Notre Dame Review*, *Eleven Eleven*, *Lyrikline*, *The Winter Anthology*, and *Hayden's Ferry Review*.

Alexandria Peary is an associate professor and the first-year writing coordinator at Salem State University. She holds a PhD in composition from the University of New Hampshire and an MFA in poetry from the University of Massachusetts–Amherst and the Iowa Writers' Workshop. She is the author of three books of poetry, *Fall Foliage Called Bathers and Dancers*; *Lid to the Shadow* (2010 Slope Editions Book Prize); and *Control Bird Alt Delete* (2013 Iowa Poetry Prize). Her poetry has received the Joseph Langland Award from the Academy of American Poets. Her scholarship on writing across the curriculum, women's writing, and the history of creative writing has appeared in *College Composition and Communication*, *Rhetoric Review*, the *WAC Journal*, *Pedagogy*, *New Writing: The International Journal for the Practice and Theory of Creative Writing*, the *Journal of Aesthetic Education*, and the *Journal of Teaching Writing*.

Contributors

Joyce Peseroff is the author of five books of poems and the editor *of Robert Bly: When Sleepers Awake; The Ploughshares Poetry Reader*; and, most recently, *Simply Lasting: Writers on Jane Kenyon*. She has received a Pushcart Prize and fellowships from the National Endowment for the Arts and the Massachusetts Foundation. Recent work has appeared in *Consequence, New Ohio Review, Ploughshares*, and *Salamander*. She is currently a distinguished lecturer at the University of Massachusetts, Boston, where she directed the MFA program for its first four years.

Jeremy Schraffenberger is the associate editor of the *North American Review* and an associate professor of English at the University of Northern Iowa. He is the author of the book of poems *Saint Joe's Passion* (Etruscan), and his other work has appeared in *Best Creative Nonfiction, Birmingham Poetry Review, Brevity, Notre Dame Review, Poetry East, Prairie Schooner*, and elsewhere.

Carey E. Smitherman is an associate professor of and interim chair of the department of writing at the University of Central Arkansas. She has also served at UCA as the director of first-year writing and the interim writing center director. Her research interests include first-year writing theory and pedagogy, writing center theory, and service learning. Her latest article, coauthored with Amanda K. Girard, is titled "Creating Connection: Conversations about Composition Theory and Creative Writing Craft in the First-Year Writing Classroom," which was published in *Currents in Teaching and Learning* (2011). Recent presentations include "Making It Real: Service Learning, Authenticity, and First-Year Writing" (Arkansas Philological Association Conference) and "Writing Hurricane Katrina: Creating Engagement through Disaster Relief" (PCA/ACA).

Stephanie Vanderslice is a professor of writing at the University of Central Arkansas and the director of the Arkansas Writer's MFA Workshop at UCA. She is a coeditor, with Kelly Ritter, of *Can It Really Be Taught? Resisting Lore in Creative Writing Pedagogy* (Boynton Cook, 2007), as well as a coauthor of *Teaching Creative Writing to Undergraduates: A Resource Guide and Sourcebook* (Fountainhead, 2011) and the sole author of *Rethinking Creative Writing in Higher Education: Programs and Practices That Work* (Professional and Higher, 2011). Her fiction and nonfiction, as well as articles and essays on creative writing pedagogy, have appeared in *College English, College Composition and Communication, New Writing: An International Journal of Creative Writing Theory and Pedagogy, Profession, Writing on the Edge*, and a number of edited collections in the United States and the United Kingdom.

Jen Webb is the distinguished professor of creative practice at the University of Canberra, Australia, and director of the Centre for Creative and Cultural Research, Faculty of Arts and Design. Jen holds a PhD in cultural theory, focusing on the field of creative production, and a DCA in creative writing. She has published widely in poetry, short fiction, and scholarly works: her most recent scholarly work includes *Understanding Representation* (Sage, 2009) and a coauthored book, *Understanding Foucault: A Critical Introduction* (Allen & Unwin, Sage, 2012). She is completing a coauthored book on contemporary Asian art (for Manchester UP) and a textbook on research methods for creative writing (for P&H Publishing). She is also working on a series of short creative pieces exploring the trope of Icarus. Jen is a coeditor of the Sage book series Understanding Contemporary Culture and of the online journal *Axon: Creative Explorations*, published out of the University of Canberra. Her current research investigates representations of critical global events and the use of research in and through creative practice to generate new knowledge.

Bronwyn T. Williams is a professor of English at the University of Louisville. He writes and teaches on issues of literacy, identity, and creative nonfiction. His books include *New Media Literacies and Participatory Popular Culture across Borders, Shimmering Literacies: Popular Culture and Reading and Writing Online, Popular Culture and Representations of Literacy,* and *Identity Papers: Literacy and Power in Higher Education.*

Index

Index

Index

Index

Index

Index

Index